GRILLING DAHMER

THE INTERROGATION OF "THE MILWAUKEE CANNIBAL"

PATRICK KENNEDY and ROBYN MAHARAJ

WILDBLUE PRESS

WildBluePress.com

GRILLING DAHMER published by:
WILDBLUE PRESS
P.O. Box 102440
Denver, Colorado 80250

Publisher Disclaimer: Any opinions, statements of fact or fiction, descriptions, dialogue, and citations found in this book were provided by the author, and are solely those of the author. The publisher makes no claim as to their veracity or accuracy, and assumes no liability for the content.

Copyright 2021 by Patrick Kennedy and Robyn Maharaj

All rights reserved. No part of this book may be reproduced in any form or by any means without the prior written consent of the Publisher, excepting brief quotes used in reviews.

WILDBLUE PRESS is registered at the U.S. Patent and Trademark Offices.

ISBN 978-1-952225-64-2 Trade Paperback
ISBN 978-1-952225-63-5 eBook

Cover design © 2021 WildBlue Press. All rights reserved.

Interior Formatting/Cover Design by Elijah Toten
www.totencreative.com

GRILLING
DAHMER

"A serial killer's victims are randomly chosen to fulfill an uncontrollable need to kill. Often he leads an ordinary life—his family and friends unaware of his homicidal passions."

Jim Kallstrom
Former FBI Assistant Director
New York City

Acknowledgments

This book is dedicated to those who serve on the front line as police officers and detectives in law enforcement.

It is also dedicated to all of Jeffrey Dahmer's victims*.

***

I would like to thank the late Patrick Francis Kennedy for sharing his story with me. Thanks to Patricia Kennedy for allowing me to share Patrick's story with others and for encouraging and inspiring me during the entire process.

Thanks to Natalie Ballard for her incredible editing skills and to her and Richard "Chip" Smith for their directional input. Thanks to Dan Zupansky for his skills and expertise during the reading stages of the manuscript.

I would like to thank the staff at Wild Blue Press for taking this book on and allowing it to reach a wider true crime audience.

I would also like to thank David and Dianne Maharaj for their love, patience, support, and understanding—always.

For Patrick

I worked on this book because I wanted to honor a man who had a story I believed needed to be told despite his sudden death. I was afraid that his manuscript might be put back into a desk drawer, never to be read again. Patty, his widow, and I both wanted his story to be available to a larger audience.

Patrick Kennedy was someone who Jeffrey Dahmer seemed to look up to and wanted to please immensely. Kennedy, who as a devout Catholic was naturally drawn to the spiritual and literal confessional model, had a gentle, unassuming, and nonjudgmental method that built a significant rapport that helped Dahmer feel comfortable with finally confiding to someone in authority. Pat demonstrated a willingness to share private truths about himself in a way that worked with this particular and unique suspect.

What drew me to tell Pat's story was his compassionate ability to see the humanity in a man who everyone in the world called evil. From the beginning, he chose to hear that man's story and not to judge him as so many people lined up to do. That man, who experts and family said would normally shut down when faced with authorities and confrontation, opened up to this particular detective—a cop he believed from the beginning he could trust to listen to him and help him take on the weight of the story about his murderous crimes.

Pat heard and saw firsthand all that Jeff had done and yet he still chose to treat him humanely, to respect him for agreeing to talk, and to help devastated families find out the fate of their missing loved ones.

Note

Since *Grilling Dahmer*'s first incarnation, there has been an even greater interest in true crime, serial killers, and crime stories. Podcasts have sprung up everywhere and true crime proves to be a popular genre of discussion from shows who profile cold cases and unsolved crimes to shows that look back on famous and infamous killers as a form of education and entertainment.

My Friend Dahmer, a 2017 film directed by Marc Meyers and based on the graphic novel by John "Derf" Backderf, came out and featured actor Ross Lynch as Jeff Dahmer in high school and his life as a young person prior to his first murder. Netflix is due to release *Monster: The Jeffrey Dahmer Story,* directed by Ryan Murphy and featuring Evan Peters as Dahmer, in spring 2022.

Dahmer has been portrayed in books, films, and documentaries since he was first captured in 1991. Dahmer, like so many others, unfortunately, inspires others to tell and retell the story in the form of literature, art, film, and stage. Hopefully something comes from the exploration of some of the most horrific crimes we have ever seen in our times – but as time moves forward, these serial killers go from becoming an article or story in the news and in magazines that we read and remember reading to people who make up the criminal history we are so fascinated by. It's interesting that some of the young actors selected to portray Jeffrey Dahmer now weren't even born when his crimes were discovered, he was caught, sentenced and eventually brutally killed in prison.

Sometimes, the further a crime gets from us, the less real it becomes. When you have actors auditioning for the roles of real people (still living sometimes), there is a weird dichotomy of reality and art occurring when true stories are told by people who are telling a story from those perspectives. How do members of the families of victims of serial killers feel about these books, movies, and podcasts? Too often we focus on the perpetrators of violent crimes and rarely the victims and we shouldn't.

I was twenty-one when I first heard the name Jeffrey Dahmer, so he was a real person to me when he was first in the news and then later when I had the opportunity to meet Patrick and work on this book. I was focused on telling the "real story" as it was coming from one of the people directly involved in the case. At the same time, I hoped to accomplish telling Patrick's story as artfully, as literarily, as truthfully, and as respectful as possible. Now, exactly thirty years later, *Grilling Dahmer*, reissued and released by Wild Blue Press, is one telling of the Jeffrey Dahmer story.

> *"Our scars have the power to remind us that the past was real."*

Hannibal Lecter, *Red Dragon* by Thomas Harris.

*List of Jeffrey Dahmer's known victims

Steven Hicks, 18
Steven Tuomi, 26
Jamie Doxtator, 14
Richard Guerrero, 25
Anthony Sears, 24
Eddie Smith, 36
Ricky Beeks, 27
Ernest Miller, 22
David Thomas, 23
Curtis Straughter, 16
Errol Lindsey, 19
Tony Hughes, 31
Konerak Sinthasomphone, 14
Matt Turner, 20
Jerimiah Weinberger 23
Oliver Lacy, 23
Joseph Bradehoft, 25

Introduction

I was first introduced to former Milwaukee Homicide Detective Patrick Kennedy during a short interview with Kennedy and Christopher James Thompson at the SXSW (South by Southwest) Festival in 2012, where Chris's film *The Jeffrey Dahmer Files* made its world premiere. I was interested in Kennedy's approach to Dahmer when he questioned him on the night of Dahmer's arrest.

Several months earlier, I had experienced the devastation of losing a family member to homicide. A paternal uncle who lived in Freeport, Trinidad, and Tobago, West Indies, burned to death in a fire that was later determined to be arson.[1] That crime is still unsolved (as of this printing), and leaves a loss, emptiness, and the knowledge that someone decided to intentionally kill a member of my family and got away with it.

Homicide fractures a family. Geographically, my uncle Vishnu and I were not close, but I felt the loss of one fewer Maharaj in the world, and my family tree is forever altered in a painful and sudden manner.

---

1. Retired teacher perishes in fire - by Susan Mohammed, susan. mohammed@trinidadexpress.com. Story Created: Oct 9, 2012 at 10:01 P.M. ECT. Story Updated: Oct 10, 2012 at 11:50 A.M. ECT. A 62-year-old retired teacher died in a fire that destroyed his home at Freeport yesterday. The body of Vishnu Maharaj, of Arena Road Village, was discovered burnt beyond recognition, in a gutted bedroom. A family of three, and another man who rented separate apartments on the ground floor of the house, has been left homeless. Freeport police said that at around 5 A.M. they were called to Maharaj's home. When they arrived, the house was engulfed in flames.

My dad, David, and his siblings lost a brother because of the destructive actions of a complete stranger, someone with an utter lack of respect or concern for the life of another person. A killer who decided that his or her wants, needs, desires, or passions were more important than a human being. When the victim is a family member, it changes the way you look at violence, victims, and the preciousness and frailty of human life.

Many of Kennedy's colleagues at the time of Dahmer's capture, and in the years that followed, credited Pat's confessional technique. He had a personal nature that encouraged people to trust and open up to him without fear of judgment, and an unflappable and unwavering ability to commit himself to suspects.

Pat didn't manipulate any frailties in someone he needed to talk to, but he did recognize and acknowledge these potential weaknesses in order to view the suspect as human, no matter what crime they were believed to have committed, and no matter what psychological trauma he faced when involved in a particularly heinous homicide case. There was something very open and encouraging about Kennedy; where anyone else might see the most frightened or delusional suspect and perhaps use that to his or her advantage, Kennedy felt a perhaps unexpected compassion.

It was this quality that allowed suspects and witnesses to count on him if they needed to talk to him. Kennedy, at one point early in his life, had dreamed of being a Catholic priest, so he seemed to have a calling to listen to troubled people or people in crisis. He never judged anyone for anything they said or did. He was able to offer hope, guidance, and wisdom at a time when only darkness appeared to prevail. How easy it might have been for Dahmer to clam up, shut down, and refuse to acknowledge the situation beginning to unfold in the small apartment that held his darkest secrets.

I believe that given their similarity in ages, (Dahmer—the older of two boys—was thirty-one, while Kennedy—

the eldest boy in a family of ten kids—was thirty-seven), plus Kennedy's genuine warmth (he insisted Dahmer call him Pat), convinced Dahmer almost instantly that he was safe and heard, but not judged, by Kennedy if he decided to divulge—for the first time—who he was and what he had done.

Chapter 1

The Hollywood blockbuster *The Silence of the Lambs*, released in the US in 1991, is considered a visually stunning and atmospherically provocative yet graphically violent film. It resonated with a generation of moviegoers who began and continued to demand a new level of sophistication, intelligence, and wit from the horror/thriller genre.

Audiences were fascinated by and yet frightened of the imposing, imprisoned psychotic psychiatrist and serial killer Dr. Hannibal Lecter, and yet may have felt an even stronger uneasiness and revulsion toward the true villain of the piece, Buffalo Bill, a killer who snatched his victims off the street, starved them, then skinned them for his own desire to be reborn as a woman.

As frightening as some scenes were, a truly terrifying aspect was the incredible and shocking inner reality and solitary emotional world that Buffalo Bill was remaking for himself, as well as the physical and visual transformation he was undertaking during his crime spree.

While fans loved echoing the now infamous Sir Anthony Hopkins' line about the fate of a census taker who tried to test Hannibal Lecter—"I ate his liver with some fava beans and a nice Chianti"—others were spellbound by the exciting new world of criminal behavior profiling. The film—a critical and commercial box office hit based on the novel of the same name by Thomas Harris—won every major Academy Award and became a favorite among legions of film critics, reviewers, and movie fans for years to come.

However, in those auspicious early days and weeks of the film's release, a different yet eerily similar kind of solitary crime spree was well underway in apartment #213 of the Oxford Apartments, located at 924 North 25th Street in the city of Milwaukee.

Milwaukee, Wisconsin, prior to the summer of 1991, was probably best known as America's leading dairy producer, as the setting for the popular seventies sitcom *Happy Days*, the Green Bay Packers, and beer production. Wisconsin State is where R&B singer Otis Redding's life ended in 1967 when his small plane crashed in Lake Monona en route to a concert in Madison. Notorious killer and grave robber Ed Gein lived in Plainfield, Wisconsin, and it was on his family farm that the atrocities he committed were discovered in 1957. Coincidentally, Gein was one of the inspirations for the Buffalo Bill character in *The Silence of the Lambs*.

June 1978

The stretch of highway was dark except for the occasional lights of a small village dotting the Ohio landscape. While the vast fields were clearly farmland, a lot of the newer villages were filled with residents who commuted to larger centers—many commuting along this stretch of connected freeways and byways. There had been a boom of sorts in the mid-sixties when urbanites, who originally left the big cities for the quieter suburbs, picked up and moved into even more remote surroundings, as developers purchased pockets of land and built grander homes than what you might expect "in the country."

While many enjoyed the convenience of the suburbs in terms of proximity to the cities, they preferred the safety of the smaller communities and family-oriented neighborhoods. Others longed for more isolated lodgings—where they could see the stars in the night sky and hear wildlife in the forested areas that connected farms, creeks, dirt roads, and fields.

Officer Richard Munsey of the Bath County Police Department patrolled a particularly lonely stretch of highway by himself. He had a thermos of coffee, heard the occasional squawk of police radio chatter and static, and once in a while, saw a lone car or truck pass in either direction. He was on a rotating duty schedule; every officer in the department of his rank or junior had a three-night (overnight) shift of babysitting these deserted roads, being there to help a motorist lost or in trouble, or other emergencies. Munsey was out in the field and ready to go "lights and sirens" in the rare event of something more serious.

There was nothing serious or sinister about the little compact car that drove quickly over one of the rises toward Munsey's patrol car one early summer night. Munsey noticed the car swerved a bit, and the driver was in a hurry. It wasn't going over the speed limit, but it was faster than most of the people who usually traveled these roads. As the car passed, Munsey's headlights illuminated the driver's side and he was able to make out the blond, wavy hair of a young man. Munsey allowed the car to pass, but decided to check it out. Could be a car of teens out drinking and driving—it was summer, after all, and most young people in the district spent a lot of time in cars traversing and racing across parts of the more rural sections of the state, burning through gasoline and killing time, usually bored and occasionally up to no good.

Munsey followed the car, flashing his lights and siren until the car slowly pulled over to the right-hand shoulder of the road. Munsey could only make out the driver, who appeared to be alone. He grabbed his police hat and radioed in his position, stating he had pulled over a suspicious vehicle. He jotted down the plate number in his notebook before exiting his car.

He walked to the driver's side of the vehicle and noted that the young, blond man had already rolled down his window.

"Is there a problem, officer?" the young, bespectacled man asked softly.

"I noticed your car swerving a bit as you came over the pass. Have you been drinking tonight?"

"I was with a friend earlier... this afternoon. We split a couple of beers, but I'm not drunk." The young man looked at Munsey. He appeared to be sober. He wasn't slurring his words and he was lucid.

"I need to see your ID," Munsey said, and the young man pulled his wallet out of his back pocket and produced his driver's license. "May I ask what you are doing out here so late?" Munsey asked. "It's well after midnight."

"I know," the man said, nodding. He looked down and then back up at Munsey. "My parents are getting divorced and I'm having a hard time dealing with it. I couldn't sleep so I just decided to go for a car ride, get some fresh air, clear my head."

Munsey had written down the details from the license and handed it back to the teenager, who didn't say anything. The young man did not live far from where he had been stopped. Munsey unstrapped his flashlight from his belt.

"Is this your car?" he asked.

He would check, of course, once he got back to the station, but something told him to engage this young man a little longer. The young man's politeness unnerved him for some reason. Munsey didn't believe that he was drunk or drugged and he seemed pretty harmless, just a lone teen driving around. The parents' divorce story seemed a bit flimsy, but he didn't really have grounds to detain him further. Munsey took a quick sweep of the car with his light and immediately noticed several large garbage bags taking up most of the backseat.

"What's in those bags?" He motioned to the back with his light.

"Oh, I decided that if I was going to go out for a drive, I might head out toward the dump and drop off these garbage bags. I had promised my mother I would, but then forgot. So I decided that I would try and get rid of all of this garbage tonight." The young man stammered ever so slightly.

Munsey's light passed over the bags and then across the face of the young driver. The boy looked up rather blankly. The young man started to say something, and then stopped. Munsey waited.

"My mom has been so upset because of the divorce. She cries a lot, she rages sometimes about how much she hates my dad. I forgot about the trash last night and when I remembered, I decided that if I could take it away before she got up, it would be one less thing for her to be upset about," said the young man.

Munsey clicked off his flashlight and stood up straight beside the car. "The dump gates will be closed at this time of night, and you aren't allowed to leave bags outside the gate. You better just go home and take the bags tomorrow once the dump opens to the public." He stepped away from the car and returned his flashlight to his belt.

The young man smiled and quickly rolled up his window. He started the car up and slowly turned around, heading back the way he came. He headed toward the address listed on the license, driving away slowly at first and then gaining some speed.

Munsey walked back to his car where he jotted down the last of his notes, reporting this innocuous traffic stop on a lonely stretch of highway. The name on the young man's license was Jeffrey Dahmer.

Sunday, May 26, 1991

911 call to report a victim of possible assault

Caller: Hi. Okay. I'm on 25th and State and there is this young man. He is butt naked. He has been beaten up. He is very bruised up. He can't stand up. He is butt naked. He has no clothes on. He is really hurt. I got no coat on. I just seen him. He needs some help.

911: Where's he at?

Caller: 25th and State. The corner of 25th and State.

***

The young boy stumbled over the sidewalk when all at once everyone on the street heard sirens in the distance.

A motherly-looking woman stood beside him. She had grabbed a windbreaker from the back of a dinette chair on the stoop of her apartment. She hustled over as soon as she sensed he was lost and in distress. She realized that the boy was completely naked, but didn't believe for a second that it was part of a prank or joke. She wrapped the windbreaker around his middle and called out to a neighbor, who confirmed that police had been called. Two teenage girls had also rushed over. The woman and the two girls tried talking to the boy, but he couldn't explain what had happened to him. He tried speaking to the woman, but the boy slurred his words. She was aware of people around them, but they were in the distance—standing in the doorways of houses and other buildings, walking and gathering along the sidewalk, looking slightly amused or puzzled, but waiting and watching to see what would happen next. She could really hear the sirens now.

The woman motioned to the police car as it rushed to where they stood, waving as it came down the street. Two policemen stepped out of the squad car and calmly walked over to where she stood. She immediately started to talk to them in a rushed, concerned manner.

She explained that she had been out on the sidewalk when she saw the boy come out of the apartment building, completely naked. She told them he looked "out of it" and confused, which was why she approached him. One of the policemen turned to the boy and began asking him questions. The boy tried to speak, but his words were slurred. The officers tried to understand him and tried to piece together what had happened. One policeman had taken out a notebook and scribbled down notes on the particulars of the scene. He turned to look at street signs, the address of the Oxford Apartments where they stood, and looked the young boy over. When the boy started to speak again, he stopped writing and tried to make sense of what the kid was saying.

The woman was getting impatient with the police. She was telling them what she had seen and her fears that someone had assaulted him, but the police weren't listening to her. A couple of other women from the neighborhood slowly walked to the little huddle and added their voices to the situation, confirming what she had told the police, stating that the boy had indeed been naked and scared, but also explaining that they didn't know exactly where the boy lived and they did not know his name.

A thin blond man with glasses had been walking down the street in their direction. He stopped suddenly when he noticed the boy, the gathering crowd, and the police on the sidewalk in front of his building.

He paused momentarily, but with a rush of confidence and bravado, walked to the small group. He smiled widely at the police and then at the boy. In a soft, calm, and reasonable voice, he explained to the police that the boy was in fact not a boy, but a man in his early twenties. He told them that he was his boyfriend and the two had been drinking and arguing earlier, and he must have decided to leave, but in his haste and drunken stupor, left the apartment without clothing. The man explained that while he too had been drinking a bit, he had left the apartment and his young lover behind to make a quick run to the liquor store—he held up the six-pack as proof—and that his boyfriend must have come to look for him. The neighbors recognized the man and confirmed to police that he did live in the apartment building. However, they balked at the idea that the boy was older than he appeared, and told police that he was a school-aged kid. The man ignored the neighbors, staring at both policemen as he repeated that this was simply a minor disagreement between two men who lived and partied together. He even explained that this had happened once before, but he had woken up and convinced his boyfriend to come back into the building before any commotion could occur. In a measured voice, the blond man assured police that the boy was in his early twenties.

He gave the police polite and reasonable answers to their questions and even smirked and chuckled a bit when he told them about his boyfriend's habit of arguing with him and then threatening to leave after removing every stitch of clothing. He also mentioned how he rescued his boyfriend when he drank too much and paraded up and down the sidewalk without clothes. The man told the police that this often occurred when his boyfriend drank. Because his boyfriend had passed out this time, the man thought he would just sleep it off.

The police escorted them back into the building. The boy tried to twist away, so they tightened their grip on his arms. The policemen decided they weren't going to return him to the apartment until they verified the young man's residence. The blond man led the police and the boy to his unit on the second floor.

The police immediately smelled a foul odor emanating from somewhere on the floor, but that wasn't unusual in these kinds of older buildings. Years of cooking, body odor, cigarette smoke, marijuana, fast food, etc. permeated and clung to the walls and carpeting of buildings where numerous people lived under one roof. It was unpleasant and off-putting, but nothing that concerned the policemen as they followed the man to his apartment door, #213.

He took out keys; however, the door was closed but unlocked. The boy had simply let the door close behind him when he left. The blond man hadn't said much as they strolled through the building but now that they were at the threshold of his unit, he began talking again. Confirming that he was who he said he was, he produced his wallet and identification, which they scanned quickly and handed back.

He produced some Polaroid photos of the young man in various stages of dress—one showed him smiling widely at the camera, wearing pants but without a shirt. The police flipped through the photos; they showed an obviously conscious and willing subject participating in the photoshoot, unrestrained and even toasting the photographer with a glass of some kind of drink, obviously in good humor.

The blond man, who had offered to show them the young man's identification, had been going through some papers on the kitchen counter, claimed now that he couldn't find it, but assured them the young man lived there willingly and that there was nothing for the authorities to be concerned about. He apologized to the police for wasting their time over a minor domestic disagreement. He promised that he would not leave the man alone again when they found themselves in this predicament. He assured them that this kind of drunken public display would not happen again.

The policemen were wrapping up the emergency call, one of them closing his notebook, the other taking a final survey of the small one-bedroom apartment. The blond man saw them both to the door. He closed the door and locked it. He didn't say anything as he turned to the weak, scared young boy now left alone.

***

Milwaukee Police Department reporting in 15 minutes later from the police car dispatched to the scene:

"The intoxicated Asian naked male (laughter in background) was returned to his sober boyfriend (more laughter)."

When the officers are dispatched to another scene, one comments, "First, my partner is going to get deloused at the station."

***

Second 911 call

Officer: Police.

Ms. Cleveland: Yes. There was a squad car, Number 68, that was flagged down here earlier this evening, about fifteen minutes ago.

Officer: That was me.

Ms. Cleveland: Yeah. What happened? I mean, my daughter and my niece witnessed what was going on. Was anything done about this situation? Do they need their names or...

Officer: No, I don't need them.

Ms. Cleveland: ...or information, or anything from them?

Officer: No, not at all.

Ms. Cleveland: You don't?

Officer: Nope. It was an intoxicated boyfriend of another boyfriend.

Ms. Cleveland: Well, how old was this child?

Officer: It wasn't a child. It was an adult.

Ms. Cleveland: Are you sure?

Officer: Yup.

Ms. Cleveland: Are you positive? Because this child doesn't even speak English. My daughter has dealt with him before, seen him on the street, you know.

Officer: Yeah. No, uh, he's uh, he's... It's all taken care of, ma'am.

Ms. Cleveland: Isn't this... I mean, what if he's a child and not an adult? I mean, are you positive that this is an adult?

Officer: Ma'am. Ma'am. Like I explained to you. It's as positive as I can be.

Ms. Cleveland: Oh. I see...

Officer: I can't do anything about someone's sexual preference in life, and if...

Ms. Cleveland: Well, no, I'm not saying anything about that, but it appeared to have been a child, this is why...

Officer: No.

Ms. Cleveland: No?

Officer: No, he's not.

Monday, July 22, 1991

Tracy Edwards knew he was in trouble. A young man who could usually talk his way out of a lot of jams, he was running out of ideas about how to keep the blond man he had befriended several hours earlier from attacking him with a knife.

In the twinkling, summery sunshine of a lazy, late afternoon, Edwards had been out with friends hanging around the Grand Avenue Mall when a good-looking man approached them. He was soft-spoken but direct, and although he appeared to be addressing the small group of Edwards's friends, he kept staring specifically at Edwards. Edwards was appreciative of the attention and interested in what the man said. The blond man complimented Edwards's appearance, his toned physique, and the lean angles of his jaw and neck, stating that Edwards was the kind of male subject he sought out for photos he liked to take. He motioned for Edwards to step aside, mentioning that he would be willing to pay up to a hundred dollars if Edwards was willing to pose for photos. Edwards recognized what was going on, and perhaps was a little intrigued and enticed—there was the lure of money, alcohol—maybe some level of mutual seduction would develop. Edwards's friends balked when he told them he was taking off with his new friend, encouraging him to stay and hang out with them, but he decided to leave.

The man, who introduced himself as Jeff, led the way out of the mall and into the sunshine. Edwards could eye the man who now walked purposefully beside him as they traveled to an apartment not too far away. They stopped at a beer store where Jeff bought a six-pack, and Edwards was able to size him up more closely. He was over six feet tall and looked to be in pretty good shape. He was blond and fair and decently dressed. As they walked and talked, Edwards began to sense that Jeff was shy and lonely and maybe didn't have a lot of friends. He talked a little about movies and even suggested that they could watch one once they got back to his place.

The building was fairly mundane—a three-story walk-up box—and the apartment much what one would expect from a one-bedroom efficiency apartment in this part of the city. The apartment was hot and smelled terrible. Edwards complained, and Jeff nodded that his landlord kept promising to fix the problem. Edwards sat down, taking in the surroundings, while Jeff fixed him a drink. Not offering him a beer or asking what he might like, Jeff simply handed Edwards a glass full of a dark liquid that smelled and tasted odd. Edwards sipped at it, disliking the taste; he noticed that Jeff took a beer for himself right from the can. Jeff put in a movie and Edwards realized that he hadn't said much to him since locking them inside the apartment. Jeff had a serious look on his face as the start of *The Exorcist III* flickered on the screen of his television. Edwards started to ask him about what work he did, but Jeff brushed off the conversation. He noticed an element of darkness in Jeff's face, and the smell of the place was making him nauseated. He didn't like the drink and didn't think he'd be able to sit through an entire movie in this horribly smelling place. He had changed his mind about all of it—the photos, the drinks, and the man beside him, who was starting to act stranger by the moment.

Jeff got up abruptly and left the room. Edwards thought about just taking off, but Jeff was back seconds later. He had his camera and a pair of handcuffs, and he asked Edwards to remove his shirt. Jeff was smiling now, but there was an edge to his voice that made Edwards feel as though he should comply. He hesitated but decided to play along. Jeff asked if he could attach a handcuff, but before Edwards could respond or resist, Jeff snapped the cuff on his wrist. He had him sit down, and encouraged him to loosen up and drink more of the strong liquid. They sat together and watched the movie, Edwards strategizing his next move while Jeff moaned under his breath and rocked back and forth. Edwards sensed that Jeff was a ticking bomb and wanted to keep him as calm as possible so he could leave without upsetting him.

The movie continued to play. When it finished, Jeff picked up the remote, rewound the movie, and started it again. Jeff switched his focus from rocking back and forth and watching the movie to looking at Edwards, who desperately tried to look calm and comfortable to keep Jeff at bay as the hours ticked by. They moved to the bedroom. Jeff pulled out a knife and pushed Edwards to the bed.

"I'm going to cut out your heart and eat it," Jeff said to him in a low, deep voice. He held the knife to Edwards's chest.

Edwards heard him but pretended he didn't. He tried to lighten the conversation by suggesting Jeff remove his shirt and perhaps they could fool around. Edwards desperately wanted him to put the knife down, but Jeff resisted every suggestion. Edwards asked if they could move back to the living room where the window air conditioner helped alleviate the heat and smell, but Jeff didn't respond. Jeff wasn't focused on the knife, but he also wasn't putting it down—all the while moaning, rocking back and forth, and slurring incoherently from several hours of near constant beer drinking.

Edwards leapt suddenly and punched Jeff full in the face. Not expecting it, Jeff fell to the ground and Edwards ran to the bedroom door and then the locked apartment door. He grabbed at the locks, feeling that Jeff was right behind him. He knew that if he didn't escape at that moment, he would likely never leave that place alive.

Edwards managed to get the door open and ran down the hallway, not looking back. He raced down the stairs and out the door into the night.

***

It must have been a strange sight if you happened to be on the darkened street that blistering hot night. A few city residents may have been out taking whatever relief possible from the night air and seen a young man with glazed eyes running down a Milwaukee street, a pair of handcuffs dangling from one wrist.

After what Edwards had experienced in the several hours before his escape, he was just thankful to be out and on the street, though frightened his attacker might have followed and would catch up to him.

Edwards flagged down the first police cruiser that he saw. The two officers recognized immediately that their keys would not remove his cuffs, as the handcuffs were not Milwaukee Police Department-issued, and it was someone other than a fellow officer who had attached them. Edwards desperately wanted the cuffs removed and for this reason alone he finally agreed, after much persuasion on the part of the police, to accompany the officers back to Oxford Apartments #213, a couple short blocks away.

The apartment threshold, unbeknownst to Officers Robert Rauth and Rolf Mueller, and Tracy Edwards, was a doorway that when crossed, usually proved fatal to most of the people who had visited in the time its sole resident lived there. That imminent moment eventually became the beginning of the Jeffrey Dahmer story—once the world learned his name.

Chapter 2

The Cop and the Killer

Kennedy: July 22, 1991 was a hot, sticky summer night in Milwaukee, one that changed the direction of my life. The heat that night was nothing new to me. I had prowled the streets of Milwaukee on many a night like this while in uniform. I spent ten years at District Five, in the heart of the central city, pounding a beat or hacking a squad, and I genuinely enjoyed being a cop there. The third shift was always jumping, as everyone knows the freaks come out at night. A fourth-generation police officer, I always believed law enforcement was my calling, but now things were different. I was in the Criminal Investigation Bureau, a detective. Assignment to the elite homicide unit only increased the perks and prestige that went along with the new promotion, and I was eager to make my mark.

Relishing the blast from the air conditioner, I drove the fifteen-minute commute to downtown from my comfortable West Side Cape Cod-style home. Although I was relatively new to the bureau, I had already obtained a few run-of-the-mill murder confessions and had established myself as a decent interrogator.

At six foot-seven, and two hundred and sixty-five pounds, my colleagues often teased that it was my size and not my technique that convinced suspects to spill their guts. Indeed, there were bullies in the bureau who pushed, slapped, and threatened suspects. I, however, took a gentle, matter-of-fact approach to keep them talking.

I killed them with kindness, shaking their hand, offering them coffee and cigarettes while I proposed a suspect-friendly scenario to the crime—one that allowed them to keep their dignity as they confessed their deeds.

A marked squad car roared past me with its sirens wailing as I stepped from my car. Crossing the street to the police administration building, I took the elevator to the fourth-floor detective assembly. My partner Mike Dubis was already sipping coffee at his desk. Mike was a Polish kid, born and raised on the south side of Milwaukee. His father was a cop, and Mike joined the force at eighteen as a police aide. He was promoted the same day as I was, and his youthful appearance made him look out of place at the bureau.

Detective Lieutenant Roosevelt Harrell had teamed us up. He was the highest-ranking African American in the bureau. He had worked through a time in the department when African American officers were routinely passed over for promotions. He prevailed because of his stubborn nature and his uncanny ability to elicit information from people. He took a liking to me during my first week in the bureau. I had been sent to a stabbing, and the investigation led to a ramshackle house where I discussed the situation with the suspect while sitting at his kitchen table. I was unaware the victim had bled out en route to the hospital, and hadn't noticed Harrell had arrived on scene and was observing my interrogation. Within thirty minutes, I had convinced the suspect that alcohol was the culprit for his deed and that no intent to kill was evident. He agreed and not only gave a signed statement, but also provided the bloody knife and clothing he had hidden before police arrival. Harrell was impressed with my work and told me so. "Kid—I like your style. That was a damn good job!" He continued his support and mentored me until the day he retired.

I poured myself a cup of coffee and started toward my desk when Harrell motioned me into his office as he hung up the phone.

"Kennedy, I want you and Mike to take a run up to 924 North 25th Street. I got a call from a couple cops up there that say they found a head in a refrigerator. Sounds like some bullshit to me, but go check it out anyway."

Rolling my eyes, I walked over to Dubis and told him about the hitch.

"You got to be fucking hosing me! Really?"

We grabbed our suit coats, made our way to the garage, and rolled to the alleged murder scene.

"I'll tell you one thing," Mike said with a smile as we climbed into our unmarked squad car and drove toward the assignment, "I'm certainly not going to lose my head over this investigation."

It was my night to drive and as we rode the twenty blocks or so to the scene, Mike remembered we had been there before. About a month earlier, we investigated the strangling death of a thirty-four-year-old Black male on the third floor. It was still an open homicide with no suspects. We pulled up to the Oxford Apartments, a three-story, thirty-six unit, white brick structure. The building was just west of the downtown area. Lower-income people of all races and ethnicities occupied it. There were some families but it was mostly people on welfare, social security, or some kind of general assistance. I remember talking to residents during the previous investigation. It had its share of alcoholics, drug addicts, thugs, and sex workers, both straight and gay.

Entering the main vestibule of the building, our nostrils filled with the sweet, putrid, nauseating smell of death, which had become so familiar to us both. The odor hung heavily in the air, intensified by the heat and humidity. We looked at each other, acknowledging the smell.

"Maybe this ain't gonna be bullshit," I said, wondering if I should have left my suit jacket in the car. The smell of a dead and rotting corpse was known to penetrate the fibers of clothing and lingered if not dry cleaned.

We took the stairwell to the second floor and rounded the hallway to unit 213. There, we met a stout, veteran copper whose wildly excited eyes were as big as saucers. He was sweating profusely and his disheveled uniform gave evidence that he had been in a hell of a fight. I knew this officer from my uniform days. He had a reputation as a take-no-shit kind of guy—not necessarily heavy-handed, but someone who responded to assaultive behavior in kind.

"What the fuck is going on?" Mike asked the red-faced copper.

"You won't believe this shit!" he responded as he led us through the apartment door.

I entered first and saw three more uniformed cops, all dripping with sweat. They were straddling a Caucasian male suspect, who lay face down on the floor, handcuffed behind his back and shackled at the feet. One officer had his knee firmly in the suspect's back, another held his leg-ironed feet, and the third cop wiped his face with a hanky. Their uniforms looked just as unkempt as the first officer's.

"Take a look in the refrigerator!" shouted the portly cop with his knee in the suspect's back.

I walked to the fridge and opened it. What I saw shot an overwhelming wave of panic and fear that rushed from the bottom of my feet to the top of my head: a clean, barren refrigerator holding only an open carton of baking soda and a cardboard box containing a freshly severed head. There was no blood and it was cut cleanly at the base of the neck. The Black man's head in the box looked back at me. His eyes and mouth were wide open as if he were surprised. It was surreal, and it appeared as if he were about to speak. I stepped back quickly, bumping into Mike, who stood directly behind me. Although there was no danger, I could barely control the thought of running away. My only thought was *Get the hell out of here!* It was irrational, and I knew it. To give in to my fear would mean the end of my homicide assignment and relegation to the ranks of the burglary and theft detail. There was an eerie silence for a moment, broken by the sweaty cop with the hanky.

"And that ain't all, Pat, look at this shit."

He handed me a stack of about twenty-five Polaroid photos depicting numerous male victims of different races in various stages of dismemberment. At first, I wondered how this guy got hold of pictures from the medical examiner's office, but as I sorted through them, it became clear to me that the background depicted in the Polaroids was the apartment I stood in. The fear returned. It seemed a while before I regained my composure and radioed Lt. Harrell that we did indeed have a homicide, and please meet us at the scene.

"Don't anybody touch anything!" Dubis shouted.

He seemed to be struggling to remain calm as much as I was. We were all satisfied to wait in silence for the lieutenant to arrive. I began to take note of the apartment; besides the obvious signs of a struggle, it was immaculately clean with good quality furniture. It was a one-bedroom place with a combination kitchen and living area, adjoining hall, and bathroom.

I looked at the suspect as he lay on the floor. His light-colored hair was greasy and wet with perspiration. The faded denim shirt he wore was drenched with sweat, and I noticed he was bleeding slightly from the corner of his mouth. There was an obvious rug burn on his right elbow, glistening blood red. He appeared completely defeated, but his condition showed that a great struggle brought him to that point. He was motionless but made an ever-so-faint crying whine, like that of a child or a cat in the night.

I entered the bedroom, stepping over four large boxes marked Caution: Muriatic Acid, and noticed a very large blue plastic drum, securely sealed. A fan stood behind it, blowing at high speed in the direction of an open window. Walking back to the living room, I checked the artwork that adorned the walls. Three large black and white portraits of long, lean muscular men, posed in various provocative positions, showing their fine form and physique. A large aquarium sat on top of a black enamel table against one wall. Several boxes of Soilex cleaning powder and an array of cleansers and air fresheners were in plain view on the kitchen countertop. I figured this guy was gay and some kind of clean freak.

"All right, what do we got?" Harrell bellowed as he entered the room, chomping on a big black cigar.

"Check the fridge, boss," Dubis said, winking at me.

Harrell opened the refrigerator door and quickly stepped back. His eyes widened and he puffed hard on his Arturo Fuente cigar, filling the modest apartment with heavy clouds of smoke.

He closed the door, took a deep breath, and said, "Okay, boys, here's what we're gonna do. Kennedy, you take this guy downtown and start talking to him. I want you with him every minute, understand? No one else. If he's got to piss, you hold his dick. Get it? I mean stay with him all the time until I get back there, do you hear me?"

I nodded in agreement.

"Dubis, you and me are going to go over this place with a fine-toothed comb." Looking at the coppers, Harrell ordered, "Get some help up here. I don't want anyone else in or out of this place!"

I directed the two coppers who held the suspect down to pick him up and follow me outside.

"I already called for a wagon," one of them said as they ushered the suspect down the hall to the stairway.

The suspect walked slowly as he tried to negotiate the leg irons. His head was bowed over his slouched shoulders, but even in this position, I could tell he was over six feet and in good shape. As we descended the stairs, I could see the bright lights of TV news cameras. The local stations all carried police scanners and routinely monitored them so they could be on the scene of breaking news, sometimes arriving even before the police. The radio call regarding a head in a refrigerator was too juicy for them to pass up. I stopped short of leaving the building and directed one of the conveying officers to move the reporters and their cameras across the street. As he herded them back, I heard a preppy newshound complain about freedom of the press.

The veteran officer responded, "Move it or you'll be free to spend the night in jail for obstructing this investigation." It was obvious he enjoyed ordering the TV talking head out of the area.

The wagon pulled up to the entrance of the apartment building, so the trip from the door was quick. I assisted the suspect into the wagon and climbed in after him. The two conveying officers got in the front and drove away toward the station. No one said a word as we cruised back downtown. I eyed the suspect as we rode. Although he was a good-sized man, he appeared almost fragile, sitting hunched over and trembling slightly. At the station, he cooperated—almost zombie-like—as I led him into the prisoner elevator and up to the interrogation rooms on the fourth floor.

Once inside, I pointed to the cuffs and leg irons and said, "Take these off him."

"Look, Pat, I wouldn't do that. I had to fight with this fuckhead and he's no pussy." I looked at the copper and his pudgy partner and I knew he was not kidding.

I turned to the suspect. "Hey, if you give me your word you won't act up, we can take these off."

For the first time, the suspect looked at me directly and I caught his steely blue eyes. He nodded in affirmation and I motioned again for the officers to remove his shackles.

The pudgy officer removed the binds and stepped outside, saying, "I'll be right here if you need me."

The interrogation rooms are about 9x12, with high ceilings and dingy beige cinder block walls. A metal table and two metal chairs are the only furniture. I extended my hand.

"My name is Pat, and I'm the detective that will be investigating your case."

The suspect looked bewildered but meekly placed his limp hand in mine. I directed him to take a seat, and he obediently sat in the corner chair.

"You're not going to let them hit me anymore, are you?"

These were the first words out of his mouth, and they came almost pleadingly. I assured him by my manner, voice, tone, and general approach that I was not there to fight, argue, belittle, or harm him in any way. He seemed to think I was in charge and had authority over the uniforms, and I let him continue to think so. From now on, he would only be talking to me, and fighting was not part of the program. For the first time, I really took stock of the guy. A hint of barely controlled hysteria was evident in his voice. The smell of alcohol was more than noticeable. His eyes were glazed and his speech slightly slurred. He appeared to be desperately trying to contain himself and talk straight.

"What's your name?" I asked, opening the interrogation.

"Jeff. Jeffrey Dahmer," he replied.

"I'm going to get a cup of coffee, would you like one? Oh yeah, do you smoke?"

A look of surprise came over Dahmer's face and he indicated he would like both. I left him in the locked room and went to my desk where I kept a pack of smokes for prisoner interviews, and grabbed two cups of coffee. I took a moment to compose myself and develop a plan for the interrogation. From my brief observations, I felt I had an intelligent, gay white man, a product of middle- to upper-middle-class upbringing, involved in at least one homicide and maybe more. He was about my age and probably shared similar values to mine. I decided to take a quiet, almost gentle approach and returned to the room.

I placed the coffee, pack of cigarettes, and a lighter in front of him. He looked quizzically at me and I encouraged him to help himself. He fumbled with the smokes and lit one up. I noted that he relished the nicotine as he inhaled deeply. He took the cup of coffee and sipped it with obvious relief. I could see he enjoyed these little niceties and was polite and thankful for this small kindness. I decided to begin.

"What can you tell me about the guy in the refrigerator?" I tried to sound as matter-of-fact as possible.

Dahmer looked startled and sat upright in his chair. He took another exaggerated pull from his cigarette and, exhaling, politely thanked me for the coffee and smoke.

"I don't want to be uncooperative, Pat, but I really don't think it's in my best interest to talk to you." I was surprised at how articulate he was. "Do you think I should talk to a lawyer?" he inquired, trying to be polite yet forceful.

Undeterred, I stretched out in my chair. "Oh, I think you'll need a lawyer eventually for this." I noticed how his eyes followed my body as I shifted back to a normal sitting position. "Hell, Jeff, it's one o'clock in the morning. Do you want to wait till the rest of the world wakes up to discuss this case?"

Dahmer seemed upset by this rebuff and inquired as to what would happen if he refused to talk any further. I nonchalantly explained the Miranda rights and began to describe the booking procedure; however, he seemed familiar with this and nervously asked if he could get his own cell instead of going to the bullpen.

I picked up on Dahmer's fear of the bullpen, a large holding room occupied by every kind of arrestee, from traffic violators to murderers and everything in between. It's a claustrophobic, smelly, disgusting place to wait for criminal justice. I decided to play off this fear. It had been a busy night and I told him so. The jail was full, so a cell to himself would not be possible. He would have to make do with the others jailed that night and get packed into the bullpen to await arraignment the following day. A look of fear struck Dahmer's face as he slunk back into his chair.

"Look, you don't have to go there now. We can talk about some general information, you know, about yourself, your education, things like that."

I had made up my mind that this guy wasn't going anywhere until he told me about that head. Working homicide, I had seen some pretty gory things but that head was tops. Dahmer lit another cigarette and asked me if he could have another cup of coffee. I obliged and returned with another cup for myself as well. I began by asking him questions about his job, apartment, and any vehicle that he might have. Dahmer was employed at a local candy company and his job was to mix ingredients during the processing part of the operation. I knew the plant well and told him I had often stopped at their retail outlet to buy treats for my kids. He acknowledged that their product was quality and seemed proud of his contribution. Dahmer stated that he chose his apartment because it was cheap and close to the bus lines and his job. He was polite in manner and spoke fluently, not using big words, but obviously had a good command of the English language.

"What about your family? Do you have any kin in this town?" I asked.

Dahmer's back stiffened; his tone became defensive. He caught me with his eyes.

"Look, Pat, what I did, I did on my own. My family had nothing to do with it and I would rather leave them out of this." He answered matter-of-factly and appeared to be sobering up. I could feel the strength of his conviction on this point; however, this was the first hint of an admission. I decided not to lie to him as I had done so many times before with other suspects.

"All right, Jeff, I'll be straight with you," I said, taking a deep breath. "You're fucked, understand? You're not going anywhere. I already saw the head. My partner and a bunch of detectives are going through your apartment right now, so I'm sure there will be a lot more evidence coming. Look, sooner or later you're going to have to talk to somebody about this whole mess, so it might as well be me. Now, you can wait till the morning and talk to your attorney, but hell, that won't be for another seven or eight hours. If you want, I can take you up to the bullpen right now and you can rot for the night with all the drunks, thugs, and crackheads, but hell, Jeff, that's not you. It's obvious that's not your crowd. At least stay a while and talk to me. You know, I can help you! I've been doing this for quite a while, Jeff, and I know that nothing is cut and dried. There's always some kind of extenuating circumstances. Hell, I can tell just by looking at you and listening to you speak that you're an intelligent, decent guy, not some freaked-out murderer. There must be a logical reason for what happened. Won't you let me help you?"

At this, Dahmer became noticeably depressed. He seemed to realize the magnitude of his situation.

"What am I going to do?" he groaned. "It wasn't supposed to end like this! No, no, I can't do this. Pat, please take your gun out and kill me. I want to die. Don't you understand? I had it all planned out. I'm not supposed to be here. I should have done it a long time ago and saved myself all of this. It's over anyways. Please, Pat, take your gun out and shoot me, just end it!"

I noticed that his gaze was locked on the chrome-plated .357 revolver still strapped to my waist. In all the excitement, I had forgotten to take it off and place it in my desk, the usual procedure when questioning a prisoner. I remembered the three coppers at the scene. I sure didn't want to get in a struggle over my gun with this sinewy suspect. That had happened once on the street when I was in uniform. I vividly recalled the fight for my life and didn't want to repeat the scenario.

"Look, Jeff, calm down," I said, placing my right hand on his shoulder and carefully shielding my revolver with my left. "This ain't the end of the world. Take it easy. What do you mean, you should have done it long ago?"

Dahmer again seemed on the edge of hysteria, about to jump out of his skin. He edged toward me with eyes wild and intense.

"Do you know what hydrochloric acid would do to you if you put it into your veins?" Looking directly at me, he continued. "That's right. Just inject some hydrochloric acid or formaldehyde into your veins by using a hypodermic needle. The acid would travel right to your heart and boom— it would be all over, no pain, no problem. I should have done it. I wouldn't be here now but I just couldn't, Pat, don't you see? I just couldn't. I wanted to so many times."

Dahmer hung his head and began to sob like a scared little boy. His shoulders heaved as he tried to catch his breath and a small puddle of tears formed beneath his chair. I genuinely felt sorry for him but saw this as a good time to break.

I stood up and hovered over him, putting my hand on his shoulder. "Take it easy, Jeff. Nobody is going to hurt you. Settle down a bit. It's going to be okay. I'm not going to leave you, and we can talk this thing through. Just relax. Look, I'm going to get another cup of coffee. Do you want one?"

Dahmer watched me, his eyes red and swollen. "Yes, please," he said faintly.

I left the room and quickly took off my revolver, glad to be out of there without a fight. I grabbed two more cups of hot coffee and returned to see Dahmer lighting up another cigarette and inhaling deeply.

"These help," he said, and took another long and deliberate drag.

I couldn't help but notice how much Dahmer seemed to enjoy cigarettes. Now, I'm not a smoker myself but I sat down, grabbed a smoke and tore the filter tip off it, lit it up, and began to puff it, cigar-like. Dahmer seemed amused by my antics and appeared a bit more composed. I pulled my chair closer to him and sat down, my knee touching his. When he lifted his head, he caught my eye.

"Look, Jeff, I'm not going to kill you." Dahmer saw that the .357 was gone from my holster. "And I'm not going to let anyone else hurt you. Because you told me of your plans to kill yourself, when you leave this room, you will be under a suicide watch, so you won't have an opportunity in the future to hurt yourself. So you can just get that idea out of your head right now, do you understand? You know, Jeff, you're still a young man, and you've got a lot of living left to do. You and I both know that you're going to have to spend some time in jail for this thing, but hell, I meet guys on the outside who have killed people all the time. Nothing is forever, Jeff. We can work this thing out, explain it the best we can, and make some sense out of it. I'll stick with you, get you through it. Come on, Jeff, what do you say?"

I reached over and put my hand on Dahmer's shoulder as I spoke.

He seemed to know, even at this point, that he would never be free again. "For what I've done, I should be killed. I know they will never let me out again."

I interrupted. "Aw, come on, Jeff, I see this shit all the time. If we explain what happened, you never know. I'm sure there are some reasons for what you did. Let me help you."

"Not for what I've done, Pat, you don't know. I'll never get out!" he said with conviction. He left his seat and began to pace the small, cell-like room, wringing his hands. "I can't believe I was so stupid! I never thought I'd get caught like this! I was always so careful. I guess I just got drunk."

I could feel the intensity growing in his voice and became uncomfortable with him standing over me. I got up and gently guided him back to his chair by grasping his upper arms. I noted that although Dahmer was not a bulky man, his arms were rock solid.

"What do you mean, you just got drunk?"

Dahmer again slouched in his chair and stared at the floor.

"I always get drunk. If not for that, I would still be out there. I got drunk and just couldn't stick to my regular plan."

There was anger now in Dahmer's voice and as he looked up at me, I could see rage in his eyes. I didn't want him agitated again, so I asked about his drinking. "Do you think you have a drinking problem, Jeff?" Dahmer nodded in the affirmative.

I sighed. I had something here I could use.

Chapter 3

I was well aware of the devastating effects of alcohol. It had taken a heavy toll in my own life. At the time of the Dahmer case, it had been six years since I took my last drink and even then, I worked daily to keep it in check. I told Dahmer that booze and cops go together, and many an officer had fallen prey to "Old John Barley Corn." I confessed that I battle the demon of alcoholism myself and it almost cost me my job and my family. Dahmer looked at me intently as I continued, explaining that alcoholism was a disease that could be treated. I shared some of my own shameful drinking episodes and told him how my father, a retired Detroit police officer and alcoholic himself, had introduced me to Alcoholics Anonymous. It was through AA I kicked the habit. For a moment, I became self-conscious and was a little surprised at my honesty, but noticed Dahmer was much calmer and appeared to empathize with my story. I said that as a detective, I had investigated a lot of homicides where alcohol was a contributing factor leading to the killing and that without alcohol, chances were many murders would not have been committed in the first place.

"So you see, Jeff, you're not a monster. You're just another guy who fell victim to the bottle. Don't you see? Without the booze, who knows? You might not be sitting here right now."

Dahmer's mood continued to soften. He felt he did have a drinking problem, but he either couldn't or wouldn't stop drinking. His father had tried many times to get him help for his drinking and had even introduced him to AA, but he just didn't get it and always returned to the booze. I could see Dahmer's family was important to him and tried to use this to further the conversation, but he was adamant about keeping them out of it.

"Look, what I did, I did alone. I don't want them to know what I've done. I don't want them involved in this thing in any way!"

This second, slight admission encouraged me to continue. I explained that it would be impossible to shield them from his actions, stating that because of the nature of the crime, it would soon be a matter of public record. The media already knew something was up. I reminded Dahmer of the news cameras in front of his apartment as we left. Dahmer was stunned momentarily and sat straight up in his chair. The realization of the coming exposure of his deeds swept a wave of panic through him.

"Oh my God! What am I going to do? What will they think of me when they find out? Pat, I beg you, go get your gun and end this thing for me right now! I can't take this, please!" Dahmer slouched further into his chair and began to cry again.

I spent the next thirty minutes or so trying to calm him down. I emphasized the fact that alcohol played a big part in his crime, that he was a young man with a long life to live, and he was going to have to find a way to accept what he had done if he was to have any peace during his incarceration. Although still shaky, he seemed to internalize what I said and calmed down a bit. By this time, he had smoked an entire pack of cigarettes and downed several cups of coffee. He was beginning to sober up and I could tell he was buying what I was selling. It was almost like we were pals—not interrogator and suspect.

There was a faint knock at the door and it quickly opened. Lieutenant Dave Vahl, a newly made lieutenant, stuck his head inside. He was acting captain for that night, and asked if he could have a word with me. As I left the room, I assured Dahmer I would return with more coffee and cigarettes.

Once outside the interrogation room, Vahl asked, "Well, is he talking or not?"

I shook my head. "No, not yet, but I think he's almost ready to crack. Why, what's up?"

Vahl told me that Dubis and Harrell were afraid to continue their search of the apartment because of the boxes marked Caution: Muriatic Acid. They wondered if anything was explosive, or if they were in danger of blowing up. Vahl was worried about the legality of the search. Would Dahmer give his consent? I grabbed a fresh supply of smokes and coffee and returned to the room.

"Look, Jeff, my partner is going through your apartment right now, but he is concerned for his safety and the safety of the rest of the building. Is there anything in your apartment that can blow up?"

Dahmer's face began to show the familiar panic. "Did you search my room?"

I told him no, but explained we would get a search warrant in the morning.

"Don't you see, Jeff, it's important for it to seem like you're cooperating with me? Besides, if there is any danger, we should get to it now before the police or anyone else gets hurt. Come on, Jeff, work with me here. Let's not make this any worse than it has to be."

Dahmer leaned back slowly in his chair and became morose. "Go ahead and search. You're going to find out everything anyway. Don't worry, nothing will explode. It's just some chemicals; it won't hurt anybody as long as it stays in the boxes."

I quickly retrieved a "permission to search" document and had Dahmer sign it.

Taking the signed form back to Vahl, I said, "You can go ahead and search. Everything is cool, just some chemicals, no explosives, but leave everything in the boxes."

I returned to the room with more coffee, but before I could sit down, Dahmer looked up at me like a child afraid of a spanking and said, "Pat, when you find out what I've done, you'll hate me. Everyone will."

I placed my hand firmly on his shoulder as I sat down next to him. I explained that as a detective, I had seen many horrible things but it was not my job to hate, love, or judge anyone. I was simply a gatherer of facts, a seeker of the truth.

Dahmer shook his head and said, "You haven't seen the things I've done."

I told Dahmer about my Catholic upbringing, how I didn't feel it was my place to judge people, and only God had the right to judge. I told him that no matter what it was that he had done, it couldn't change my belief in that. I firmly believed there was a God, and that He was an all-knowing and all-forgiving God. I believed if we admitted our wrongs, changed our behavior, and led different lives, we would be forgiven. This idea seemed to appeal to Dahmer and his mood changed again, sparking a lengthy conversation about the existence of God, religion, and the hereafter.

Dahmer was brought up as a member of the Lutheran faith, but he hadn't been a practicing member of any religion in a long time. He stated that he wanted to believe in a loving, caring, and forgiving God, but felt it was too late for him. I could sense Dahmer was getting comfortable with me and getting out of himself. As a matter of fact, we were chatting and exchanging ideas like two old friends.

We finally agreed that there was a power in the universe greater than man, and that most people called that power God. Dahmer was obviously searching for a way out of his predicament, and he seemed to be picking my brain for the answers.

Finally, he said point-blank, "Pat, how will I ever be able to live with myself, or face my family again, after everyone finds out what I've done?"

I looked at his pleading face and told him that the first and most important step was to admit to God, himself, and another human the exact nature of his wrongs. He nodded as I continued. "Second, you must say and be truly sorry for your actions, ask forgiveness of God, yourself, and those you hurt." Dahmer searched my face as I spoke. "Third, you must make some kind of amends for your actions." I again reassured him I was not there to judge, only God had that power, and nothing he could tell me would change my mind about that. "Jeff, I know that I am here to get information from you, but I can be the other human being in that equation. Don't you see? You can start right now. What do you say?"

Dahmer looked at me with a sigh and said, "You know, Pat, this is nothing like I thought it would be." I asked what he meant, and he went on. "I guess I just never imagined that my interrogation would be like this. You're going to find out everything now anyways. I can't stop the news media, so I might as well tell you everything, but if I'm going to tell you, I should start at the beginning. Pat, when I tell you what I've done, you'll be famous." I chuckled at the statement, tore the filter off another cigarette, lit it, and inhaled.

I settled back in my chair. The nicotine and caffeine had begun to work on me and I was buzzing. I expected to hear about the head in the refrigerator, but instead Dahmer began to talk about an incident that occurred in Bath, Ohio, his hometown. It happened, he said, when he was just eighteen years old. I wanted to direct his attention back to the head in the refrigerator, but thought that since he was freely talking, I should just shut up and listen.

Dahmer said that when he was a senior in high school, his mother and father had gone through a messy divorce with lots of shouting and arguing. His mother packed up his younger brother, who was her favorite, and moved to

Wisconsin. She left him with his father, who was already seeing another woman and very busy with his job as a chemist. It was summer and he was alone a great deal. He mused that he was lonely most of the time and had not really made any friends in school. He described the place where he lived, stating it was a new and comfortable home located on a large wooded lot. One day, as he drove down a town back road, he picked up a hitchhiker, a white man in his late teens. He invited the young man to his house, saying there was plenty of beer and booze.

The young man accepted and upon arrival, they drank quite a bit of alcohol. They were getting a little drunk when the guy began to kiss Dahmer deeply by sticking his tongue in his mouth. Dahmer said this was not the first time he experienced gay tendencies. He knew he was attracted to men and had an earlier encounter when he was younger, making out with the neighbor boy in a tree house. He said, though, this was the first time he ever engaged in any true physical, intimate sexual activity, and he liked it.

He said that he felt this guy must really like him and he enjoyed the attention and the company. After a few hours of touching and kissing, the guy announced it was time for him to go home. Dahmer pleaded with him to stay until the morning, and told him he would not drive him anywhere until the next day. The guy became upset and said he would leave whether Jeff gave him a ride or not. As he tried to walk out the door, Jeff stopped him and a fight broke out. The guy was a little bigger than he was, and was getting the upper hand in the struggle as they rolled on the floor. The fight ended up in a corner of the room where a barbell set, given to Jeff by his father in an attempt to "make a man out of him," was located. Dahmer said he grabbed a loose hand bar without weights and struck the guy in the head with it. The fight ended right there, as he lay motionless.

Dahmer tried to wake the guy up, but even in his drunken stupor, it was apparent to him the hitchhiker was dead. At this point, I grabbed a sheet of blank statement forms and began to write.

"Go on, Jeff," I said.

Dahmer said he was surprised he didn't panic. Even in his intoxicated state, he realized he had to do something with the body. He dragged it outside to a remote wooded area of the property and hid it under some heavy brush. Dahmer was comfortable leaving the body there, as he had never seen anyone walking through their property. He left the body to rot for several weeks while he tried to figure out what to do with it.

One day while checking on the body, he noticed that most of the flesh had rotted away or been eaten by animals and insects. Handling the corpse, he noted that the bones appeared to be brittle and wood-like, so he decided to get his father's sledgehammer from the tool shed and smash the bones into small pieces. He was surprised how easily the skeleton came apart, smashing and splintering with each blow. Dahmer eventually spread the bones and remaining body parts all about the wooded lot, throwing them as he spun in a circle.

I noted that Dahmer appeared excited. He was out of his alcohol-induced state and buoyed by the massive amounts of coffee and cigarettes he had ingested. He said he had recurring feelings of remorse for the dead hitchhiker, but they were overshadowed by the excitement he felt when he remembered the physical sex and warmth of the guy's body. He was surprised that he didn't worry about being caught. He felt a strange amount of inner power, knowing he had done something no one else knew about.

His eyes stared off into space as he told the story, a strange look of contentment on his face.

"You mean to tell me that nobody ever found out about this guy?" I asked with disbelief.

"No," Dahmer replied, and said he regularly checked the local paper and watched TV news reports for information concerning him, but nothing surfaced. He said that he felt it was just an accident anyway; he didn't mean to kill the guy, so decided he should just forget it.

But he couldn't forget, and the haunting thought of the hitchhiker's bones spread all about his property caused him to seek solace in more alcohol. Besides that, his father was always gone and he was still lonely. The alcohol seemed to help, beer mostly, but any kind of liquor would do.

His drinking was becoming a problem, as his father often came home to find him drunk. In the autumn after his graduation, Dahmer enrolled at Ohio State University but spent most of his time drinking and drunk. He rarely went to class and never completed assignments. He was kicked out of school after the first term.

His father and he began to argue about his drinking and his father threatened to throw him out of the house. During one of their discussions, his father mentioned that the military might provide some direction to his life, thinking it would make a man out of him. Dahmer never wanted to become a soldier, but he loved his dad and wanted to please him; besides, he thought it would be an opportunity to see the world and maybe forget about the dismembered body in the woods. Jeff signed up for four years and received training as an army medic. Boot camp was difficult, but it challenged him mentally and physically. He began to feel good about himself and was too busy to think about his secret. He deployed to Germany and bunked with several other soldiers. After his shift, he had a lot of free time and began to frequent the beer gardens.

His drinking soon accelerated and eventually got him into trouble. The thought of the dismembered hitchhiker remained, and alcohol was the only way he knew to dull the pain. He was disciplined numerous times before receiving an honorable discharge.

After a short stint in Hollywood, Florida, where he drank away the remainder of his military pay, he returned to Ohio to live with his father and stepmother. By now, he drank every day, which caused a stir in the household. His father convinced him that he'd be better off if he moved in with his grandmother. She owned a large house in the Milwaukee area and lived all alone. He could be his own man there and look after his grandmother in her old age. Jeff felt this would be an opportunity for a new start and moved in with his grandma.

He recalled his grandma with obvious affection. She was very religious and had a strong Lutheran faith. She was kind and loving toward him, and encouraged him to accompany her to church on Sundays, as well as prayer meetings during the week. He thought this might be a way to dispel the memory of his murder and keep his drinking and growing sexual fantasies in check. He knew he was gay, but realized this was not acceptable to his grandma or the church they attended. He thought that by immersing himself in religion, he could turn the corner and live life anew.

I was engrossed in Jeff's story and had stopped writing. I listened intently but couldn't help but think this was all bullshit. We had talked for about three and a half hours; I needed a break and said so. Dahmer butted his cigarette and said he needed to use the bathroom. I directed him to a holding cell, and we took turns using the toilet. After returning him to the interrogation room, I went for more coffee and wondered how to steer him back to the head in the refrigerator. I found him patiently waiting for me, and more energized. As I took my chair, he continued his story.

"Pat, I think it all started again one day while I was reading a book at the Wauwatosa library." As Jeff sat quietly reading, a young man walked by and dropped a crumpled piece of paper in front of him. He opened it to find a note: *"If you want a blow job, meet me in the men's room."* He was shocked at the bluntness of the note, and began to feel he was wasting his time on his newfound "right living." He

GRILLING DAHMER | 53

wasn't fooling anybody; even this stranger knew he was gay, and thoughts of the dead body in Ohio remained.

Dahmer took a pull from his smoke and said, "This is when I decided to give in to my sexual urges."

He began by purchasing gay pornography and satisfied himself with masturbation. He frequented the taverns in Milwaukee and discovered a lively gay nightlife on the south side. He didn't own a vehicle and because of his excessive drinking, he always took a cab or used the bus. His grandma was asleep when he got home, so no mention was made of his intoxicated state. After learning the ins and outs of the gay bar scene, he found it surprisingly easy to meet and spend time with other gay men, often bringing them back to Grandma's basement for sex. Other times, he secured a hotel room downtown to take his one-night stands. Dahmer told me that one night, he met a young, slim, smooth white man at a local transgender hangout. After drinking all night, he invited him back to his room at the Ambassador Hotel[2], a cheap dive just west of downtown.

At this point, he stopped and looked at me earnestly. "This is the truth, Pat. I really don't know what happened. The last thing I remember, we were lying naked in bed. I must have blacked out because when I came to the next morning, the guy was dead. My hands and arms were sore and bruised, and his face and chest were black, blue, and bloody. It looked as though he had taken a terrible beating. I swear, Pat, I don't remember what I did, but I figure I must have beaten him to death in a drunken rage when he tried to leave. I quickly got up and cleaned myself off, trying to figure out what to do with the dead guy.

"As a matter of fact, it was Thanksgiving morning. I know because I had to get back to Grandma's for dinner, as my father, stepmother, and younger brother were all coming

---

2. The Ambassador Hotel has since seen a major remodel since the mid-1990s, and is once again a very impressive hotel.

into town for the holiday. I remember calling a cab and had him take me to the Grand Avenue Mall. It was open until noon that day. At a department store, I bought the biggest suitcase I could find. It was the kind that had the side zipper feature, making it easy to fill with large items; it came equipped with little rollers on the bottom. I took the cab back to the hotel and told the driver to wait. I went up to my room and carefully folded my dead roommate and all his belongings into the suitcase. I know it sounds strange, but the guy folded right into the thing, just like it was designed for him. The cab driver helped me carry everything out to the car and placed the suitcase into the trunk. Then he drove me to Grandma's house."

"Wait a minute, Jeff," I interrupted. "You mean to tell me you got this cab driver to help you load this body-filled suitcase into the trunk of his cab and he never asked you any questions?"

"Yes," he replied. "I thought he would, but he didn't. He was an Arabian guy and spoke in broken English. Actually, he was very helpful." After getting home, Dahmer took the suitcase down to the basement and put it in the fruit cellar. His family had already arrived, so he left the guy down there in the suitcase and enjoyed his Thanksgiving meal. "It was strange, Pat, but I wasn't even nervous. Nobody had the slightest idea what was going on."

The next day, his family left for Ohio, and Grandma went to a play with some friends. Jeff thought this was a good time to dispose of the body. He explained how he placed the dead man over the drainage grate on the basement floor. He used one of Grandma's butcher knives to cut the flesh and muscle from the body and into fist-sized chunks, allowing the blood to flow down the drain. He placed all the severed flesh into four or five double-wrapped garbage bags, believing that one large squishy bag might draw attention from city workers. He then got an old bed sheet from upstairs and wrapped the freshly skinned skeleton into it. He remembered seeing a sledgehammer in Grandma's garage and recalled how easily it had broken up the bones of his first victim. He pounded away at the bones engulfed in the sheet, smashing them into tiny pieces. He then wrapped the splintered bones into another double-wrapped garbage bag and placed everything into the large green city-owned dumpster behind the garage. He used a hose to wash the basement floor and poured some bleach down the grate, destroying any evidence of his work. Dahmer told me that in the weeks to come, he ventured out to the gay bars, picked up men, and brought them to Grandma's house for sex.

"It was easy and exciting, Pat, but when they left in the middle of the night, I always felt empty and alone. I hated that."

I studied Dahmer as he spoke. His eyes were constricted now and I noticed he was no longer drunk, but appeared high on all the caffeine and nicotine he had consumed. I matched him in the coffee and cigarettes department and felt a bit stoned myself. I wondered if Dahmer was taking me for a ride. His tale was incredible, but he recalled it now with such enthusiasm that I decided not to interrupt him. He had now, according to his story, killed two men without detection, but was haunted by his crimes. During the day, he fluctuated from the sheer terror of exposure to the exhilarating high of recalling his deeds. He stated that just thinking of these events gave him great pleasure and he masturbated as he did so. The fact that he had gotten away with it made him feel powerful, almost God-like. Nobody knew what happened; he had his little secret, his own little world that no one knew about, and he was in complete control. He began to feel that he couldn't be caught, that since he had already gotten away with killing two people, he could do it again. He wondered about the killing part of it. Was it subconscious, deliberate, or what? He decided to kill again, only this time, he'd plan the whole thing. Jeff said that he became aroused just thinking of what he planned to do and how he planned to do it.

Dahmer was a third-shift worker at a chocolate factory and found it difficult to sleep during the day. He remembered reading in the newspaper that President George H. Bush used a new drug called Halcion to help him sleep during the tension of the Gulf War. Jeff went to a doctor and convinced him to give him a prescription for the sleeping pill. It worked like a knockout drug, putting him to sleep quickly. He wondered how these pills might work on his weekend pickups.

"Why would you want an unconscious lover?" I asked.

Dahmer took a moment. "Well, Pat, most men that I have been with want to have anal sex with me. I enjoy all the touching and kissing. I love giving and getting oral sex, but anal sex is uncomfortable and hurts. I know it sounds selfish, but I thought if I could render them unconscious, I could spend hours pleasuring myself and not have to reciprocate."

He seemed earnest as he spoke, eyes now glazing over as if in a trance. He mechanically opened the third pack of smokes as he told of a night about two months after the Thanksgiving Day murder. He was at Club 219, a gay bar on South 2nd Street, where he met a young man. Dahmer remembered him as possibly Hispanic, young, long, lean, and attractive. He invited him to Grandma's for additional cocktails and sexual intimacy. They took a cab and once inside the house, Jeff fixed him a drink of rum, Coke, and about five crushed Halcion tablets. Within fifteen minutes of drinking the concoction, the young man was out cold. Dahmer had sex with him and said he enjoyed it immensely. He was pleasantly surprised to find out that even in his drug-induced state, the young man was able to obtain an erection as Dahmer kissed and fondled him for hours before falling asleep.

Upon waking, he noted the young man was still unconscious. He feared he might go to the police and tell them about being drugged, so Dahmer decided to kill him. This time, he used his bare hands to strangle the young man, keeping pressure on his throat until he could no longer see his chest rise and fall. He hid the body in the fruit cellar as before and left it there until the following day. Grandma never missed Sunday services or the fellowship afterward, and he felt this would be a good time to dispose of the body. Like clockwork, he said, Grandma left for church and he proceeded in the same fashion as before, carefully cutting the flesh from the young man's body as it lay over the drainage grate, smashing the skeleton with the sledgehammer, and throwing the entire mess, wrapped in four or five garbage bags, in the trash.

Dahmer's face looked incredulous as he said, "Pat, I almost couldn't believe what I did, yet just thinking about it gave me great pleasure."

He explained that he constantly checked the papers and TV newscasts for any kind of story regarding his victims, but nothing, not a word. Nobody even knew they were missing. This thought gave him a strange feeling of superiority and power. For the first time in his life, he was in complete control. He knew what he did was wrong, but there weren't any consequences, no punishment, no one to answer to. How could there be? No one knew but him.

As he spoke, he looked off into the distance as if he could actually feel the power. He figured the reason no one mentioned his deeds was because of the way in which they were committed. His victims were anonymously picked up in a bar or on the street, taken to a place that nobody knew about, killed, and disposed of—no evidence, no witnesses, no nothing. He mentioned how the feeling of power was intoxicating. His job at the chocolate factory was pretty mundane and ordinary, but at night, especially on the weekends, he could cruise the gay bars looking for a suitable victim. It was exciting, and he decided to kill again.

We sat in a thick cloud of smoke as he continued his tale, and I started to feel nauseated. *This couldn't be true,* I thought. Besides, I really needed a break and said so. I stepped into a nearby holding cell with a toilet and took a piss, then walked into the detective assembly for a breath of fresh air. Lt. Vahl approached me. He seemed excited and wanted to know if the suspect was forthcoming with any information.

"Yeah, he's talking," I said with exasperation. "But I don't know, Dave; I think this guy is full of shit. He's admitted to three homicides and wants to tell me more, but hasn't even mentioned the head in the refrigerator. He must be fucking nuts. I don't think he's going to help us."

Vahl could hardly control his voice as he squealed, "No, Pat, he's for real. I just got off the phone with Harrell. He's back at the scene and you won't believe what they're finding—four skulls and several frozen heads. There are human bones all over the joint. He's not fucking with you, Pat. Now get back in there and keep him talking!"

I dropped the coffee cup I had just filled, and it ran down my shoes. "You're kidding me? This guy is for real?" I could tell by the look on the young lieutenant's face that he was in earnest. I poured two more cups of coffee and returned to the interrogation room with renewed vigor. Now, pen in hand, I dutifully waited to record every word.

Dahmer noticed my change in attitude and asked if everything was all right.

"Oh yeah, I think I'm just a little revved up on all the coffee, that's all," I said.

He agreed and said he felt better about his situation, but wondered about something. I put my pen down and asked what he meant.

"Well, you know how we talked about admitting what I did and being truly sorry?" I nodded. "Well, you mentioned that amends would have to be made if I was to have any serenity in my life."

"That's what I believe. Why?" I said, wondering where he was going with this line of thought.

"Pat, how will I ever be able to make amends for what I did? I mean, I don't even know the names of these guys, and who should I make amends to?"

I sat back in my chair and thought for a moment. Dahmer sat upright, alert and inquisitive, like a college kid wrestling with a new concept and looking for a solution. Sipping my coffee, I tried to formulate an answer to satisfy him, and then it came to me.

"Jeff, you just answered your own question!"

"What do you mean, Pat?" Dahmer pulled a fresh smoke from the pack and lit it. His eyes searched mine.

"Well, Jeff, it would be a long, difficult task and quite time-consuming, but if we could identify each and every one of your victims, at least their families would know what happened to them." I noticed that he winced at the word *victim*, but I gained confidence with my statement as I spoke. "I'm sure you've heard about the anguish of the families whose sons went missing in action or taken as prisoners of war without notice in Vietnam?" I mentioned the black and white flags representing these men that still fly on flagpoles along with the Stars and Stripes. "If we could do that, Jeff, we could eliminate the uncertainty they faced in not knowing. They could finally put them to rest."

Dahmer seemed satisfied with this idea and studied the smoke as he exhaled. "I think you have something, Pat. It's the least I can do, maybe the only thing I can do."

Chapter 4

This acceptance of the "plan" brought a sense of relief to Dahmer, and it lightened the atmosphere in the room for the first time. He continued now with a sense of purpose, and we returned to his story.

He explained that about a month after the last incident, he was drinking heavily at a local gay joint that catered to the more outrageously dressed, many of them in drag, complete with makeup and heels. Dahmer enjoyed watching the campy activities and drag shows; however, he was only attracted to straight-looking guys. While there, he struck up a conversation with a young, smooth-skinned, muscularly built guy of mixed race. He was immediately attracted to him for he was young, alone, and on the hustle, like himself. He convinced this fellow to accompany him home to Grandma's for some after-bar activities. Once there, Dahmer prepared the Halcion concoction for him, and soon the young man was fast asleep. Dahmer spent the entire night having sex with his unconscious partner before strangling him to death in the early morning hours. He waited for Grandma to attend church that Sunday and disposed the body as before. Dahmer's mood seemed to change during this part of the story, and I sensed a bit of remorse about his actions. *Was this guy for real or what?*

"Pat, I was mixed up about the whole thing," Dahmer said, looking at me sincerely. "I loved having these guys with me and making love to them. Their warm bodies were under my complete control, but after killing them, I felt empty, and the task of disposing their bodies was no easy job. When it was done, I felt empty and alone." He explained that because of his unresolved feelings about the killing, he played it straight for a while by meeting guys and trying to have relationships with them. However, they always left in the morning, and he felt hollow and alone.

"Pat, no one really wanted a relationship. Just quick, anonymous sex and that's it. It was over in an instant and they were gone. I struggled with these feelings for about a year and felt lucky that I had not been found out. I continued to cruise the gay bars, picking up guys to have sex with, but it was shallow and unfulfilling."

He kept cruising the gay bar scene, keeping his dark secret while trying to find someone who would love him, but it didn't happen. The memory of his dead lovers stayed with him, and he masturbated daily thinking about the unrestrained sexual control he'd had over them. "I knew I was lucky to go undetected and I was afraid my luck would run out. I feared that I would be caught, but the allure of a warm body, one that would not leave at the end of the night, stayed with me, and I constantly thought about killing again."

Dahmer took another cigarette, inhaled deeply, and watched the smoke as it funneled from his nose.

By now, I had finished page one of the initial confession report. It was a skeleton account, not containing his musings or feelings, but an attempt to chronologically record days, dates, times, victims' physical appearances and eventual demises.

Dahmer seemed to settle in at this point and looked as if he enjoyed telling his shocking story. I had recorded three homicides and wondered where this would end. It was unbelievable, but I continued to write without interruption. Jeff struggled with his conscience for about a year, trying to find a lover who would stay with him, but to no avail.

"It was during this time that I met a guy at the bus stop outside Club 219. He was a young Mexican man; he was nice looking, long and lean, with jet-black hair and smooth skin. I wanted to be with him. He was alone, and I struck up a conversation as we waited for the bus. I invited him to come home with me and he jumped at the suggestion. On the trip to Grandma's, I decided I wouldn't let this one leave. Down in the basement, I gave him the Halcion-filled cocktail; I made love to him and kept him alive until morning. I heard my grandma moving around upstairs, so I strangled him and hid his body in the fruit cellar. After Grandma went to church, I dismembered and disposed of the body as before."

The fear of being found out was constant, but it excited him and he felt compelled to continue. The pleasure he experienced at every level—from the planning to the pickup to the complete control over someone—was overwhelming, and Dahmer enjoyed recalling these events over and over, usually masturbating as he did so.

"I knew that if I really was to have control over my situation, I needed my own apartment space. I rented a place not far from the chocolate factory. It was a cheap one-bedroom deal and I was there for about a year. I brought several men home for sexual activity, but I didn't kill them." He said he used to enjoy sitting in the food court of the Grand Avenue Mall, drinking beer and watching people.

"One day as I sat and drank, I saw this young Asian male. He was a little younger than I would have liked, but he was eager and willing. I offered him fifty bucks to come home with me and let me take some nude photographs of him. We drank some rum and Cokes and I took some Polaroids, but he was very young and not that developed sexually, so I didn't kill him. He must have told his parents because about two hours after he left, the police were at my door, found the photos I took, and arrested me. I thought this was it, that everything would come out, but the cops were only interested in the photos I took of the Asian kid and nothing else. I remember that my father was upset when I called from jail, but he got me a lawyer. I made a plea arrangement in court and was put on work release for about a year."

Dahmer thought it was weird to report to jail after work every night, but his army experience helped him play the game. He simply did whatever the corrections people wanted him to do, and he had no trouble at all. He moved to his apartment upon release. Within a week, he resumed his old habit of frequenting the gay bars. It had been a year since he had been able to do so, and he was glad to be free to roam and meet guys again. He was very relaxed when talking about his sexuality, and seemed to genuinely enjoy the gay nightlife. His mood was light and accepting as he recalled the campy activities and sexually charged atmosphere of the club scene.

I took stock of him as he spoke. Even in his disheveled condition, you could see he was a good-looking man, tall and well built. He was polite and well spoken, and it was easy to see how he could meet and engage his victims in conversation.

A knock at the door interrupted my thoughts. Lt. Vahl entered and said that the identification unit needed Dahmer's clothes. He handed me a county jail jumpsuit and left.

In all the excitement, I had forgotten about that. Dahmer looked at me quizzically, so I explained that they needed to check his clothes for forensic evidence. "You know, hair, blood, semen, fibers, like on TV."

As he stripped naked, I observed that he was physically cut and muscular, with no body fat and well-defined arms. I handed him the jail suit as I collected his clothing and he dutifully climbed into it, pulling the long zipper up the front. I stepped out to the hallway and met a police aide holding an evidence bag. He was grinning from ear to ear, obviously pleased he had a part in this investigation. I stuffed them in without saying a word and returned to find Dahmer sizing up his new wardrobe. After we settled into our seats, I began again.

"So nothing happened while you were on work release?"

He pulled another smoke from the pack and shook his head no. "But I remember that shortly after that, I came home one night after not meeting anyone that I found appealing, when I ran into this Black guy in front of the bookstore on 27th Street."

I immediately knew the place he was talking about—a newspaper and porno bookstore that catered to a sleazy late-night crowd. It was stuck in between taverns about two blocks from Dahmer's apartment. It was a late-night hangout for bums, sex workers of all genders, dope heads, and winos. The area was frequented at night by suburban white guys looking for a quick blow job.

Dahmer continued, "This guy was big, strong, and well built. He said he was a player and I asked him if he would come home with me. I told him I would give him fifty bucks if he let me perform oral sex on him and take some nude photos. I don't think he was gay, but he was really nice looking and his body was lean and attractive. One of the best-looking guys that I had ever met."

"What do you mean, you don't think he was gay?"

"Well, when we got back to my apartment, he took off his clothes and I began to go down on him, but he made it clear that he wasn't a fag and said that if I didn't pay him the money I offered, he would kick my ass and take everything I had."

"Wow, Jeff, weren't you afraid?" I asked, starting the second page of his confession.

"No, not really. He had already drunk the potion of Halcion and I knew that within minutes he would be mine. After he fell asleep, I made love to him for hours. I enjoyed him so much that I kept him alive a little longer than usual. In the morning, I could tell by his breathing that he was coming out of his drug-induced state, so I began to strangle him;

but the drug had worn off and as I choked him, he began to struggle with me. I panicked, realizing that I was not strong enough to overcome him, so I grabbed a knife and stabbed him in the carotid artery."

Dahmer noted that I had stopped writing. "I'm sure you know, Pat, that's the main artery that allows blood to flow to your brain." I acknowledged his gaze by nodding, and he continued. "After that, I took several nude photos of him in various positions and then cut up the body."

Dahmer described his knife as a special one he had purchased at a cutlery shop in the downtown mall just for this purpose. He discovered through trial and error at Grandma's that a good knife was mandatory for the job. It was a six-inch serrated blade with a black plastic contoured handle, and he kept it razor sharp. He placed the body in the bathtub, letting the blood flow down the drain as he severed the flesh from the corpse. He cut the flesh into small pieces and flushed them down the toilet. He told me that the skeletal remains were the most difficult to dispose of, so in preparation for his next kill, he purchased a large plastic garbage pail.

"I cut the cartilage and tendons at the joint and pulled the bones apart, placing them in the container. Then I covered them with several gallons of muriatic acid. That's what's in those boxes you asked about," Dahmer said.

He explained that after a few days in the acid, the human remains became like a mush and he could easily flush it down the toilet. This eliminated placing the discarded body in the trash and lessened his chances of discovery. "I knew now that I was in it till the end, and this one was so sexually satisfying that I began to feel remorse that it was over so soon. It seemed a shame to get rid of the whole body, so I decided to keep his head."

I looked up from my report to catch his steely gaze. He sat motionless, staring, watching for some sign of disapproval. Finding none, he relaxed again, butting his cigarette as he pulled another from the pack.

"Yeah, Jeff, what's with the skulls?" I told him the lieutenant had said they found skulls and heads along with other body parts all over his apartment. He seemed eager to continue.

"Well, I wanted to keep those guys with me," he said nonchalantly. "But after a while, they gave off an awful smell; as a matter of fact, the smell was a problem that I constantly had to deal with. So I bought a large ten-gallon soup kettle at the mall and began boiling the heads in a solution of hot water and cleansing soaps. After being in the solution for about an hour, the hair and flesh just boiled right off and left the skull. I kept the finished ones in my closet. Any clothing, jewelry, identification, or other property of the guys that I brought home, I cut up and threw out."

He continued. About a month after this incident, he met a Black man while walking on Wisconsin Avenue. The two talked for a while, and Dahmer asked him back to his apartment for sex and drinks. Of course, he used the sleeping pills to drug him, had sex with him, killed him, and disposed of the body as before.

I observed that Dahmer's voice tone changed. It was becoming emotionless and monotonous. The nonverbal cues were gone, and his eyes glazed slightly. I did not know it at the time, but this was to become the norm whenever he described his deeds. I finished writing his last statement and motioned for him to go on.

"About a month later, I was having cocktails at a place called La Cage, a gay dance club in a relatively straight neighborhood. I met a tall Black man and convinced him to come home with me. I was out of Halcion, so we drank into the early morning hours until the guy passed out. I just lay with him for a while listening to his heart, feeling his chest rise and fall. Then I had oral and anal sex with him and decided to kill him. So I strangled him. I remember I didn't keep any part of that guy. He wasn't that good looking and I had time constraints."

I stopped writing and looked up from my notes. "What do you mean, time constraints?"

Dahmer explained that most of his pickups occurred on Friday nights. That way, he could keep the body around and have sex with it until Sunday evening, when he cut up the body. The trash men came early Monday morning and took away everything. At times like this, he just cut up the body into fillets to throw out and placed the disarticulated skeleton into the rubber trash container with the acid until it became sludgy and then he could flush it down the toilet.

The confession was starting to come together. It was sketchy and sparse, but I felt the judge would get the general idea. I leaned back in my seat as if to take a break and Dahmer did the same, taking a slow drag off his cigarette. He held the nicotine-filled smoke in longer than usual as he studied my face.

"Pat, this next guy I almost got caught with." I motioned for him to go on. "I met this really nice-looking Asian guy one afternoon while I was at the mall downtown. I like going to the mall. There are always so many different types of people, all races and ethnic backgrounds, every size and shape."

It was obvious that Dahmer liked variety and even seemed to like people. I wondered about him. One moment he seemed like a regular, likable person, and the next, he coldly recited a litany of horror. I picked up my pen and returned to my notes.

"I was getting my knife sharpened at the cutlery shop in the mall," he said. It was where he originally bought the knife. The store had a policy of keeping your purchase razor sharp, so he occasionally brought it back in for a free sharpening.

"Anyway, it was that day that I met this Asian male. He was alone and really nice looking, so I struck up a conversation with him. Well, I offered him fifty bucks to come home with me and let me take some photos. I told him that there was liquor at my place and indicated that I was sexually attracted to him. He was eager and cooperative so we took the bus to my apartment. Once there, I gave him some money and he posed for several photos. I offered him the rum and Coke Halcion-laced solution and he drank it down quickly. We continued to drink until he passed out, and then I made love to him for the rest of the afternoon and early evening. I must have fallen asleep, because when I woke up it was late. I checked on the guy. He was out cold, still breathing heavily from the Halcion. I was out of beer and walked around the corner for another six-pack but after I got to the tavern, I started drinking and before I knew it, it was closing time. I grabbed my six-pack and began walking home. As I neared my apartment, I noted a lot of commotion, people milling about, police officers, and a fire engine. I decided to see what was going on, so I came closer. I was surprised to see they were all standing around the Asian guy from my apartment. He was standing there naked, speaking in some kind of Asian dialect. At first, I panicked and kept walking, but I could see that he was so messed up on the Halcion and booze that he didn't know who or where he was.

"I don't really know why, Pat, but I strode into the middle of everyone and announced he was my lover. I said that we lived together at Oxford and had been drinking heavily all day, and added that this was not the first time he left the apartment naked while intoxicated. I explained that I had gone out to buy some more beer and showed them the six-pack. I asked them to give him a break and let me take him back home. The firemen seemed to buy the story and drove off, but the police began to ask more questions and insisted that I take them to my apartment to discuss the matter further. I was nervous but felt confident; besides, I had no other choice. One cop took him by the arm and he followed, almost zombie-like.

"I led them to my apartment and once inside, I showed them the photos I had taken, and his clothes neatly folded on the arm of my couch. The cops kept trying to question the guy but he was still talking gibberish and could not answer any of their questions, so I told them his name was Chuck Moung and gave them a phony date of birth. I handed them my identification and they wrote everything down in their little notebooks. They seemed perturbed and talked about writing us some tickets for disorderly conduct or something. One of them said they should take us both in for all the trouble we had given them.

"As they were discussing what to do, another call came over their radio. It must have been important because they decided to give us a warning and advised me to keep my drunken partner inside. I was relieved. I had fooled the authorities and it gave me a tremendous feeling. I felt powerful, in control, almost invincible. After the officers left, I gave the guy another Halcion-filled drink and he soon passed out. I was still nervous about the narrow escape with the cops, so I strangled him and disposed of his body."

The story left me in disbelief. "Come on, Jeff. Are you telling me these police officers brought him back to your apartment that night and left him there?"

Dahmer could tell by my vocal inflection that his account distressed me. "Yes, Pat, that's what happened. Why, is there a problem?"

"No. Not really," I said, returning to my normal voice. "But this is important, Jeff. Can you remember when or what time of year this was?"

He paused and sipped his coffee. "Well, let me think. I have been trying to tell you things in the order they occurred. I believe this happened around May or June of this year."

I queried him further, but he felt sure about the time. I later learned, as we worked to identify each of his victims, that Dahmer had an incredible memory for the times and dates of his exploits.

I stood up and mentioned that I needed a break. I noted that we were out of cigarettes as well. I walked to my desk and called a clerk at District Three. I asked her to check for any calls to the area of 25th and State after midnight during the months of May and June of this year. Within minutes, she returned and announced that a squad was sent to investigate a "man down, Asian male" in the vicinity of 25th and State on Monday, May 27. She added that the disposition was marked advised. I told her that I needed the names and phone numbers of the officers that responded. She looked at squad assignments for that day and provided me with the information. I was familiar with the names; they were both good officers, real go-getters who frequently covered me when making a house arrest for homicide suspects. I called the senior of the two and explained that we had a problem I could not fix. I needed him to contact his partner and come down to the detective bureau immediately.

Chapter 5

I returned to the interrogation room with a fresh pack of smokes and two more cups of coffee. Dahmer anxiously waited for me.

"Is everything all right?" he asked, looking at me with concern. I handed him the pack of cigarettes and set the two coffees down.

"Yeah. No problem. How about you? Do you need a break? Are you hungry?" He shook his head and opened the smokes. I took up my pen again and he continued.

He found out there was an area called Boystown in Chicago, with many nightclubs that catered to the gay population. On occasion, Dahmer took the bus there Friday nights after work. About a month after the incident with the young Asian, he sat at a bar called Carol's. There, he met a light-skinned Black man. During their conversation, he learned the man was also Jewish and Puerto Rican. He was personable and very good looking, so Dahmer convinced him to take the bus back to Milwaukee.

"We spent the whole weekend together, almost like a real relationship, Pat. We made love and went to the mall, shopped for food to make dinner and everything. For a while, I thought that maybe this one would stay." Dahmer lowered his head and sighed as he continued.

"But then Sunday night came. He said he had a job in Chicago and had to catch the bus in the morning. I knew it couldn't last, so I made him the Halcion drink that night before we went to bed. After he passed out, I had oral and anal sex with him and killed him, just like the others."

Dahmer pulled a smoke from the open pack as I completed writing down his last statement.

"A week or so later, I met this guy while I was waiting for the bus on Wisconsin Avenue. After striking up a conversation, I offered him fifty bucks to come back to my place for sex and drinks. He accepted and we took the bus to my apartment. Once at my place, I made the Halcion drink for him, and after he passed out, I made love to him and disposed of the body in the usual way."

At this point, he became methodical in his descriptions and explanations, almost monotonous. He quickly rattled off several more homicides in similar fashion, staring straight ahead as he spoke, motionless. I wrote without interruption, hoping I could fill in the blanks later, but I kept wondering about the head in the refrigerator. By now, he had told me about fourteen homicides and still no mention of it. I couldn't erase the picture in my mind of the head, staring back at me with its surprised look.

Dahmer interrupted my thoughts, as if he knew what I was thinking. "I suppose you're wondering about the guy in the refrigerator?" There was feeling in his voice again and he looked at me with a slight smile.

"Well, I was starting to think that maybe you forgot about him," I replied, relieved that we might be coming to the end.

"I met him a few days before my arrest. That's why he looked so fresh." Dahmer kept the heads in the refrigerator to preserve them for as long as they appeared lifelike. "He was extremely handsome, the nicest looking man I had ever met. I think he was a model or something, because he showed me some pictures of himself in professional poses.

"He was smooth-skinned and muscular, and more than willing to come home with me for cocktails and sex. I took my time with this one. Just looking at him gave me great pleasure. I hated to kill him and tried to keep as much of him as possible." Dahmer seemed genuinely depressed as he talked about this, slouching in his seat. "I even kept his ID. You'll find it in my bedroom drawer."

He sat and smoked deliberately, as if he were finished with his recital. I directed him to tonight's activities. "Tell me about tonight, Jeff. What happened?"

He sat up again and appeared eager to tell me. "Well, Pat, it's weird. I was out of Halcion, but I still wanted to be with someone warm and alive. I went to the mall downtown and started drinking at a pub on the third floor. I met the guy there; we had a few beers together and talked. I figured that he was a willing prospect, so I offered him fifty bucks to come back to my apartment and let me take some pictures of him in the nude. He agreed. I figured I'd ply him with booze until he passed out and then I would kill him, but this guy could really drink. I was getting drunk and knew that if I wanted him, I would have to try something else. I asked him to let me take some bondage pictures of him, thinking that if I could handcuff him behind his back, he would be mine. Then I could knock him out by hitting him over the head or something, I don't know. I was drunk and not thinking straight. Anyway, I got one cuff on him but he wouldn't let me cuff his other hand. I got mad and tried to force his other arm behind his back and into the handcuffs. We began to struggle, nothing big, just some wrestling around on the floor. Even though he was a little guy, I couldn't get the best of him, so I grabbed the knife to stab him, but he got loose and ran out the door.

"I was too drunk to chase him. What else could I do? I don't really remember what happened next. I think I passed out for a while until I heard a knock at the door. It was two big policemen and they were asking for the handcuff key. I could see the little Black guy behind them. He had the one cuff on and said that he didn't want to prosecute—he just wanted the cuffs off. I fumbled around but couldn't find the damn key. The cops were getting impatient waiting at the door, so they entered and began to look around. I think one of them found my Polaroids and said something to his partner. The fat cop walked over to the refrigerator and started to open it, and I knew this was it, so I tried to stop him. I'm not sure what happened next; I just know that I got the shit beat out of me. I tried to fight back but it didn't seem to faze them, and now here I am with you, Pat."

Dahmer settled back in his chair and took a long, satisfying drag. We had been at it for a little over five hours by now and the cigarettes and coffee had given me a queasy feeling in my stomach. I shuffled the five-page confession and placed it in front of him. "Take a look at it, Jeff. If you agree with it, sign your name."

He picked up the last page and quickly signed without looking at it. I urged him to take his time and read it over completely, but he responded, "Why, Pat? You got me. It's over. I'm just going to have to learn to live with what I've done. It's funny, but in a way, I almost feel relieved. You know, this is nothing like I thought it would be."

I gathered the confession and stood up. "What do you mean?"

He paused and looked at me. He was relaxed and smiling. "I don't know, I just never thought my interrogation would go like this."

There was a knock at the door and I opened it to find a police aide. "Pat, those coppers you asked for are here."

I excused myself and stepped into the hallway. There stood the senior squad man with a worried look on his face. Unbeknownst to me, local news organizations had covered the story since the early morning. A virtual media circus had sprung up outside Dahmer's apartment complex to record the massive police presence.

Some information leaked to the press, and rumors of what detectives found were already circulating.

"What's up, Pat?" asked the senior squad cop.

I thanked him for coming down so quickly and asked if he punched in. He nodded and asked what I needed. I told him the story about the naked Asian male on 25th and State. His eyes grew wide, and I could tell he recalled the incident.

"He says he killed the guy after you left."

My comment stunned the officer, and the color faded from his face. I assured him that he was not in any trouble as far as I was concerned, but I needed him and his partner to file detailed supplemental accounts of everything they did and said that evening. I advised him to say nothing to anyone not involved in the incident. He acknowledged that, and I returned to the interrogation room to find Dahmer smoking leisurely. I advised Jeff that I needed to give his statement to the lieutenant and I would return.

As I entered the detective assembly, a host of my brother and sister detectives engulfed me. Many were called in to assist and some, hearing the reports on TV, voluntarily offered to help. There were even a few who cancelled vacations and days off, hoping to catch a portion of the investigation. The place was jumping with personnel from all three shifts, and they pounded me with questions. Some patted me on the back; others openly stated that I was lucky to get the assignment. I walked to my desk and sat down, a little surprised at all the attention.

As usual, there was a lot of jocularity. Some of my colleagues opined I must have let the guy suck my cock in order to establish rapport. They chomped on their morning hard rolls and as I sat there and enjoyed the camaraderie.

Lieutenant Vahl waded through the crowd and motioned for me to follow him. As I walked into the captain's office, I noticed Dennis Murphy, an old, day shift homicide detective, whose athletic build and boyish face didn't scan with the number of years he had on the job. Murphy was the top interrogator of the unit and had vast experience in homicide investigations. He was especially known for his attention to detail. Vahl told me that Murphy would take it from here.

He said the day shift lieutenant feared my inexperience might jeopardize the case. I was a little surprised they would switch interrogators, an unusual move, but I was bushed.

"You can have it. I've been talking to this goof for the last seven hours." I shared the confession with Murphy and mentioned Dahmer's affinity for cigarettes. "A real nicotine freak," I said.

A knock at the door revealed a uniformed officer. "Pat, that Dahmer guy is pounding on the interrogation room door and asking for you."

Vahl looked at Murphy and said, "You're up."

As Murphy left, I walked to the window overlooking State Street. I couldn't believe my eyes. There must have been fifteen different TV news vans and trucks. Satellite dishes, wires, and technicians were everywhere.

"I know," Vahl answered my thoughts. "They've been coming in a steady stream since the case broke."

The door opened and in walked Harrell. His sleeves were rolled up, his tie hung loose, and his shirt was covered with perspiration stains. He puffed on his trademark cigar and looked as though he had done some heavy lifting.

"Hey, kid, I heard you did a nice job. Where is he? I thought I told you to stay with him until I got back!" Vahl sheepishly advised him of the switch. Harrell exploded. "What the fuck are you talking about? You don't switch interrogators!" Vahl explained he was ordered to do so.

"Who?" Harrell bellowed. Vahl told him of the day lieutenant's concerns and Harrell stormed out of the room. He must have found his day shift counterpart in the corridor, because even with the door closed, I could hear Harrell chastising him. "Who the fuck do you think you are? This is my case! You don't change interrogators in the middle of an investigation!"

I looked at Vahl and could tell he was embarrassed. There was no love lost between Harrell and the day lieutenant. The voices muffled slightly, and I could tell others had

GRILLING DAHMER | 77

joined in the discussion. Again, the door opened and Captain Don Domagalski walked in, followed by the two bickering lieutenants. Domagalski was a crusty old copper with a face red from hard drinking, smoking, and homicide investigations.

"Good job, kid!" he said with a graveled voice as he sat in the plush leather chair behind his desk. Before Harrell could lodge another complaint, Murphy walked in. "What's up, Murphy?"

"The guy won't talk; he won't even look at me," said Murphy.

Harrell, feeling vindicated, glared at his counterpart. Domagalski wearily rubbed his face with both hands before speaking. "Pat, get back in there. I don't know what's going to happen, but you're going to need help on this. See if you can get him to cooperate with both of you."

I walked back to the interrogation room and found Dahmer pacing back and forth. "Hey, Jeff, they said you wanted to talk to me about something?"

Dahmer stared at me. "Who was that guy? You said that you would stick with me! What's going on?" There was an uneasy feeling in the room that had not been there since the early hours of the morning.

I sat down and explained the case was too big for me to handle alone. "Look, Jeff, this guy is all right. I've worked with him a long time and he's totally cool. I told him what we've been talking about and he's not freaked out or anything. He's been around a long time and has a lot more experience with this sort of thing. I really feel he can help us tell the story and put it in a way that will make the case better for you. Really, Jeff, it's the best thing all around. I have to have a partner working with me anyway, and this is the guy I would pick. You're going to have trust me on this, Jeff. I'm telling you it's all right, he's okay."

Dahmer looked up at me with pleading eyes. "But, Pat, you said that I would only have to talk with you. I only want to talk to you. I trust you. You're not like any cop I ever met. Why do we have to have someone else with us? Will I have to start all over again?"

I pulled my chair closer. "No, Jeff. He's just going to help us prepare the case. I need him. Jeff, can't you see that I can't do it all myself? If we are going to present this case properly, we are going to need someone that is experienced. I've known this guy for years, Jeff, and I trust him. He's an understanding guy. He won't judge you or treat you any differently than I do. Come on, Jeff, what do you say? Can I let him back into the room?"

Dahmer seemed to accept the situation and nodded reluctantly. I opened the interrogation room door, and there stood Murphy with three fresh cups of coffee and an unopened pack of Camel straights. Dahmer studied the pack of Camels and said he had never tried one before.

"Well, Jeff, let's have one!" We each took one and lit up. I was really flying now as the fine Turkish tobacco swirled around my head. "Now, what was it that you wanted to tell me so badly?"

The three of us sat around the small metal table in silence for a moment before he spoke. "I forgot to tell you about two more. I don't know how I forgot about them. I guess I was pretty drunk when we started. Anyway, if I'm going to come clean, I should tell you everything."

Murphy grabbed a supplemental report, and Dahmer studied him as he began to write. Murphy was an old pro and no look or sense of disgust would cross his face. He had dealt with child killers and thugs of the worst kind during his career. Noting his indifference, Dahmer continued. He began to tell us the details of the remaining two homicides. I sat quietly, listening, relieved to share the burden of such a confession with another. I put my feet up on the table and took an exaggerated puff of my Camel straight, causing Dahmer to look at me and smile.

I was relaxed and it was evident from Dahmer's gaze that he had developed affection for me. A knock at the door brought me to my feet. Opening it, I saw Harrell. He looked tired and worn but still smoked that black cigar. He motioned for me to come outside.

"How did you do, kid?" he asked.

"Okay. He's telling us about two more homicides. Can you believe it? He says he forgot! Hey, what did you find?"

Harrell shook his head and sighed. "You wouldn't believe it, kid. A fucking nuthouse, a chamber of horrors this guy was running. What kind of freak do we have in there?"

I was deliberate in describing the suspect and secretly glad that I was not part of the search team going through the apartment, knowing the gruesome findings would have colored my attitude and the way I interrogated him. Although the human genome had been broken down, at that time, DNA was still in its early stages and not yet routinely used for identification purposes in law enforcement. We needed Dahmer's complete cooperation and a little luck if we had any chance of identifying his victims. The bond built between us during the initial interrogation would continue to grow in the coming weeks and was invaluable in keeping him on task.

Harrell continued, "We found a bunch of heads and skulls but three of them look as if they have been altered in some way. Ask that crazy fuck about the skulls. Are they real or what?"

I returned to find Dahmer and Murphy sitting in strained silence.

"Hey, Jeff, the guys are going through your apartment and they are finding all sorts of things that they don't understand. Can you help us out with some of it?" Dahmer seemed glad that I was back in the room and nodded his head. "They found these three skulls that look different from the rest."

"Oh those," Dahmer said. "They were some of the first ones I decided to keep. I wanted to keep part of them and decided on the skulls, but I was afraid someone might see them and detect what I was doing, so I bought some spray paint, a kind of fake granite color, and painted them to look like fakes. I wanted the skulls to look like Halloween decorations. One I did in gray, one in green, and the other in a kind of brown-beige color. Those were the only shades available so I thought I would try each one. I did those when I was living at my grandma's because I feared that she might accidentally stumble on them while I was out of the house. After I got my own apartment, I had a security system, so I no longer had to paint the skulls anymore."

As he told us this, I noted a slight change in his demeanor. He had again slipped into the deliberate, almost robot-like tone I had encountered earlier in the interrogation. This became the norm for the remainder of our time together whenever Dahmer explained his murderous deeds. It was only in between questioning, when we relaxed and conversed, that his emotions and gestures returned. Murphy continued to write, not looking up or asking any questions. He seemed to understand that Dahmer was not comfortable with him yet, and savvy enough not to force it. I asked about the apartment and stated that I was surprised to see so many cleaning agents.

"Yeah, that was a constant problem for me. The smell was awful. I tried to keep the bodies with me for as long as I could after I killed them, but after a day or so, they started to rot, depending on the temperature of my room. Summers were really the worst because I didn't have air conditioning. When you fillet the flesh from the body, it gives off a horrendous odor. Several times the neighbors complained of the smell, so I constantly had air fresheners around. I even kept a fan going, using it as an exhaust for the fumes, pointing it out the bedroom window."

I interrupted, "I suppose all the cleansers I saw were used to clean up the blood?"

Dahmer shook his head no and said that cutting up the bodies was a dirty job, but after a while, he had it down to a science. "I cut the body open in the bathtub and let gravity work to draw the blood down the drain."

As he spoke, I recalled the many autopsies I had witnessed and remembered how no blood splattered as the medical examiner did his work.

Dahmer continued. He purchased a ten-gallon soup kettle that could easily hold a human skull. He boiled the heads in a solution of Soilex and water for about an hour. This effectively boiled off the flesh and hair, leaving slurry in the kettle that could be flushed down the toilet. After that, he used a large serving spoon to dig out the brain matter, which became a mushy substance during the boiling process. He explained that if you severed the head correctly at the base of the neck, you could easily fit a serving spoon in the inner cavity, like cleaning out a cantaloupe. Then he placed the skull in another solution of Soilex and boiled it an hour or so, finishing it off in the oven on low heat for about twenty minutes, leaving it bone dry. He also used the kettle to boil flesh and sinew from other body parts he had decided to keep with him. He described the process almost mechanically, studying our faces as he spoke. He seemed to be looking for some sign of disdain or horror from us, but he found none.

"Pat, remember the one I had to kill with the knife? Well, I decided to keep all of him. I filleted his flesh, muscles, and tendons, and then boiled his whole skeleton." He seemed almost proud of his accomplishment.

"But how did you fit that big guy into a ten-gallon kettle?" I asked in disbelief.

He looked at me, detecting the air of incredulousness, but said simply, "Pat, it's not hard if you know what you're doing. If you cut the joints properly, slicing the cartilage and tendons, the bones come right apart. After boiling and drying all the parts, I could place the entire body back together if I wanted to, and I did on occasion. Sometimes, after putting him back together on the floor of my apartment, I relived mentally what happened with him. I fantasized the whole scenario and got really turned on, and masturbated as I fondled his bones. I thought that this would be enough to satisfy me, and that maybe I wouldn't have to kill again; but after about a month or so, the urge to have another warm, live human being under my complete control returned. It consumed me, and soon I was out looking to kill again."

Dahmer sat back in his chair. I checked my watch. It was two o'clock, and I had been working on this for fourteen hours. I was burnt out. All three of us sat in silence as Murphy finished writing the last statement, and, clearing his throat, spoke for the first time. "Are there any more incidents that you want to tell us about?"

Dahmer shook his head no. At this point, I recalled the still-unsolved homicide at the Oxford Apartments.

"What about the Black man who was killed on the third floor of your building?"

Dahmer appeared to perk up a bit at this question. "Pat, that's really weird. I remember that day very well. It was about a month ago. I answered a knock at my door and there was a detective. I almost panicked, figuring, *this is it, I'm caught,* but he started asking me questions about some guy on the third floor. The name was not familiar and to tell you the truth, I wasn't involved with anyone in the building. I tried to be pleasant and polite, but I never tried to pick up anyone where I lived; too risky. I was always very careful when I picked someone up."

Again, Murphy asked if he had told us everything. Dahmer seemed exasperated by the question and looked at me plaintively.

"Pat, honest, I told you everything I did. Why would I lie now? After everything I told you, why would I not admit to more if I did them?" His face showed a sincerity I had not seen since he broke down and began to tell me of his crimes many hours ago.

I decided not to pressure him anymore. "I need a hot meal and a few hours' sleep," I said, stretching my six-foot-seven-inch frame in front of Dahmer, who watched me attentively.

Murphy took note of his gaze and winked at me as he shuffled his reports. Dahmer stated that he too was done in and needed some sleep.

"Will I have to go to the bullpen now?" he inquired with a look of worry on his face.

"No. No way, brother, you get the special treatment now, Jeff," I said as I stood. "I told you I would take care of you, pal. It's not over yet. Remember, we've got work to do. We're all in this together, Jeff; you, me, and Dennis." Murphy nodded in agreement, and we led him to the prisoner elevator and up to the fifth-floor jail.

After talking with the sergeant in charge, we placed him in an isolation unit located in the back of the cellblock. A young officer was assigned to sit outside his cell. Dahmer said that it wasn't necessary because he no longer wanted to kill himself. I reassured him this was just procedure; this was not just to keep him from harming himself, but also to keep other prisoners and police officers away from him.

Pointing to the rookie cop, I said, "This guy won't bother you, Jeff. I'm going home for a few hours' sleep. I suggest that you do the same." I noted a forlorn look on his face as the cell door slammed. He gestured a sad goodbye as Murphy and I walked back to the elevator.

As soon as the elevator door closed, Murphy slapped me on the back and said, "Good job, Pat, that fucking freak loves you. Did you let him suck your cock or what?" I looked at Murphy, who grinned from ear to ear. "You'll be famous for this, kid; this is the biggest thing ever to hit Milwaukee!"

We walked to my desk in the back of the detective assembly and as we sat down, a throng of older day shift dicks surrounded us. An ancient burglary detective, about forty pounds overweight, wearing an outdated plaid suit jacket and smoking a pipe, quipped, "Well, kid, you went from a zero to a hero in just one night. Yesterday you were nobody and today you're top dog."

I was exhausted and felt a bit overwhelmed with all the attention. All I could do was sit and smile. This was unusual, for I always had a quick comeback or smartass reply to the playful ribbing that occurred constantly in the detective bureau. Besides, I was done in; I just wanted to call in my reports and go home. It had been an exciting but draining night. I sat at my desk and wondered how I would call in my reports with all the commotion going on around me. Suddenly, the sea of wrinkled-faced detectives parted, and I heard the graveled voice of Captain Domagalski.

"All right, you assholes, get back to work! Who called this coffee klatch anyway?" The older dicks scattered back to their desks, leaving Murphy and me alone with the captain. "That was a nice bit of work, Kennedy. Come on, you two, let's go back to the inspector's office where we can have a bit of privacy."

The three of us walked toward the front of the detective assembly and into the inspector's office—a place most detectives entered only if they were in some kind of trouble.

Once inside the captain asked, "Well, how many homicides do we have?"

"Seventeen," I answered.

"Yeah, but one of them happened in Ohio," Murphy added.

"Seventeen, eh," Domagalski said, biting down on a fresh, hard roll. "You know, Pat, your partner and Harrell have recovered all kinds of body parts and unexplainable evidence from that freak's apartment. They took everything.

There's nothing left but the floor and walls. Do you think he'll help us identify the bodies?"

Murphy interrupted. "Are you kidding, Cap? That fucker loves Pat. You should see the way he looks at him! I think he wants to do him!"

I slouched in my seat, trying to remember Dahmer's gaze and wondering if Murphy was right. Finally, I spoke up. "I don't know, Cap. He seems to want to cooperate. We talked about making amends to the dead victims' families by identifying everyone."

"How in the fuck did that conversation come up?" the captain asked, scratching his head.

I continued, "Hell, Cap, we talked about everything under the sun before the guy crapped out. I tried to tie it in with MIAs in Vietnam. He seemed to bite on that idea and wants to help us."

"Well, good," Domagalski said. "Because we got a big job ahead of us. Now look, you two, the press is all over this story. I don't want you talking to anyone. From now on, Kennedy, you're working days. You will call in all your reports from this office. I have already assigned steno girls to the case; as soon as they are typed, you review and bring them to me. No copies until I have everything. Do you understand?"

Murphy and I both nodded as the captain walked out and closed the door. "Well, kid, welcome to the day shift. You finally made the big time."

I smiled and picked up the phone to dictate my report, wondering if this was really such a good thing after all.

"Hello, this is Gloria," the voice at the other end of the line answered. "I guess we will be working together awhile."

"I guess so," I said in response.

I dictated my report from the mass of notes I had taken, reading verbatim from the original confession. When I was done, I walked to Domagalski's office with the finished reports.

"All right, Pat," the captain said. "Go home and get some rest. I'll see you in the morning. You've got your work cut out for you."

I took the elevator to the ground floor and walked into the blazing afternoon sun. Personnel from every radio and TV station in the city and half the state were outside the police administration building. I was stunned as a reporter approached me and called me by name, asking if there was anything I could tell her about the case. I had watched this petite little blonde on the tube many times while dressing for work at night.

"No comment," I said, wading past TV cameras, technicians, and reporters to the parking lot.

I smiled to myself, thinking how easily the phrase had come out of my mouth. Like a detective in one of those classic murder mysteries I enjoyed watching so much late at night. I had worked up a sweat just walking to my car and the air conditioning felt good as I took my time driving home.

Chapter 6

I walked in the front door and noticed my wife sitting on the couch. She was wide awake; her eyes bugged out and a worried look on her face.

"I just saw you on TV! Please tell me you're not involved in this thing?" The television was on as the camera panned the front of Dahmer's apartment building. Some talking head questioned a neighbor, asking if there was anything he could tell them about the man who lived next door.

"This is unbelievable," I said as I walked down the hallway. I put away my revolver and cuffs and hung up my suit. Standing in the bedroom in my underwear and socks, I answered my wife. "Involved? Are you kidding? I was there right from the beginning. I was there for the arrest. I mean, I am the man. I've been with that nut all night; hell, I took his confession. And that's not all; I've been assigned to the day shift until this whole thing is over. I can hardly believe it myself." I looked at her as she put her head in her hands and sighed.

"What's wrong?" I asked.

She had a panicked look now. "That's all that's been on TV! Is it true what they are saying about this monster? That they found severed heads in his refrigerator and that he might be involved in several murders?"

"Several?" I said, showing the excitement in my voice. "More like seventeen. I saw the head in the refrigerator. Man, it was freaky. We have to identify all the victims they found and I think we can do it. The guy loves me."

I was disappointed that she didn't share my enthusiasm. I figured she thought this could lead me back to the bottle. It had been six years since my last drink, but she never really forgot. Suspicious looks and comments were the norm, and she constantly wondered if I would drink again. I had kicked the habit cold turkey, I went to AA meetings, and attended daily mass. I felt blessed that the compulsion was gone and was confident that with the grace of God, drink would never be a problem again. I walked into the kitchen, made myself a sandwich, and guzzled down a glass of milk. I jumped in the shower and quickly lathered up. Before going up to bed, I motioned for her to join me.

"No, no way," she said. "This whole thing has got me too upset."

I climbed in the bed and quickly fell off to sleep.

***

The next morning, I was up early and had a good breakfast of bacon, eggs, toast, and coffee. I felt great about my new day shift assignment and was eager to get to work to see what the day held. For the first time in my career, I encountered rush hour traffic. The freeway was virtually empty on my way to work during the third shift. I smiled, thinking that I was just another working stiff on my way downtown. I parked my car and walked to the police administration building. By now, news organizations from all over the country had set up shop right across the street. It was as if a small network city had sprung up overnight. Stepping off the elevator on the fourth floor for the detective assembly, a horde of reporters rushed me.

"Detective Kennedy, we understand that the suspect has been asking for you all night. Is there anything that you can tell us about his character or the crimes he's involved in?" The same little blonde who had accosted me the day before shouted.

"You know that I can't say anything," I quipped as I entered the assembly and quickly closed the door behind me.

I saw Captain Domagalski and Murphy sitting in the inspector's office having coffee and waving at me to enter.

"Yes, sir, what's up?" I asked.

"Your friend has been asking for you since five o'clock this morning. I sent Murphy up to talk to him, but he says he wants to talk to you. I hope you haven't been talking to any of those reporters?"

"No, sir, I know better than that," I answered.

The captain shook his head and said, "Well, somebody has. They know too much already. We have a leak up here. But don't you worry about that. Just don't talk to anyone about this case but me, and I'll take care of the rest. Now go and get him down here. We have a lot of work to do."

Murphy and I took the prisoner elevator to the jail and walked in the back to the seclusion area. The young, fresh-faced officer who sat outside Dahmer's cell got up immediately upon seeing us and took me to the side.

"He's been asking for you all night, Pat."

I nodded my acknowledgement and strolled to Dahmer's cell. "Good morning, Jeff. How did you sleep last night?"

"Okay, I guess." He seemed relieved to see me.

"I told you that I would be back," I replied as I led him down the corridor. Murphy followed behind and we took the quick elevator ride down to the interrogation room.

Directing Dahmer to a seat, I asked, "How about a fresh cup of coffee and a doughnut?"

But before he could answer, Murphy threw an unopened pack of Camel straights on the table and encouraged Dahmer to help himself. He picked up the smokes quickly and opened them, explaining that he was having a nicotine fit and that the coffee and doughnut sounded good. We left him sitting at the interrogation table enjoying the smoke and walked to the coffee bar.

"Pat, I've been talking to the captain, and he wants us to try to identify each and every one of the victims. Harrell and your partner Mike found all kinds of bizarre shit and they want us to find out about it."

I nodded and added, "I know. I talked to Harrell a little bit yesterday and he said it was a fucking nightmare in there. How do you figure we should begin?"

Murphy's face became serious. This was his forte. "I figured that we start with his first victim and go through them one by one, in chronological order. If we can establish a season or date, along with a location of where he met his victims, then we can use departmental missing persons reports and try to match family photos with his Polaroids. The captain is setting up a task force to do the legwork. All we have to do is get the information out of him, and it looks like he wants to play ball."

Murphy grabbed a handful of doughnuts, and I picked up several cups of fresh coffee. Returning to the interrogation room, we observed Dahmer finishing the first of what would be many cigarettes that day. I set a cup of coffee in front of him and he quickly picked it up, sipping it carefully. Murphy put the doughnuts on a napkin, and before either of us could sit down, Dahmer bit into a large, jelly-filled pastry.

"Hungry?" I said with a smile. He nodded and continued eating. I decided to begin. "Well, Jeff, remember how we talked about making amends? Here is what we have in mind. We thought that if we could go back to the beginning, starting in Bath, Ohio, we could try to tell your story in a logical way, to make some sense of what happened to you."

Dahmer finished his coffee and I pushed my untouched cup in front of him, urging him to take it before I continued. "It will be time consuming, but if you can remember the approximate day or time of year that you met each of your victims, along with an accurate physical description, we can try to match them with existing police files."

Dahmer picked up the fresh cup of coffee and sipped it as he thought.

"I'm willing to try, Pat. It all happened over a thirteen-year period, but I do know that the first one happened in October of 1978."

"How do you know that for sure?" Murphy piped up, speaking for the first time that day. "You always remember your first one?"

Dahmer set down the cup of coffee and stared directly at him. A stony silence settled over the room until I broke the uneasy quiet.

"Well, good, Jeff, then let's get started, but let's do it right. I don't want you to be uneasy or hold anything back. What do you think?" I reached over and placed my hand on his arm as I spoke.

He looked at me sincerely. "Pat, I've been thinking a lot about what you said last night, and you're right. I'm not going anywhere, and I really don't want to kill myself anymore. I feel like I should be killed for what I did, but I don't want to do it. It's apparent to me that I'm going to have to learn to live with myself in prison. What you said about admitting my crimes and making amends makes sense. I know that whatever I do, I can't bring those men back, but if I identify each one, at least their families will know what happened to them and they can put them to rest. Like you said, Pat, that's the least I can do; maybe it's the only thing I can do."

Murphy placed a pack of blank supplementary report forms on the table. He mentioned that we should probably start with Dahmer's home life, and we both pulled out our pens. Dahmer took another cigarette from the pack and began.

"I remember my early childhood as being one of extreme tension. I never really felt at ease or comfortable. It wasn't that my mom and dad didn't love me; I knew that they did. They told me so. They took care of the house and showed me love, but it was never peaceful. I could feel it. My mom and dad were always at each other's throats. They fought all the time, not physical fighting, although there was some pushing and shoving that went on. It was mostly a lot of arguing and screaming."

He talked as if he were in a therapy session and I wanted to direct him to his first homicide, but I noticed that Murphy recorded his every word so I didn't interrupt.

"My mother did a lot of the screaming, and I would go to my room when they fought, but I could still hear it. I remember trying to put it out of my mind by daydreaming, making up a little fantasy world of my own. Later on, I found out that my mother had a mental problem and was treated by a doctor. There were times when she was gone for extended periods. She was never mean or unkind to me. Actually, she could be very comforting, but she was gone a lot. I remember staying with my aunt and overhearing her talking to some relatives, saying that after I was born, my mother suffered a severe case of postpartum depression and had to be hospitalized. I didn't know what that was at the time, but I do remember feeling responsible for it, like I had done something to cause her illness." Dahmer paused to take a sip of coffee.

"My senior year in high school, Mom and Dad went through a divorce. After I graduated, my mother took my brother and moved to Wisconsin. We had relatives there. My dad was always busy at work, and I was left alone most of the time. I had the house all to myself. I never really had any close friends in school; I was kind of a loner and pretty shy around people. My parents were not big drinkers, but they kept a fully stocked bar in the home. I was lonely and started to drink. It made me feel better; I could talk to people and fit in, but I wasn't that good at it and I'd usually end up drunk and alone in my house. I'm sure it was at this time that I began to develop feelings of not wanting to be alone, especially at night. It seemed as if everybody was leaving me. My father had started a new relationship with my current stepmother and spent a lot of time at her house. He said that I was old enough to take care of myself, so I ended up alone. I hated it. I didn't like sleeping alone in that big house. It made me angry. I started to have fleeting fantasies of killing someone. I don't know where they came from, but they did. They were always intertwined, sex and killing. I tried to get them out of my mind, but the sexual fantasy was powerful and I masturbated for hours thinking about it. The fantasy was always the same. I met a good-looking man, brought him home, had sex with him, and then killed him.

"In my fantasy, I always strangled them as they slept. I don't know why, but it seemed the most humane way. I knew from my earliest sexual awakenings that I was gay. I was always attracted to men and never really questioned why. I just accepted the fact that I liked men and not women. I was raised Lutheran, and I knew the faith frowned on gays. I saw that openly gay people could have a tough time of it, so I decided to keep this my little secret. This wasn't hard, since I kept most thoughts to myself.

"I don't know why, but my fantasies always included cutting into the dead bodies of my lovers. I sliced their torso from chin to crotch and pulled out their inner viscera, laying it on their chest. The thought of the warm inner cavity excited me tremendously, and I masturbated thinking about it. The orgasm was always pleasurable and intense. I'm not sure, but I think this was an extension of something I got involved in as a kid. When I was lonely or when my mom and dad fought, I walked the country roads by my house in Bath. I noticed that occasionally there were dead animals along the roadside, hit by cars. I was interested in what they looked like on the inside. At first, I brought them home and cut them up, examining their insides, not telling anyone. But the more interested I became, the less pleasure I got from just cutting into them.

"The inner workings of these creatures fascinated me and I wanted to preserve their bones. I remember that I talked to Dad about my interest. I told him that I would like to preserve the bones in some way for future study. Dad was a chemist and knew all about chemicals that could clean off the dead skin. I wanted to sterilize the bones so they could be handled safely. I actually think he was proud of my interest. He helped me by providing various solutions, and even helped me build a little cemetery along the side of our garage to bury my experiments after I was finished studying them. This phase of finding dead animals along the road lasted until I was about fourteen. I actually had the complete set of bones from a large dog I found dead along the side of the road. It was a beagle, and I severed all the flesh from its body, cleaned and polished the bones with various solutions, and reassembled the animal on a large piece of wood. It was just like something in a museum.

"I think this early interest was the beginning of my obsession. My sexual interests and cutting up dead animals slowly merged. I don't remember being sexually stimulated as a kid when I was engaged in this behavior, but I do know that it gave me great pleasure and that it consumed a lot of my time and thoughts. At any rate, the two thoughts became one, and I couldn't think about sex with a man without also having thoughts of cutting open his human body and examining the insides."

Dahmer looked at his coffee cup and noted it was empty.

"I could use some more coffee," I said, getting up and reaching for Jeff's coffee cup. "How about you, Murphy?"

Murphy nodded, and I quickly left the room to retrieve some more coffee and smokes. I returned and Dahmer eagerly grabbed his coffee and continued.

"When I was eighteen, my parents went through the divorce. Mom took my brother and left for Wisconsin. Dad was under court order to stay out of the house. He took a room at a motel just outside of town. That's when it began.

I was alone. I had access to the family car and drove the back roads when I was lonely, listening to music. On a few of these occasions, I saw the same guy jogging. He was nice looking and I fantasized about being with him. I actually thought up a plan to wait for him in the bushes and strike him in the head with a baseball bat as he ran by. I thought I could pull him into the bushes and have sex with him before he woke up. I know it sounds stupid, but one day, I took a baseball bat and lay in wait for him, but he never jogged by." Dahmer smiled and chuckled slightly, thinking back on this foolish early plan.

"Then it happened. My dream became reality. I was driving to town one afternoon and came upon a hitchhiker. I pulled over and he got in right away. He was a good-looking white male, five foot ten inches tall, thin build, with straight, brown, collar-length hair. I think he was my age. I told him that I lived alone at my folks' place and asked if he would like to come over and have a few drinks. To my amazement, he said yes."

Dahmer retold the story of his first kill. I checked my notes from the night before. The story was the same, only this time he added that before he pulverized the skeletal remains, he used a kitchen knife to cut the flesh from the body, placing it in plastic garbage bags. That night, he loaded the bags into the car and made for the county dump, thinking it was a good time to dispose of the body.

"I drove along a back road but was pulled over by a Bath police officer. I was terrified and afraid that this was the end. The officer approached the car and shined his flashlight into the interior, lighting up the whole car. He spied the large garbage bags in the back seat and inquired as to what they were. I told him it was garbage and I had forgotten to take it to the dump. He seemed to buy it, because he wrote me a citation for crossing the yellow line and sent me on my way. That was my first encounter with the authorities. It was nerve-racking, but when it was over, I felt a rush. I had fooled him."

Dahmer stopped at this point and finished his coffee. He sat there staring off as if remembering how it all began. "Pat, it was weird. Living in that house by myself and knowing that a young man's body was lying out there in my woods. Nobody asked about him. I checked the news stations—nothing. My dad came over to check on me and make sure that I had enough to eat, but he never looked around outside. I was alone with my thoughts most of the time."

Murphy continued to write as Dahmer talked about not wanting to be alone at night and being unable to sleep. I watched him as he spoke, trying to get a handle on his character. His eyes were red and drawn, and his manner and voice were calm. I wondered what really went on behind those blue eyes of his.

He interrupted my thoughts. "Pat, this is when I really started drinking a lot. I couldn't sleep, thinking about that guy out there in the woods. I started drinking early in the afternoon, and by nighttime, I would be so drunk that I would pass out."

He reminded me of the night before when we discussed the scourge of drink and how it wrought havoc in both our lives. It had been quite a while since I delved that deeply into my past drinking episodes. I told my tale to him in an effort to build rapport, but our examination of the subject, along with his gruesome narrative, left me with an uneasy feeling. I recalled my early days on the job. Many a morning I came home still hyped from the night's activities. I poured myself a glass of Canadian Club on the rocks and sat in front of the TV sipping it until my eyes became droopy and I could fall asleep.

There was a knock at the door and a young police aide stuck his head inside, stating there was someone who wanted to talk with me. I followed the aide into the outer hallway. There was an attractive young woman, with collar-length blonde hair, wearing a light blue business suit. She introduced herself to me.

"Hello, Detective Kennedy. My name is Wendy Patrickus. I am a lawyer out of Gerald Boyle's office, and I'm here to represent Mr. Dahmer."

I took her extended hand and shook it.

"I'm pleased to meet you, counselor, but Mr. Dahmer has not requested an attorney at this time."

She stepped back and looked at me strangely. "Well, I was told by Mr. Boyle to come over here and talk with his client." She stood straight and tried to exhibit her best professional posture, hoping I would admit her into the detective assembly.

I again politely told her that Dahmer had not requested an attorney and she would not be allowed to talk with him. She gave me a perturbed look and asked for the name of my commanding officer. I gave her Captain Domagalski's name and disappeared behind the door.

I walked back into the interrogation room to find Murphy and Dahmer sharing a laugh. Obviously, he had broken the ice with Jeff and the two were getting along well. I sat down as Jeff said that his first victim wore a braces retainer on a chain around his neck. Jeff had worn the chain for a few days, then thought better of it and threw it in a shallow river near his house. We continued to take as much information as possible, which we then conveyed to the Bath Police Department. They would check against their missing persons files from that time and with any luck, send photographs of anyone matching that description.

Another knock on the door interrupted us. This time, Lieutenant Raymond Sucik, a ranking day shift homicide supervisor, entered and ordered both Murphy and me to follow him. I stepped out of the room and around the hall to see the chief, Philip Arreola, standing with an inspector of the Criminal Investigation Bureau, Vince Partipilo, and Captain Domagalski. They were huddled around a middle-aged, gray-haired, portly man dressed in a light blue seersucker suit. They talked as if they all knew each other. The man in the blue suit extended his hand and introduced himself.

"How do you do, Detective Kennedy? My name is Gerald Boyle. I am Jeffrey Dahmer's attorney, hired by his father Lionel Dahmer. I would very much like to speak with him."

I shook his hand and acknowledged the chief's presence. I then boldly stated that Mr. Dahmer had not requested an attorney and that we were not finished interrogating him. I said that I was under the assumption that unless a defendant requested a lawyer, one was not permitted until the police finished their investigation. I noted some raised eyebrows from the chief, but felt I was correct in this assumption.

Boyle's face turned beet red and it appeared as if he were going to explode. "Now see here, rookie. Maybe you don't know who I am, but if you want to jeopardize this case, just keep talking that rot. I am duly appointed, and I demand to see my client."

I looked to the captain for support. Domagalski smiled. "He's right, you know, Gerry. The guy has not asked for counsel."

Boyle spun around and faced the inspector. "Vince, do you hear this? I'm not going to let this go. Is this the way you're going to play it?"

The chief finally spoke up. "Now, settle down here a minute—let's talk about this. You two are excused," he said to Murphy and me as he directed the attorney and company to a room farther down the hallway. We walked back to the interrogation room to find Dahmer kicked back in his chair and enjoying a smoke.

"What's going on? What's all the yelling about?" he asked.

Murphy explained that an attorney named Gerald Boyle was out in the hall asking to speak with him. "He said that your father appointed him," Murphy said.

Dahmer nodded in acknowledgement, stating Boyle was the same lawyer hired by his father to represent him in his last arrest with the Asian boy. He said it was all right and he would talk with the lawyer. Murphy quickly sat down next to him and said, "Hold on a minute, Jeff. I thought you said that you were going to help us to identify each and every one of your victims?"

Dahmer looked at me. "That's right. Pat; you said that was the only way I could possibly make amends for my actions. I want to help in any way I can."

Murphy continued, "Good, that's what I wanted to hear, Jeff. But you see, if we let this guy in here, he's going to tell you to clam up. You have to understand that it's his job to defend you; he won't want you to talk to us anymore. They'll haul you off to county jail and that will be the end of our little talks. You'll rot in a cell until your trial."

Dahmer's eyes got wide and he cried, "But I want to talk with you guys! I need to identify those men. I believe what Pat said about being sorry for my actions and trying to make some kind of amends. What can I do?"

At this point, I pulled out my memo book from my back pocket. I opened it to the day's date and handed it to Dahmer. "Look, Jeff, why don't you just write in this book that you want to continue talking with Murphy and me, and when we're finished, you can talk with your lawyer. That way we can finish identifying all of the victims and clear this whole mess up."

This lightened the mood and he took my memo book, writing in it that he wished to talk with Murphy and me. He would contact Mr. Boyle afterward. He then signed and dated under his statement. I left the room and returned to the meeting room where the chief and company were still discussing the matter. I handed my open memo book to Boyle.

After reading it, he looked at me with disdain and showed it to the inspector. "Is this the way it's going to be?"

The inspector shook his head no and stated, "Detective Kennedy, we have decided to allow counsel to speak with his client. Since he is already here and hired by the defendant's father, I feel he should be allowed in."

Boyle brushed by me and headed to the interrogation room. It appeared as if he knew where he was going and had been there before. He asked Murphy to step out and closed the door behind him. Murphy and I stood together as the commanding officers huddled about, talking. Murphy confided in me that Gerald Boyle was a powerful defense attorney who had once run for district attorney. Boyle had also been a close ally of the police in the past, and many an officer who found themselves in need of legal assistance had called upon him.

"I just hope we convinced Jeff to stay with us," he whispered.

A moment or two passed, and Boyle reappeared from the interrogation room looking stressed and disgusted. He had in his hand a waiver form stating he had advised his client not to talk with us; however, Dahmer told Boyle of his intention to finish the task of identifying all the victims. Jeff signed the release, despite Boyle's advice not to.

Boyle looked directly at Murphy and me. "Okay, look, you guys. He wants to cooperate, but I want one of my associates in the room with you while it's being done. I'm sending over an associate to sit in on your sessions." He then walked away in the direction of the inspector's office.

Murphy slapped me on the back. "We did it," he said, and we both walked back to the interrogation room. We opened the interrogation room door and found Dahmer smoking contentedly.

"Well, what's going on?" he asked.

"It's all cool," Murphy said, smiling. He sat down next to Dahmer and slapped him on the back. "Now we can take all the time we need to identify each victim."

Dahmer seemed a little taken aback at Murphy's outward display of male bravado and was clearly bothered by the term *victim*, wincing at the word. I asked Dahmer as to the nature of his discussion with Boyle.

"Well, what did you say?" I queried.

Dahmer took another smoke from the pack, lit it, and said, "I told him everything that we talked about last night, Pat. I told him that I had already told about all my crimes. That I felt the only way I could prove to the world, my family, and myself that I am truly sorry for what I did was to cooperate with you. I told him that I wanted to continue talking to you guys until we had identified everyone."

We all sat quietly for a moment. Murphy smiled widely, and it appeared as if Dahmer was glad that we were pleased with the outcome of the situation. We were interrupted by another knock at the door. It was the captain again: Ms. Patrickus was outside and needed to sit in with us as we continued the interview. I left the interrogation room and went to the visitors waiting area, where I found the associate counsel.

She stood up as I entered and extended her hand. "Shall we try again, Detective?"

Taking her hand, I asked her to call me Pat, and tried to explain the reason for my previous curt behavior. She brushed off my attempts and in a professional demeanor said that Boyle wanted her to sit in on all our conversations with his client. I led her through the detective assembly and back into the interrogation room. I opened the door and found Murphy and Dahmer trying to pin down an exact date when Jeff met the first victim. Dahmer looked up and appeared startled by the sight of the woman standing next to me. Wendy entered the room and took Dahmer's hand.

"Hello, Jeff. I'm Wendy Patrickus. I work for Gerald Boyle, and I'll be sitting in on your interviews with these two gentlemen." She looked around the room for a place to sit and I quickly offered her my seat, leaving the room momentarily to retrieve another chair. We all sat down and Murphy explained that we were trying to come as close as possible to the dates when Dahmer met his victims. If we could ascertain a relatively close date of encounter, we could then sift through missing persons reports filed by the families just before and after this date. Murphy figured that if we got a detailed description of each victim and matched them to the dates given, we could obtain photos of these men through police or family and show them to Dahmer for positive ID. It was a brilliant idea.

Dahmer continued to stare at Wendy and seemed unsure of the situation. She pulled out a notepad and pen and began writing in it, oblivious to the hesitation in his demeanor.

Murphy nonchalantly continued. "Jeff, you were saying that you thought it was in the early fall of 1978 that you met the hitchhiker?"

Dahmer still stared at the newcomer. She never looked up from her pad, and after a moment of silence, he said, "I was really drunk that night. But now after thinking about it, I'm quite sure it happened in June, not too long before I was stopped by that cop for crossing the yellow line on my way to the dump."

A check with the Bath police revealed that Dahmer was issued a citation on June 25, 1978. The Bath police department was helpful, and said they would send photos of all missing persons matching Victim One's description from that time. We were well on our way.

By the time we finished, it was going on four o'clock. Patrickus announced she was returning to her office. Murphy said that we too were wrapping up for the day and we would take Dahmer back to his cell. I showed her to the elevator and said we would start again at nine o'clock in the morning. I returned to the room and found Murphy good-naturedly questioning Dahmer regarding his feelings about Ms. Patrickus.

"She's a fox," I interjected, curious at what Jeff's reaction might be.

Dahmer shook his head and looked down at the floor. "I guess she is pretty, but I'm not really attracted to women."

He asked if he could have another cup of coffee and a smoke before we took him back to his cell, and said he wanted to sit and talk for a while without a bunch of writing and questions going on. I told him we would be glad to, and this became a pattern with us throughout the investigation. Murphy stepped out to get some more coffee, and Dahmer lit up a smoke. I kicked back in my chair and extended my leg onto the one vacated by Patrickus. I studied Dahmer as he smoked.

He sat rigidly in his chair, back straight, knees and feet together, one arm at his side and the other slightly bent to hold a cigarette. He seemed relaxed, but his body language betrayed him. He had been in police custody two days now, and because our city jail was not equipped with shower facilities, he was beginning to smell a little ripe. We had taken every stitch of clothing he had worn, and the gray jumpsuit he wore was soiled and stained. His hair was greasy and stringy; a three-day beard was evident. The black rubber flip-flops we gave him were too small, and his toes and heels hung over the ends. I remarked upon his disheveled condition and he smiled slightly, not looking in my direction.

"You know, Jeff, tomorrow you will go for your preliminary hearing. After that, we will turn you over to the county sheriff's department. They have all the comforts of home over there, and you will be able to get showered, and given a clean jumpsuit and socks to wear."

Dahmer looked at me directly and a wave of panic crossed his face. "What do you mean you will turn me over to the sheriff? I thought you said that you would be with me the whole time?"

I took my foot off the chair and leaned forward. "Hold on, Jeff, I'm not going anywhere, but you can't stay here. We don't have the facilities to accommodate prisoners on a full-time basis. Hell, aren't you getting sick of those bologna sandwiches they've been giving you?"

Dahmer butted the cigarette with his hand and reached for another.

"But how will we continue our task? And where?" he asked with a bit of anxiety in his voice. I explained that the sheriff's department was in the building directly west of us, and a walkway on the fifth floor connected the two buildings. We could walk back and forth from building to building without ever having to go outside. This seemed to appease him. He took a long drag off his smoke and held it in for a moment before exhaling.

"What about the court hearing?" he inquired. "Will it be open to the public?" I explained the preliminary hearing was indeed open to the public, and that the press would probably make a big deal of it, considering the nature of the case. He stood up and paced the room a bit. "Is there any way that I could shower and change into some clean clothes before the hearing? I hate this dirty feeling."

Murphy returned and placed the coffee in front of Dahmer and stated, "Well, it looks like things are starting to come together. I just talked with a lieutenant from Bath, Ohio, and he said that he'll be here the day after tomorrow with some files and photos."

I told Murphy about Dahmer's concerns regarding his court appearance and said that my son, Patrick, a sophomore in high school, was about the same size as Jeff. I wondered if we could give him some clothes before the hearing. Murphy didn't see why not, but said we should talk with Boyle beforehand to see if it was all right. We all stood up and walked to the prisoner elevator.

On the way up to the jail, Murphy reminded Dahmer that he must request to speak with us every morning in order to be let out of his cell. "Just tell the officer that you want to talk with us, like you did this morning."

We explained his Miranda rights. If he called for us, there could be no question as to the voluntary nature of his information. Dahmer seemed to understand and was more than willing to accommodate. He sheepishly waved goodbye as the cell door slammed. Murphy and I went back down to the detective assembly. I called in my day's reports to Gloria and waited for them to be typed. After checking them for accuracy, I handed them to the captain and said I was going home for the day.

Chapter 7

Leaving the police administration building, I again encountered a cavalcade of reporters. Their numbers had swollen and I saw vans with satellite dishes representing news organizations from around the world. I was surrounded by reporters of every size and shape. Someone thrust a microphone in my face as I waded through the crowd.

"Detective Kennedy, we understand that the suspect asks for you by name. What does he want to talk to you about? Is there anything that you can tell us?"

I continued walking and answered, "You'll have to talk with the chief about that. I have nothing to say." I climbed into my car and drove off.

By now, my three children—ages fifteen, eleven, and eight—were well aware of the media circus and quite excited about my role in the investigation. As I entered the house, they bombarded me with questions. My wife quickly intervened, shooing them away. She was concerned the horrific story might disturb them and told me so.

"I don't think you should tell them anything. This can't be healthy for them or you."

There was a cool distance in her voice, and I decided not to argue. The kids returned to their homework and television shows. I changed clothes and motioned for my eldest son Pat to come with me to his bedroom. I explained Dahmer's concerns regarding the following day's preliminary trial and asked if he had any clothing he was willing to part with. He went to his closet and pulled out a pair of black Levi's jeans.

He said they were a bit tight. Then he handed me a blue-and-white-striped short-sleeved shirt I had bought him but he had never worn.

"I don't really like this style, Dad. Do you think these will be all right?"

They looked as if they would fit perfectly, and I placed them in my police closet. Pat was excited about his contribution to the case and couldn't wait to tell his friends that Jeffrey Dahmer would wear his clothes. No more questions regarding the case were allowed, and we ate dinner, discussing the kids' school and sports activities. Afterward, I retreated to the basement television. I wanted to see what all those news outlets were saying about the investigation. My wife followed me downstairs with an unhappy look on her face.

"Pat, I want to talk with you about how you're going to handle this."

"What do you mean?" I said, lowering the volume.

"You are going to need some psychological help."

She was a big believer in therapy and had seen a therapist ever since I quit drinking. This had caused stress in our relationship, especially when I was drying out. She had insisted I enter rehab to stop my drinking, but my pride wouldn't allow it. I felt that the time away from the job would only cause rumors to spread about my affliction, and I was determined to quit on my own. Thank God, my father, also an alcoholic, introduced me to AA. The program worked for me, but she was always uncomfortable that I wasn't getting "professional" help.

"Look, I'm fine; I'm just excited, that's all. Why don't you sit for a while and we can talk about it?"

She shook her head and headed back upstairs. "This thing is just too much for me right now."

It was eleven o'clock before I retired for the night. I fell asleep wondering what the new day would bring.

***

I woke up, shaved, showered, and dressed in a hurry. I couldn't wait to get to work. I parked my car in the police lot and waded again through the media encampment, reeling off the obligatory "no comment" as I entered the assembly.

A day shift lieutenant saw me and shouted, "Your boy is calling for you!"

I let Murphy know I was going to get our new best friend. I walked to his cell. "Good morning, Jeff. How do you feel?"

Dahmer stood up and smiled. He seemed relieved to see me. As we walked toward the elevator, he sheepishly asked if I could do something for him.

"Sure, Jeff, anything you want. What is it?"

"Well, I don't want to get anyone in trouble, but do you think you could keep some of the other police officers away from me?" he asked, looking at the elevator floor. The door opened and we walked to the interrogation room.

"What are you talking about? What police officer? Who's bothering you?"

Dahmer sat down just as Murphy entered the room with three cups of coffee and a fresh pack of Lucky Strikes. Dahmer nodded a good morning to him, and stopped telling his story long enough to open the pack and light up.

"Wow, I never had a Lucky Strike before." He inhaled with relish and Murphy smiled widely.

"Go on, Jeff," I said.

"Well, there is this very young-looking officer that is in the jail at night. He brings other officers to my cell to look at me, and this morning he brought in a copy of the *Milwaukee Sentinel* with a big headline about me and my crimes and asked me to autograph it for him."

Murphy set down his coffee. "Did you sign it for him?"

Dahmer, startled by Murphy's abrupt action, stammered, "Well, yes, I did."

Murphy motioned for me to come with him. "We'll be back in a minute, Jeff, just relax."

Together we rode the elevator to the jail and strode into the sergeant's office.

"Who's been assigned to watch Dahmer the last few nights? And is he still here?" Murphy asked.

The lockup desk sergeant was an ex-motorcycle cop with a face like leather. He fumbled through his roster and said, "Yeah, he's still here. Why?"

"Get him," Murphy ordered, and I tried to explain the problem. "And let's get that newspaper. That's the last thing we need leaked to the press."

Murphy sat down and shook his head with disbelief.

I told the sergeant, "Look, we don't want to get him busted. We just want him to leave Dahmer alone."

The offending officer appeared at the door. When he saw us, he seemed to know what was coming.

"Where's the paper?" the sergeant demanded.

An embarrassed smile broke the officer's face, and he answered, "It's in my locker."

"Go get it!" the sergeant snarled as the rookie fled and returned quickly with the signed 'Jeffrey Dahmer' newspaper copy. Murphy and I left as the sergeant tore into the red-faced rookie. We could hear the sergeant's voice trailing off as we entered the elevator and returned to the interrogation room to find Dahmer finishing his first cup of coffee and lighting another cigarette.

I told them I was going for refills and walked from the room to the coffee bar. I observed Captain Domagalski waving to me, and I entered his office.

"Kennedy, how many copies of that original confession did you make?" he barked.

"Two copies, sir. I gave you the original, I burned one copy for the report, and of course made a copy for myself," I replied. "Why?"

"Those pricks at the press have gotten a hold of a copy. Do you know anything about it?"

"No, sir. You know me better than that."

Domagalski nodded. "Good. I was just checking. There is an internal investigation going on. They think it's somebody in the district attorney's office. Other than that, how's it going?"

"Fine, sir. We got word that someone from Bath, Ohio, is coming with pictures tomorrow, and we'll turn him over to the sheriff after the preliminary hearing this afternoon." I fidgeted with my tie as the captain answered the ringing phone on his desk.

"Well, let me know if you need anything," he said, swiveling away from me in his chair.

I grabbed three more cups of coffee and returned to the room. I placed the coffee in front of my companions and took a seat. Murphy talked to Jeff about his tour of duty in the army. Dahmer really didn't want to join, but his father talked him into it. He found he actually enjoyed the routine and structure of boot camp and started to feel good about himself. He trained as a medic and was so busy he had almost forgotten about the dead man's bones scattered in his backyard at home. The army sent him to a base in Germany, where he had a lot of free time on his hands. He spent it in the local beer gardens getting drunk on beer. Dahmer never formed any relationships in the army, gay or otherwise, and satisfied his need for sexual intimacy by masturbating. He appeared genuinely disappointed that he was dismissed before finishing his tour of duty; however, thoughts of what happened in Ohio continued to haunt him and alcohol was the only way to dampen the memory. He was disciplined numerous times for being drunk on duty, and eventually given an honorable discharge.

Dahmer continued, "After I was released from the army, I used the voucher they gave me and flew to Miami, Florida.

I was tired of the cold winters in Germany and decided to go someplace where it was always warm."

While in Miami, Dahmer got a job in a submarine sandwich shop, but he didn't make enough money to live on. He drank continuously, and for a time, he slept on the beach. He lived there about six months, and soon his lack of money had him calling his father for help. Dad refused to send him any cash but suggested he come home and sent a plane ticket instead. Returning to Bath, Dahmer moved in with his father and stepmother. However, it was not long before his excessive drinking got him in trouble with the law. In October 1981, he was arrested for disorderly conduct and resisting arrest. His dad tried to get him some help and introduced him to Alcoholics Anonymous, but it didn't take. Thoughts of his earlier deed refused to go away, and his drinking caused conflict in the home. To appease his wife, his father suggested Jeff move in with his paternal grandmother in West Allis, Wisconsin—a working-class suburb of Milwaukee. His father felt it would serve two purposes: Jeff could look after his grandmother, who was getting on in years, and with him gone, there would finally be peace in their home.

Dahmer's move to Wisconsin was the beginning of some real soul searching. His grandmother was a very religious woman. He loved and admired her and felt she could help him get control of his life. She was kindly, loving, and tolerant, and she had a quiet serenity about her that he craved. He felt that religion might provide a way out of his predicament. They discussed religious matters, and he began to accompany her to Sunday service and weekday Bible study. This kept him sober during the day, but when Grandma retired for the evening, he began to drink again. He knew he had an alcohol problem, but felt his need to drink arose from the horrible memory he carried with him. He could never get it out of his mind. No matter how hard he tried, the knowledge of what he had done stayed with him.

Dahmer remembered the early days at Grandma's house as a lonely, empty time. He made no friends and constantly battled his fantasies of sexual activities, always fused with the urge to dominate, kill, and dismember the men he was intimate with in his dreams. He masturbated constantly to alleviate his urges, but this was only a temporary solution for the problem that haunted him. The turning point came one day while he was reading in the Wauwatosa public library, a suburb just west of Milwaukee. A young man walked by and dropped a balled-up piece of paper on his desk. He opened it to find a note:

If you want a blow job meet me in the men's room, five minutes.

He looked for the young man, but he was gone. The note disturbed him and he began to wonder if he fooled anybody. It seemed his attempts at straightening out his life were futile; he would never be able to forget about the dead man he left in Ohio. He also felt his attempts to deny his sexuality were a mistake.

At this point, Dahmer looked at us with complete honesty in his voice and said, "This is when I decided to give in to the dark side. Grandma's way was not working; I was miserable and lonely, so I decided to indulge my sexual lusts and fantasies."

The first thing he did was buy some gay porn magazines. He kept them in a suitcase hidden in the fruit cellar. He spent hours viewing and masturbating to the images of lean, muscular men performing sexual acts, but over time, this proved unfulfilling. He learned about Milwaukee's gay bar scene through these magazines, an area just south of downtown with a cluster of taverns and dance clubs catering to the gay community. Dahmer began to frequent these clubs on weekends, enjoying the drinking and lifestyle. He discovered a gay bathhouse on Wisconsin Avenue, where he paid for a separate cubicle to store his clothes, using it for extracurricular activities with other patrons. His fantasies of dominating, killing, and dismembering were still with him; however, he managed to control himself and tried to enjoy being with men and indulging in sexual activity. He never had a lasting relationship with anyone he met there, and often felt lonely and empty.

During this time, he worked a series of odd jobs—a stint at a plasma center and then a temporary job service—but his chronic drinking and attitude always cost him his employment. Eventually, he got a job working third shift at the Ambrosia Chocolate Factory in downtown Milwaukee. His new job provided him with an ample salary, but third shift was hard on his body and he found it difficult to sleep.

He went to a doctor about his insomnia. The doctor gave Dahmer a prescription for Halcion, a sleeping pill. The drug, he said, worked dramatically.

"It didn't slowly put you to sleep; it knocked you out quickly."

He wondered what effect the drug might have on sexual partners, and brought crushed-up portions to the bathhouses. It worked like a charm. The drug rendered his partners unconscious, and Dahmer had his way with them. This satisfied his urge to dominate, as Dahmer now had complete control and did not have to reciprocate sexually in any way that he didn't want. However, this solution was short lived because several of his pickups woke up with terrible headaches from the drug and complained. There was an episode where Dahmer gave a guy too much Halcion and he stopped breathing. Someone called an ambulance and the victim was revived, but after, management barred Dahmer from entering the bathhouse.

He simply made other arrangements.

Dahmer left Grandma's house early in the evening on a Friday night and rented a room at one of the cheap hotels just west of downtown. There, he had a supply of alcoholic beverages and crushed Halcion tablets waiting for any pickups he might persuade to accompany him for the night.

Jeff said it worked well, and he spent many a Friday and Saturday night sexually dominating men he had picked up and drugged. He left early in the mornings before his partners woke. This way, he avoided hassles or charges that he had slipped them some drug.

Murphy interrupted, "When did you meet the second victim, the one from the Ambassador Hotel?"

Dahmer's demeanor changed. He had been reliving the days of freedom and sexual pleasure as he told his story, and Murphy's question brought him back to the reality of the situation.

"It was November of 1987. I remember because it was nine years after the first one." Dahmer hung his head as he continued. "It was the day before Thanksgiving. I met him at Club 219. I already told Pat about it. He was really nice looking and we both got drunk; I took him to the hotel and gave him the mixture of sleeping pills and rum, but I don't remember anything after that. I swear. When I woke up, he was dead. There were bruises all over his face and chest. My arms were all sore, and black and blue. I must have beaten him to death in an alcoholic blackout or else I gave him too much of the sleeping potion, I don't know. All I know is that he was dead.

"The story about the suitcase is true. I put him in the fruit cellar in Grandma's basement and waited for my family to leave after the holiday. It all came back to me quickly. Just like when I was a kid. I severed the flesh from the bones and inspected the inside viscera. It was sexually exciting and I masturbated several times while disposing of the body. I placed the severed flesh and bones into several double-wrapped plastic bags and dropped them into the trash barrels behind Grandma's house. It was so easy. The garbage men came and took all the evidence away: nothing was ever said, no one ever knew. I had gotten away with murder for the second time."

Chapter 8

A knock at the door produced a deputy from the jail. The sheriff's department was ready to take custody and present Dahmer for the preliminary hearing.

"Oh yeah, I've got something for you, Jeff." I left the room and went to my locker. I retrieved the pants and shirt that my son had given to me and returned to the interrogation room. "Here, Jeff, try these on for size." I gave him the clothing and he held them up to himself.

"Thanks, Pat. I think these will fit fine." He looked at me and smiled. It was a warm smile, and for a moment, I almost forgot his monstrous crimes. It gave me an eerie feeling to think he could be so normal in some ways yet responsible for the murders of seventeen people.

Murphy broke my train of thought. "Okay, Jeff, things are going to be a little different from now on."

"What do you mean?" Dahmer replied with a hint of anxiety.

"Well, Jeff, once we turn you over to the sheriff, you will be in his custody. The only way you'll be able to talk to us is if you make a request to do so. Then Pat and I will get an 'order to produce' from a judge and we will be able to come and get you, but you must request to see us every day. The only change will be that instead of sleeping in our jail, you'll have all the comforts of the county lockup. Clean sheets and blankets, shower facilities, and three hot meals a day. We will pick you up in the morning and bring you back when we're through for the day."

Dahmer nodded his understanding and seemed pleased with the arrangement. We walked the back hall to the prisoners' elevator, went up to the fifth floor, and took the hallway connecting the police administration building with the county jail. At the end of the walkway, we pressed an intercom and announced our presence. In a moment or two, the large metal door opened and a deputy took him into custody.

"We'll see you in court, Jeff," I said, as we walked back through the enclosure and down to the assembly. Once we arrived, Murphy put in a request for all missing persons reports and pictures that might match Victim Two, and we both walked to the courthouse.

The courtroom was located on the fifth floor of the Safety Building near us, so the walk was short. Inside was a flurry of activity. Reporters and technicians scrambled for space. The hearing was open to the public, but with limited room, so a huge line had formed and deputies found it difficult to maintain order. Murphy and I slipped in through the jury entrance and proceeded to the back of the courtroom. It was a large one, decorated with lavish wooden wall carvings.

The judge's area formed an elevated majestic centerpiece. The spectator gallery could accommodate about seventy-five people and was separated from the trial area by a wall-to-wall, ceiling-to-floor, unbreakable glass divider. An electronically operated locked door, manned by a deputy, was in the middle. A large painting of Lady Liberty adorned the wall above the judge's seat. To the right, a doorway led to the bailiff's office, prisoner holding area, and the judge's chambers.

Murphy and I stepped into the back; in the bailiff's office, we could see Dahmer huddled with Mr. Boyle, Ms. Patrickus, and several other members of the defense team. I was pleased to see Jeff wearing the clothes I brought for him. Then E. Michael McCann, the DA for Milwaukee County, and several of his chief assistants entered and walked over to Boyle.

I looked in the courtroom and noticed it was filled with spectators. Six or seven TV cameras on tripods were set up with their lenses pushed against the glass divider. Reporters were everywhere, and many of them I had seen at crime scenes or on nightly newscasts. It was all quite exciting and impressive, and I couldn't believe I was in the middle of it.

A bailiff stepped out of the judge's chambers and announced the judge was ready and everyone should take their places. The DA and his entourage all walked into the courtroom and settled at the prosecution table; Boyle led the defense team, and Dahmer smiled slyly at me.

"The clothes fit fine. Thanks, Pat," he whispered as he passed through the doorway and into the waiting courtroom.

There was a hushed silence as he entered. Spectators strained their necks to get a good look at Dahmer. Camera operators were busy adjusting, zooming, and focusing on the defendant as he walked to the defense table and sat down. Dahmer himself was emotionless. He stared straight ahead and appeared not to notice everyone's obvious attention on him.

"All rise," the bailiff commanded as the judge took his seat overlooking the courtroom.

The court proceeding was short. Boyle and the defense team decided to enter pleas of not guilty and not guilty by reason of mental disease or defect[3]. There was no objection by the district attorney, and the hearing was over within fifteen minutes. The insanity trial date was set for January 13, 1992. Dahmer was ushered into the back room and returned to his holding cell. McCann and Boyle, along with their associates, huddled together to discuss the coming trial date.

---

3. Because Jeffrey Dahmer confessed, the trial was to determine his mental capacity, not his innocence or guilt.

Reporters, microphones in hand, stood in front of their cameras recapping the events as spectators noisily jammed the hallway. I walked into the judge's chambers to find Dahmer already dressed in an orange Milwaukee County jumpsuit.

"Here, Pat, thanks a lot." Dahmer held my son's clothes, neatly folded.

"No, that's okay, Jeff. You keep them. They don't fit my son anymore."

Murphy joined us and said, "So far, so good, Jeff. Remember, you have to tell the deputy that you want to speak with us in the morning, so we can come get you."

Dahmer nodded. "Don't worry, I will. Hey, do you think you could bring some menthol cigarettes tomorrow? That's what I usually smoke."

Murphy replied, "You got it, Jeff."

Two deputies arrived and took Dahmer to his secure cell in the lockup area. Murphy and I strolled back to the assembly and discussed where we should begin the following day.

"I noticed you didn't take your kid's clothes back." Murphy chuckled.

I nodded in agreement. "Can you believe it? Who would want to wear those clothes after Jeff Dahmer had them on?"

Back at my desk, I called in my reports for the day and was ready to leave. I looked up and noticed Captain Domagalski standing over me. "Yes, sir?"

"You know that little matter of your original confession getting leaked to the press? Well, I just thought I'd let you know you're off the hook. A night janitor cleaning the DA's office saw your confession on McCann's desk, made a copy, and sold it to the press. He copped out to county investigators this afternoon and he'll be charged with theft tomorrow."

Domagalski smiled, turned, and walked away, obviously pleased the leak didn't come from our department. I waved goodbye to Murphy and walked to the parking lot. The media

GRILLING DAHMER | 119

circus was still going on outside, but nobody approached me this time as I left for home.

Chapter 9

My family sat at the dinner table eating as I walked through the front door. "Dad!" they all screamed. "We saw Pat's shirt on TV!"

I took off my gun and cuffs and sat down at the table.

My eight-year-old, Maureen, touched my hand as I sat down. "He's a scary-looking guy, Dad. Are you afraid of him?"

Alex, my middle son, quipped, "No way. You know Dad is the biggest and the strongest." He smiled at me, knowing this was my usual answer to questions concerning danger and police work.

"That's enough, now. Let your father eat," my wife said with the same concerned look as the day before. The evening passed quickly, and I retired after watching coverage of the preliminary hearing on the late news.

***

The next morning, I didn't see Murphy at roll call. I picked up the ringing phone on my desk and a deputy informed me that my "star witness" had asked for me. I said I was on my way and hung up. Just then, Murphy appeared with someone dressed in a suit and tie. I figured he was a copper and stood, extending my hand.

"Pat, this is Lieutenant Richard Munsey of the Bath County Police Department," Murphy said.

We shook hands and sat down. I told them Dahmer had already requested us and was ready to go.

Murphy smiled and pulled out a fresh pack of Newport menthols. "I'm ready too."

Munsey looked perplexed, and we explained that Dahmer was a nicotine freak; cigarettes were the key to keeping him with us during the investigation.

The lieutenant followed us through the maze of hallways and elevators en route to the county jail. Jeff was waiting for us. We introduced the lieutenant and mentioned he was from Bath. Dahmer acknowledged his presence but said nothing as we walked to the interrogation room. Murphy pulled out the pack of smokes and threw them on the table in front of Dahmer. He immediately opened the pack and lit one up, inhaling deeply and obviously enjoying his first hit of the day.

"Thanks, Dennis," he said.

Murphy grabbed a chair and sat down next to him. "Jeff, today we want to try to identify the first guy back in Ohio."

Before Dahmer could answer, there was a knock at the door and a day shift detective opened it, stating that Ms. Patrickus from Boyle's office was outside. Murphy left the room to greet her, and I explained to Munsey that the defense wished to be present during questioning. The door opened and there was Murphy and the defense counsel. After introductions, we all took a seat. Munsey had come with the aerial photographs we had requested of the Dahmer residence at 4480 West Bath Road in Bath, Ohio. Munsey had been informed of the date established for the first homicide in 1978 and told us he had gone through all the outstanding missing persons reports filed with his department at that time. Only one fit our profile. Munsey produced a photographic array containing the suspected victims and handed it to Dahmer, who studied the photographs as he smoked. In less than a minute, Dahmer picked out a photo and set it on the table.

"That's him," he said.

Munsey gave Dahmer the name of the person in the photograph. He then asked, "How can you be sure? It's been thirteen years."

Dahmer leaned back in his chair and replied, "That's him. I didn't remember the name until you said it, but I remember it now. I took his ID and burned it in the trash barrel along with his clothes. I remember reading the name in his wallet before I burned them."

Munsey looked on in astonishment. "But how can you be sure?"

Dahmer put his smoke out in the ashtray and repeated the earlier retort from Murphy. "You always remember your first one."

Munsey acknowledged this was indeed the only photo in the group to correspond with an outstanding missing persons report filed at the time; the other photos were of people known to be alive. We had identified our first victim, Steven Hicks, now presumed to be dead since June 1978.

Everyone sat in stunned silence for a moment until Murphy mentioned the other photos Munsey brought. He reached into his briefcase and took out several large pictures depicting an aerial view of the Ohio Dahmer residence. He handed them to Dahmer and asked if he could point out where police should look for his remains.

Dahmer was impressed with the pictorial view of his childhood home in Bath and said so. He perused the large glossy photos and pointed to a wooded lot adjacent to his house. "This is where I scattered the broken bones. All the flesh I threw into garbage bags and took to the dump."

"Tell him about the cop who stopped you, Jeff," I interjected.

He retold the story of his late-night traffic stop and his first narrow escape with the authorities.

"And the retainer," I continued.

Dahmer explained he kept the chain with the bent retainer for a time but thought better of it, and one day disposed of it in the river by the sewage plant.

Munsey nodded in acknowledgement as he furiously wrote all Dahmer said. "I know that place. Is there anything else?"

Dahmer, smoking deeply, shook his head no. The familiar stoic tone in his voice was back again. His eyes stared straight ahead and he seemed to be in a far-off place, especially when someone else was in the room. When he finished his explanation, his gaze broke and he was back with us again. Ms. Patrickus cleared her throat to break the silence and announced that Boyle had scheduled numerous appointments for Jeff. He was to be evaluated by a battery of psychiatrists and psychologists, and his first appointment was two o'clock that afternoon. She needed to help coordinate these appointments, and started gathering her paperwork. Lt. Munsey stood with a strange look on his face and explained that he needed to call his department for additional information. Murphy offered to escort Wendy to the door, and all three left together. I stood up.

"Well, Jeff, I guess that's it for today. Come on, I'll take you back so you'll be on time for that hot county meal." Dahmer stood up and obediently followed me through the hallway. Murphy met us at the elevator.

"When will I see you guys again?" Dahmer asked, a hint of anxiety in his voice. We explained we were off for the weekend and would not return until Monday morning.

"Make sure you request to see us, Jeff, or else we won't be able to come get you," Murphy said as we crossed the tunnel toward the county lockup. The large metal door opened and a heavyset female deputy stood waiting with handcuffs. Dahmer looked sullen as he entered the jail and her custody.

"I think it's going to be a long weekend," he said mournfully.

"Don't worry, Jeff. We'll see you Monday," I said with a smile. The deputy looked at me and shook her head in bewilderment as she closed the door.

Chapter 10

Murphy chuckled as we went back to our department. "It's going to be a long time in between smokes for that guy." Stepping off the elevator, we met Lieutenant Munsey. His eyes were wide and his face had lost its color.

"Hey, are you okay?" Murphy asked as we walked into the assembly. We sat around my desk.

Munsey hung his head for a minute, then spoke. "You know, I thought that story about his traffic stop in 1978 sounded familiar, but I didn't want to interrupt him. I just called my department to search computer files for all traffic citations issued at that time." He took a breath and sighed before continuing. "You're not going to believe this, but it was me. I'm the officer that stopped him that night. I remember shining my flashlight on those garbage bags. I just can't believe it."

Murphy howled with laughter. "No wonder you look so white! You could have stopped this whole thing at the first homicide?"

I looked at Munsey. It was clear he didn't see the humor. I explained how the initial confession sparked an internal review on the officers who responded to the naked Asian male. They were suspended with pay, pending an investigation into any wrongdoing. Munsey looked as if he were going to be sick. Murphy slapped him on the back.

"Ah, come on! Let it go! How could you have known there was a chopped-up body in those garbage bags?"

Murphy shook his head as he stood up and announced he was going to inventory our first successful photo array.

I could see that the lieutenant was still in a state of shock. I tried to take his mind off the matter by explaining our plan to use the original Polaroid pictures found in Dahmer's apartment the night of his arrest. The Polaroids depicted ten of the seventeen victims, taken before and after death, and would be used along with police mug shots and any possible family photos for identification purposes. Munsey gathered his papers and informed me his department was already checking into the information Jeff had given concerning the location of Victim One's remains. He had a flight back to Ohio in the morning and intended personally to check out the story regarding the retainer on the chain.

Murphy returned in time to shake Munsey's hand goodbye, and said, "Hey, Lieutenant, I was only kidding you about that shit. Don't take it seriously. Let us know what you find out."

Munsey smiled in resignation as he walked out.

Murphy sat down and spread the sixty-two Polaroid copies on the desk. It was a gruesome sight and many appeared surreal. There were shots of several freshly severed heads placed on a countertop. Others showed bodies hanging by a strap from a showerhead in various stages of dismemberment, along with severed hands and penises. The most shocking depicted the victims lying on their backs in the bathtub, slit open from neck to genitalia, with the viscera pulled from the body and exposed on their chests. Many victims, both alive and dead, posed in positions highlighting their long, lean, muscular, naked bodies. I noted several photos of the man whose head had stared back at me from the refrigerator. He had the same look of shock on his face. We both sat silently, looking at the photos in disbelief.

"Well, Monday we'll start trying to match these up with our own police pictures and anything we get from the families. I'm going to call in my reports and go home on time for a change, how about you?" Murphy eventually said with a slight smile.

"That sounds good to me," I replied. "I could use a couple days off. The last few have been pretty exciting, but I could use a break."

Murphy took the photos and walked back to his desk. I sat motionless, letting the day's events soak in before calling in my reports. After checking them for accuracy, I handed them to the captain.

"So, it looks like we got Victim One identified, eh, kid?" Domagalski said in his usual gruff tone.

"Yes, sir. We'll know for sure on Monday."

"Well, get some rest this weekend. We've still got a lot of work to do."

I nodded as I walked away, barely hearing the captain's words. I slipped by the press on my way to the parking lot and sat for a while before starting the car. I didn't want to go home. I was elated but restless, and wanted to talk, to brag, to release. My wife's insistence on not discussing the case around the kids was a good idea, but her chilly attitude about my situation was uncomfortable. The events of the last few days tumbled in my head and I found myself driving toward the lakefront. En route, I saw a good friend of my brother's entering his East Town basement flat. I had known him since we were kids.

He waved for me to stop. "Hey, man, I've been seeing you on TV. What a trip."

I exited my car and followed him into his apartment. We talked about the case, the news coverage, and my part in the investigation. I left the apartment about an hour later, but before I could get to my car, a voice called to me from a block away. It was a clerk from the district attorney's office. She was with a group of friends leaving an upscale, East Side watering hole. She was an attractive young woman with long, silky, sandy brown hair and a nice figure. There was always a long line of coppers at her window in the DA's office clamoring for her help. I walked across the street to greet her and she left her entourage to meet me.

"What are you doing here?" she said, placing her hand into mine.

"Oh, I don't know. I guess I just didn't want to go home." I told her I was on my way to the lakefront and ran into a friend.

"Well, if you don't want to go home, let's have a drink. I would love to hear about Dahmer from the horse's mouth," she said, taking my arm and leading me back into the tavern. I could tell she had been drinking by her unsteady walk, and I let her direct me to a table. She pulled a chair next to mine and sidled up to me, smiling. "So, what's it like to look into the face of evil?"

I was a little taken aback by her sudden attention, and she sat close enough for me to catch her perfume. Our collaboration at work was always cordial and professional, but now she seemed almost flirtatious. *Was she hitting on me?* Without going into specifics of the case, I told her about some of Dahmer's quirks and emotions.

"What really stands out about him is how very much like you and me he is." I explained how at times his persona was normal and even likable. She hung on my every word and I enjoyed her attention. I sipped a Coke as we talked until I noted the time. It was going on eleven o'clock and I had to get home. We left the tavern together and I walked her to her vehicle.

"Maybe I'll see you at work," she said, reaching up in an attempt to kiss me.

I didn't hesitate and kissed her back. I wrapped my hands in her long hair as we embraced. Driving home, I was surprised that I didn't feel guilty. I rationalized that a kiss was just a kiss, but I wondered about the young clerk's unexpected attention.

The house was dark when I arrived home, and everyone was asleep. I drank a glass of milk and watched a bit of an old movie before going to bed. I drifted off to sleep with the smell of silky brown hair fresh in my mind.

＊＊

The next morning, I woke up to find my wife packing an overnight bag. No mention was made of my late-night return.

"I'm taking Maureen with me to Fond du Lac for the weekend. I don't want her exposed to any more of this. Alex is getting ready for his game, and Pat is weight lifting this afternoon with the football team."

Her folks still lived in Fond du Lac, and it was our favorite getaway. They were out the door before I could pour my first cup of coffee.

It had been a week since the news hit about Jeffrey Dahmer. The newspapers and tabloids couldn't get enough information on the "Milwaukee Serial Killer." The latest issue of *People* magazine prominently featured Dahmer on the cover wearing the blue-and-white shirt I gave him for the preliminary hearing. My son Pat was ecstatic and took a copy to school to extol his part in the unfolding drama that was prevalent in our city and all over the world.

People, the week of August 12, 1991, featured the Dahmer story, with an eighth of the cover devoted to the upcoming nuptials of actress Liz Taylor to Larry Fortensky, complete with a small photo of the happy couple: "Leaping Liz! Taylor sets the date for hubby No. 7!" Below and taking up the balance of the cover is the large headline "Horror in Milwaukee," with a photo and description: "He was a quiet man who worked in a chocolate factory. But at home in apartment 213 a real-life 'Silence of the Lambs' was unfolding. Now that Jeffrey Dahmer has confessed to 17 grotesque murders, his troubling history of alcoholism, sex offenses, and bizarre behavior raises a haunting question: Why wasn't he stopped?"

In an article by Paula Chin called "The Door of Evil," Shari Dahmer (Lionel Dahmer's second wife and stepmother to Jeff) spoke about his senior year of high school at the time of his parents' separation. Jeff's mother had left Ohio for Wisconsin with their younger son, and Jeff was alone in the family home. "Jeffrey was left all alone in the house with no money, no food, and a broken refrigerator," said Shari. "The desertion really affected him."

Lionel never believed Jeff was a monster and always maintained his son was insane. "There's no doubt he is insane," said Lionel. "Jeffrey was not born a monster. He is not a monster."

It was a real circus, and there was nowhere to go to escape the story. A corps of news organizations remained in front of the police administration building. I parked my car and walked past them without incident. By now, many knew I was involved in the case and under orders not to speak with the press. I entered the assembly and saw Murphy at his desk with two technicians from the photo lab.

"What's up?" I asked, strolling over to them.

"Look. Quite a few already correspond with the dates Jeff gave us." Murphy handed me a stack of mug shots. They were arrest photos of people now listed as missing. Many of them disappeared around the dates Dahmer provided.

The phone rang at my desk and I picked it up. "Homicide, Kennedy." The deputy on the other end informed me that Jeff requested to speak with me. "10-4. I'll be over in a minute."

I hung up and looked at Murphy. He asked, "Is that our boy calling?"

I nodded, and together we navigated the winding maze of hallways and elevators to the county lockup. After announcing our presence on the intercom, the door opened, and there was Dahmer, handcuffed behind his back and standing with a deputy. She unshackled him and he walked into the hallway.

"Well, Jeff, how was your weekend?" Murphy asked, patting him on the back.

He was wearing an orange county jumpsuit, white socks, and black flip-flops. He looked terrible. His eyes were drawn, his hair still greasy and unkempt, and he was sporting a week-old beard.

"Jeez, Jeff, why didn't you take a shower?" I said, sizing up his disheveled look.

Dahmer looked embarrassed. "They said they were so crowded that the deputies never had time to take me. They said I would have the whole shower to myself tonight."

We started down the enclosed bridge between the two buildings. About midway, we passed a line of handcuffed sex workers led by two officers.

"Oh my God! It's Jeffrey Dahmer!" one of the ladies screamed.

At this point, all hell broke loose. I heard wails and shrieks, and the women tugged at their handcuffs, jostling the officers as they pushed through the narrow corridor. We quickly ushered Dahmer through the bridge and into the elevator.

As we took the short ride down to the interrogation room, Dahmer stated, "I know it's been a while since I had a shower, but I didn't think I looked that bad."

I studied Dahmer in amazement. "Jeff, you made a joke."

He grinned at us and asked, "Have you got any cigarettes? I've been having nicotine fits for two days."

I retrieved a pack of Camel straights from my shirt pocket and Murphy pulled some fresh Newports from his pants. Dahmer was delighted and said he was ready to go to work. We left him in the room lighting up his first smoke of the day and returned to Murphy's desk to get the pictures. Before we could get them organized, Captain Domagalski called us into his office.

He hung up the phone when we walked in. "Well, that was your pal from Bath, Ohio. They found the bone fragments right where that freak said they would be. They even found the retainer on the chain he threw in the river. The family positively identified the chain and bent retainer as belonging to their son thirteen years ago. Munsey is flying back tomorrow with a family photo for ID."

He informed us that Boyle set up another psychiatric meeting for Dahmer and the DA had scheduled a few sessions with his own experts.

"Looks like there are lots of people who want to see what makes this guy tick. What do you think? Is he crazy or what?" Domagalski looked to me for an answer.

"I don't know, boss. To do what he's done, he must be crazy, but when you sit down and talk to him, he appears as normal as you and me. He's almost pleasant at times. It's a little weird."

Murphy agreed, but pointed out that in Wisconsin, the determining factor for insanity is whether one has the ability to determine right from wrong at the commission of the crime. "He certainly knew what he was doing and he knew it was wrong. Or else why did he go to such great lengths to conceal his crimes?"

We agreed that the insanity hearing would be an interesting one, and returned to Murphy's desk.

Chapter 11

After picking up the pictures provided by Missing Persons, we walked back to the interrogation room. I stopped and grabbed three cups of coffee. We found Dahmer sitting in a cloud of smoke, obviously making up for lost time. Dahmer took his cup and thanked me.

Murphy began, "Jeff, we want you to look through these photos and see if there is anyone that you recognize."

Dahmer picked up the stack of photos deliberately, taking a drag off his cigarette. The first one he set down, saying, "This is definitely not one of them."

Likewise for the next eight, until he came to the tenth photo in the array. He stopped and stared for a moment. "This looks like the first Hispanic guy I met. I think he was the first one I killed at Grandma's. I remember because it was only a few months after the incident at the Ambassador Hotel. After that, I felt it was stupid to try to control my desires. It seemed as if life conspired to allow my lusts. The situation just kept presenting itself. More importantly, there were no consequences. All I know is, after that, I had to disconnect with my conscience. I no longer felt any sense of remorse."

He looked at the photo again. "Yeah, I'm pretty sure that's him."

Dahmer described how he had been at Club 219 waiting at the bus stop when he met the man. Dahmer said that he was young, attractive, and lean. He struck up a conversation and offered him fifty bucks to come home with him. They took the bus to Grandma's where they engaged in light sex, which Dahmer described as kissing, body rubbing, and masturbating. He offered the young man the Halcion, rum, and Coke concoction and the guy was soon out cold. Dahmer usually waited about an hour for the Halcion to take effect and then had sex with the drugged victim. He recalled that he must have used too much Halcion with this victim because he was unable to arouse him through oral sex. Dahmer was disappointed because he really enjoyed making his victims hard and felating them in this state.

He decided to strangle him.

"I remember that after I strangled him, I had anal sex with him and felt that it was a shame that it was all over so soon. I wrapped him in a sheet and lay him in the fruit cellar. I returned several times throughout the week to kiss, rub, and have anal sex with him. When he began to rot, I severed the flesh from his body with a knife, double-wrapped it in garbage bags, and threw them in the trash. I wrapped the skeleton in a sheet and used a sledgehammer from Grandma's garage to smash the bones and dispose of them in the same way. I kept his head. He was real nice looking and I wanted to keep part of him. Later, I used the spray paint I told you about to make it look fake."

He leaned back in his chair and took another smoke from the pack. He was already falling into that robotic, monotonous demeanor.

Murphy stopped writing and asked, "Jeff, is there anything else that you can remember about this guy? We have no missing persons photos to correspond with the time you say this one happened."

Dahmer inhaled deeply as he smoked and pondered for a bit. Then he leaned forward and said, "Yeah, there is. I remember that this guy had some unusual scars on his body. He had one that looked like he might have had his appendix removed, and two other scars that could have been burns. They were on his breast. It almost looked like he had four nipples. I remember because it looked so weird. Does that help?"

I told him that anything he remembered was helpful, and he was doing a great job. He looked at me and smiled, like a child trying to win approval from a parent. I left the room and went to an office right off the interrogation room hallway. It had been set up as a command post for this investigation, and it was already known as the Dahmer Room. It was the clearinghouse for all information regarding the case, staffed by two old, sour-faced detectives. They were poring over mounds of missing persons reports. If they could match one with the information Dahmer gave to us, we could locate the family and obtain a photograph for Dahmer to identify.

Over the course of the investigation, sixty-eight investigators had to verify everything Dahmer said. I gave them the photo Dahmer identified and told them that the victim was from January 1988. The detectives looked into a pile from that time period and quickly produced a match; however, it did not indicate any unusual scars. They said they would get someone on it right away.

Before I could return to the interrogation room, I was called into the assembly. "Hey, Kennedy!" a clerk yelled from across the room. "There is a lawyer out in the waiting room. She says she wants to come in."

I walked to the waiting room door and opened it to find Wendy Patrickus. "I'm sorry I'm late. Did you start without me?"

I told her we had just begun, and we walked back to the interrogation room where Murphy and Dahmer were enjoying a light moment.

"Jeff, you remember Wendy?" I said, as we entered and sat down.

"Yes, good morning," he responded politely.

Murphy brought her up to speed on the last victim and showed her the photos.

"Shall we begin again?" I said, handing some more pictures to Dahmer.

He began to sift through them, taking his time and deliberately studying each photo before discarding it. After about five minutes, he stopped and placed one picture on the table.

"This one looks familiar. I remember because about two weeks after I killed him, I was reading the paper as I always did, looking for any information about my victims. There was a photograph of him in the personal section listing a number to call if anyone had seen him or knew of his whereabouts."

Dahmer told us he met this victim around March of 1988. He was drinking at the Phoenix Tavern, a local gay bar on South Second Street. He began a conversation and asked the young man if he were willing to come home with him, watch some videos, drink some cocktails, and engage in sexual activity. The guy accepted, and they took a cab to the corner of 57th and Lincoln. Dahmer said he always walked the last few blocks to Grandma's house. This way, the cab driver would not have a record of the address. Once they arrived, Dahmer offered the man the Halcion concoction and they engaged in kissing, rubbing, and mutual oral sex. After the drug took effect, Dahmer performed both oral and anal sex before strangling him. He lay with the dead man until he fell asleep. He woke up just before Grandma did and wrapped the body in a sheet, placing it in the fruit cellar. Sunday morning, when Jeff's grandmother went to church, he severed the flesh and smashed the bones, but kept the head. He threw the remainder of the body in the trash, and the garbage men hauled it away that afternoon.

I looked at Wendy as Dahmer spoke; she wasn't writing notes, just sitting wide-eyed listening to his tale. She caught me watching her and dropped her eyes to the table in disbelief. Murphy got up and left the room to give the new information to the crew in the Dahmer Room. I asked

Dahmer why he started keeping the heads. He answered that it was a shame to go through all the trouble of meeting them, bringing them home, killing them, and cutting them up, just to throw everything away. He wanted to keep some part of the men with him. Besides, he could then bring out the skulls later and masturbate while thinking of the time he had spent with each lover.

Murphy returned with coffee for everyone and sat down. By now, it was close to noon and Dahmer had an appointment to meet with the defense team's psychiatrist. We decided to return him to the county lockup and work on the information we had obtained. Patrickus told Dahmer that she would see him in jail before his interview and left. Dahmer asked if he could have another smoke before going back, and we sat down to accommodate him.

"You know," he said, "there were several guys I brought back to Grandma's for sex that I didn't kill."

Murphy leaned forward with interest. "Really? What do you mean?"

"Well, I didn't kill everyone."

Dahmer told us he met many men who were willing to be with him. He enjoyed their company, especially if they let him have his way sexually, but he only killed the ones he found the most beautiful. Those he wanted to keep with him. He said that one time he was so drunk, he passed out on a possible victim. He woke up alone and relieved of the three hundred dollars in his pants. On another occasion, a victim woke up from the drug before he was able to kill him. He made such a commotion that Grandma came down to the basement. She saw the naked Black man and was not happy that Jeff had visitors in her home without her permission. The victim was still wobbly from the drink, and Jeff had to help him to the bus stop. He must have made a complaint because the following day; a West Allis police officer came to his grandma's house to question him. Dahmer told the cop that he was gay and denied drugging the man. He told the officer that they were both extremely intoxicated and that's why he walked him to the bus stop. It must have accorded with the victim's account, because the West Allis police never contacted him again. After that, Grandma told him he had to get his own apartment.

"Well, that should be easy to check out," I said, thinking it unlikely that Grandma Dahmer had easily forgotten the incident of a strange naked man causing a ruckus in the basement of her house. I got up and went to the Dahmer Room with the new information. Dahmer finished his last smoke for the day, and he and Murphy waited for me by the elevator. We walked him back to the county jail and reminded him to call for us in the morning.

"Don't worry, I will see you guys tomorrow," he said as the large metal door closed behind him. Murphy and I returned to the detective assembly where we were informed that the FBI wanted to talk with us.

A detective assigned to the Dahmer Room approached, saying, "He wasn't lying, Pat. West Allis has a report on file from 1988, April 4. It's a report listing Grandma's house and Dahmer as a resident at that address. The report says that the officer was unable to substantiate the complainant's story and without further information, the case was put on hold."

This was the first solid confirmation of Dahmer's exploits. We had yet to catch him in a lie, and there was no choice except to continue as if everything he told us were true.

Chapter 12

We walked to my desk where two special agents of the FBI met us. "We are the serial killer experts from the bureau. We need to look over your reports and interrogate the prisoner."

Murphy, who had been involved with the FBI on other cases, was not impressed and said, "Well, you can't talk with him, but we can tell you what he's said. Maybe you can give us some information on serial killers that will be of value to us."

The two agents looked surprised at Murphy's negative answer and asked why they could not talk with the suspect. I explained that Murphy and I were the only cops Dahmer was willing to talk with. Murphy added that when we were through with him, they could request an interview, but currently our investigation was active. One of the agents got up in a huff and, without saying a word, went to a nearby phone. The other agent produced charts regarding known serial killers and their patterns of behavior.

We looked over the charts but found that they didn't really depict any of Dahmer's behaviors. In 1991, Dahmer seemed unique because he was willing to work with us to identify his victims. Not only did he confess, but also told us how and why he committed his crimes.

It was not long before the other agent returned, shaking his head. "They're right; we can't talk to him. Did you get anything that will help us?"

His partner looked at me with disdain. "You don't know what you have here. You are going to need our help. There is a good chance you are suffering from Stockholm syndrome."

This was psychological babble. His implication was that we were too close to Dahmer, that we identified with him, could possibly begin to justify his crimes, and obviously could no longer be objective. Murphy blew off the remark as ridiculous and said that we would be glad to ask Dahmer any questions the FBI may have, but this would remain a Milwaukee Police investigation.

The two agents shared a look of resignation and huddled. They returned and reluctantly shared the rest of their information on known serial killers before getting up to leave. They appeared a bit dejected as we shook their hands goodbye.

Once they left the assembly, Murphy muttered, "Those arrogant bastards. Do you believe it? They thought they could take over our case." He said his prior involvement with the FBI was not positive. He felt they were glory hounds who couldn't investigate their way out of a paper bag. They had a bad reputation for taking other investigators' information and claiming it as their own.

"I wouldn't trust those guys as far as I could throw them," Murphy said in disgust.

I was surprised to hear this. I had never worked with the FBI before and thought they were supposed to be the best. Murphy laughed aloud at my remark and explained that FBI agents were usually college graduates with degrees in history or accounting with no real police experience. He believed they were all bumblers and was glad we could put them off.

We returned to our desks and called in the day's reports. I waited to check my copies when the phone rang. Gloria, the steno assigned to type my reports, was on the other end.

"Hey, Pat, do you have a minute?" she asked.

"Of course, Gloria. What's on your mind?"

She wondered if what she had been typing was true. "Did he really say this?"

"Well, of course he did. I couldn't make this up. Why?"

She told me that after typing my reports for the day, she went home and thought about it. It was too much for her to believe, and she said she was having trouble eating and found it hard to sleep at night with all this going on in her head constantly. I reassured her that everything I reported was how Dahmer had described it. I told her that I also thought about what he said after I got home, so her reaction was probably pretty normal, even reasonable, and would hopefully disappear once the interrogation portion of the case concluded. We chatted a bit more about the news coverage and the hoopla surrounding the case before I hung up. I thought I should tell the boss about my conversation with Gloria and walked to his office.

"Hey, Cap, can I talk to you?" I advised him of the situation with Gloria and her comment about having trouble eating and sleeping. He put down the report in his hand.

"Thanks for letting me know about that. How did everything go with Dahmer today?"

"Fine," I answered. "I think we will get a few more identified tomorrow."

He told me I was doing a good job and said he would look into the problem with Gloria. I finished my paperwork and went home.

※ ※ ※

I was awake and out of the house early the next morning. I entered the detective assembly and noticed Captain Domagalski seated at my desk.

"Two things, Pat. First, a deputy called and said that your boy is requesting you. Second, Munsey is back from Ohio with a family photo and will be here shortly." He dropped a new array of pictures on my desk, put together by the Dahmer Room detectives, based on information from the previous day's interview. "I hope they will be useful," he said, and walked away.

Murphy was not in yet, so I walked to the county lockup to retrieve my new best friend. The jail door opened, and Dahmer stood with the same overweight female deputy. She said nothing as she uncuffed Dahmer and turned him over to me. He was showered and shaved, and wearing a clean, orange jumpsuit, white socks, and brown flip-flops. His hair had been shampooed and neatly combed.

"Well, Jeff, you look like a new man," I said as we walked the enclosed maze back to the interrogation room.

"Yeah, I feel much better. They gave me the entire shower room to myself. It felt good to clean up."

We rode the elevator, and I observed that Jeff was indeed a good-looking man. He carried his muscular build well on his six foot one inch frame, and when freshly coiffed, he presented a handsome figure. No wonder he had so much luck meeting and picking up men. The elevator door opened and Murphy stood there. He held a fresh pack of Newports in his hand.

"Good morning, guys," he said with a smile. "Hey, Jeff, you look like a million bucks when you're all spruced up!"

Dahmer smiled sheepishly and blushed at Murphy's comment. We all entered the interrogation room together. Dahmer immediately opened the pack of smokes and lit one up, inhaling deeply.

"Thanks," he said. "Well, what's on the agenda for today?"

He picked up the coffee, which Murphy had already placed on the table, and sipped it with obvious delight. We told him the Bath police were arriving shortly with a possible photo of Victim One, and we wanted him to view photo arrays put together from information given to us the day before. These contained photos obtained from the families of Victims Three and Four. Detectives used information from outstanding missing persons reports to locate family members and advise them of the situation. Interviews with these families garnered personal information and family pictures.

Detectives followed a lead regarding Victim Three: Jamie Doxtator. The family they located confirmed their loved one was still missing, provided a photo, and said that he had an appendix operation when he was thirteen. The mother said that her son was also the victim of child abuse as a baby; her boyfriend at the time was caught burning the boy on his chest with a cigarette, leaving two permanent scars that resembled nipples. Detectives also discovered the possible victim was Native American, not Hispanic, and was actually only fourteen when reported missing. Dahmer picked up the array and began looking through it deliberately, stopping when he came to the photo provided by the family.

"This is him," he said. "He's the Hispanic guy from the bus stop, the one with the funny scars."

Murphy and I looked at each other triumphantly. We told him about the appendix operation and that he was only fourteen. Dahmer looked surprised and said he knew the guy was young, but figured that since he was at the bus stop by the taverns at such a late hour, he must be of age. We told Dahmer that he was actually Native American, and the scars that looked like extra nipples were the result of burns suffered as a child by an abusive parent. Dahmer sat silently, listening, staring straight ahead, and smoking. Murphy gathered the array and left to inform the captain of our success. He returned with another photo array and a yellowed newspaper article, placing them in front of Dahmer. Dahmer looked through it, stopped, and placed a photo on the table.

"This is the guy I met at the Phoenix Tavern. He's the one I saw in the newspaper a few weeks after I killed him."

I picked up the yellowed newspaper article listing the missing subject and the photo that Jeff had selected together.

They were a match. I showed the article to Dahmer and he agreed. "Yeah, that's the guy. I remember the picture of him in the paper." He took the newspaper article and studied it momentarily before concluding, "That's him."

Detectives had followed our lead regarding the article and contacted the family. He was still missing, and the family had provided the newspaper article and a family photo. We had our second positive identification of the day: Richard Guerrero.

Before we could digest our victory, there was a knock at the door. An officer informed us that an attorney and an officer from another jurisdiction were waiting for us. Murphy left to tell the captain about Victim Four, and I stepped into the visitors' area to find Wendy Patrickus and Lt. Munsey waiting. I told them of our two identifications as we walked to the interrogation room. Murphy had already returned and engaged in a conversation with Dahmer. He held a copy of the *Milwaukee Journal* in his hand. It contained an article about a self-styled street preacher, who said he ministered to the gay population. In the article, he claimed he knew Jeffrey Dahmer and tried to counsel him in the way of the Lord.

There was a picture of the preacher, and Murphy showed it to Dahmer. "Do you know this guy?"

Dahmer took the newspaper and studied the picture. His eyes widened as he viewed it. "Wow, I can't believe it. Yeah, I met this guy once."

On Thanksgiving night of 1990, Dahmer went to a local West Allis bar, where he drank heavily. From there, he took a cab to the gay strip south of downtown Milwaukee. There he met the "preacher" depicted in the newspaper article. The two hit it off right away and began drinking Jim Beam. The preacher invited him to his place, where they continued to drink until Dahmer passed out. When he came to in the morning, he found himself hogtied: his hands were tied behind his back, and he was face down with legs spread apart and his feet bound by rope. The rope connected to some hooks fastened in the ceiling, and he was slightly elevated from the bed. The preacher stood next to him, ramming a long white candle up Dahmer's anus. It was painful, and Dahmer began to scream and holler at the top of his lungs, struggling with the ligatures. The preacher became alarmed at the commotion, quickly untied him, and let him down from the apparatus. The preacher tried to calm him down and offered to make breakfast. He was afraid of being reported to police and wanted Dahmer to stay and talk about the incident. Dahmer was too freaked out by the whole experience and once untied, quickly dressed and left without saying a word. About two days after the encounter, he excreted a six-inch portion of candle. Dahmer never reported this experience to the police.

"This is the price you pay for engaging in a high-risk lifestyle." He paused and took a long pull from his cigarette. Looking at me in all sincerity, he said, "You know, Pat, there are some really weird people out there."

Murphy cracked up with laughter, breaking the silence. The rest of us stared at one another, unsure how to respond to the fantastic story. Dahmer blushed, realizing that Murphy was laughing at the absurdity of his last statement.

Munsey cleared his throat. "Jeff, I brought a photo array with me for you to look at. Is there anyone in it that you recognize?" Munsey handed him the pictures and Dahmer looked through them intently, stopping to hold a single photo.

"This is him, the first guy in Bath, Ohio. I'm quite sure."

Munsey took the picture and looked at it, confirming that it was indeed obtained from the Hicks family, the only man reported missing in Bath at the time. He also said the chain with the retainer the victim wore had been recovered from the river, right where Dahmer said he had thrown it. We now had Victims One, Three, and Four identified.

It was lunchtime, and a deputy sheriff was outside the interrogation room door with a hot county meal for Dahmer.

We decided to let him eat in peace and walked to the assembly.

Wendy inquired, "Do you believe this guy? I mean, is he telling the truth?"

I answered that he had not given us anything we could disprove so far, and everything he told us was confirmed through investigation. Munsey said he had to catch a flight back to Bath. He thanked us for solving their homicide and was grateful we had not leaked his earlier late-night encounter with Dahmer to the press. He gave Murphy and me baseball caps with the Bath, Ohio, Police patch on them and two coffee mugs with the same insignia as reward for our work. We thanked him and I walked him to the door.

"Don't feel too bad about being duped by Dahmer," I said as he left. "You're not the only one he fooled."

I returned to find Murphy eating a sandwich and Patrickus nibbling on some carrot sticks. After lunch, the three of us returned to the interrogation room where Dahmer waited, smoking a cigarette. Murphy placed another array in front of him. This one contained police identification photos we had matched to Dahmer's Polaroids, and he sifted through them. We purposely placed pictures of known living people in each array in an attempt to catch him in a lie. Within minutes, he picked out a police photo and asked for the corresponding Polaroid. Murphy handed him copies of his Polaroids and he looked for a match.

"Yes, here he is. I thought that was him." Dahmer held up the matched photos confidently and placed them in front of Murphy. He met this victim in front of the bookstore on 27th Street. "I'm quite sure it was in September of 1990. I think he's the eighth guy I killed."

Dahmer had offered Ernest Miller one hundred and fifty dollars to come home with him. "Remember, Pat? This is the guy I told you about. The one built so nice and muscular. I don't think he was gay, so that's why I offered him so much

GRILLING DAHMER | 147

money. I remember he threatened me as I performed oral sex, but he drank the concoction so I wasn't worried."

Dahmer recounted his earlier tale, detailing how he was so enamored with this victim that he had sex with his unconscious body for hours before passing out. When he came to, Dahmer decided to strangle him, but the victim came out of his drug-induced state and struggled. Dahmer was outmatched, so he grabbed a knife and slashed at the man's carotid artery. Blood splattered all over his bed. "It was quite a mess and I never really did clean it all up," said Dahmer.

This man was most attractive, and Dahmer wanted to keep him. He took pictures before and after cutting him up, and Dahmer pointed out the Polaroids depicting the victim in various stages of dismemberment. He used Soilex and water to boil the victim's skeleton and skull, reassembling him on occasion to fantasize and masturbate. I took the photo array and set it aside, and Dahmer picked up another stack of pictures. He smoked nonchalantly, sifting, stopping momentarily, and then continuing. Finally, he dropped a photo on the table.

"I'm pretty sure that this is the guy I met the night before Easter in 1989. You see these?" He picked out Polaroids depicting a severed penis, a black male's scalp with a large Jheri curl still attached, and a painted skull. "These belong to him."

This was the first time he kept his victim's body parts. He met Anthony Sears at closing time in front of a dance club called La Cage. He was with a friend, a white man, and after accepting Dahmer's offer to come home with him, the friend gave them a ride to 57th and National. They walked the remainder of the way to Grandma's, and Dahmer gave him the drink mixed with Halcion. He had sex with him before and after death. On Easter Sunday, while Grandma attended church, Dahmer dismembered the body by severing the flesh, keeping the individual's scalp, genitals, and skull. He wanted to preserve these body parts, so he went to a hardware store and told the clerk he was interested in drying and treating a wild rabbit pelt. They informed him that acetone would do the trick, and he purchased some. After cleaning the body parts, Dahmer treated them with the acetone for preservation.

"It actually worked quite well, as you can see from the pictures. When they were dried, I wore his scalp. It helped me to fantasize and remember the night I was with him. I could suck on his penis and masturbate."

His eyes shifted to Patrickus, who wrote furiously in her notepad. Finding no look of disapproval, he coolly finished his coffee.

We now had five of the victims identified, and it was getting late. Wendy said she was calling it a day and got up to leave. Murphy escorted her to the door and Dahmer finished his last cigarette. We walked him to the county lockup and reminded him to call for us in the morning. Back in the assembly, we called in the day's reports. As we waited for our dictation to be typed, an aide informed us that we were wanted in the captain's office. We found him talking with the chief, Phillip Arreola.

"Well, gentlemen, how's it going?" the chief asked.

"Fine, sir," we answered in unison. We told him of the day's developments and that we were making good headway.

The chief looked seriously at both of us and asked, "Are you feeling all right? I mean, are you handling everything okay?" Before I could answer, he continued. "You know, Kennedy, I talked with Gloria and she has been referred to a psychiatrist to help her cope with all of this. What about you guys? Are you having any trouble?"

Murphy and I looked at each other in astonishment.

"Well, no," I said. "I mean, Murphy and I talk about it all the time, but I don't think I'm having any trouble. I mean, you know, I don't have any problems eating or sleeping if that's what you're referring to."

GRILLING DAHMER | 149

Murphy chimed in, "No sir, I'm fine. I know this case is a little unusual, but I've been doing this for years; it doesn't bother me. Besides, anything that's on our minds, Pat and I talk about at the end of the day, so it's been okay."

The chief nodded, not saying a word. Domagalski broke the silence. "Okay, gentlemen. Good work. Let me know if you have any problems. I'll see you tomorrow."

Murphy and I walked back to our desks and prepared to leave.

"Can you believe that?" Murphy asked.

I told him about the conversation I had with Gloria, and that I had mentioned it to the captain. "Maybe that got him thinking about us?" I suggested.

We walked to the elevator, and on the way down Murphy retorted, "Hell, if anyone needs a shrink, it's Dahmer, not you and me." Murphy was like a pit bull; nothing seemed to bother him, but I wondered about myself. I felt fine, although viewing the gruesome Polaroids did seem to diminish my appetite for red meat.

Chapter 13

I let the air conditioning flow over me once I was in my car. I didn't want to go home. The kids were busy with summer activities, and spending another evening alone in the basement was not appealing. I drove toward the lake. It was beautiful. The sun was setting, and worshippers catching the last rays scattered the beach. I decided to stop at Victor's for happy hour. It was a lounge that catered to an eclectic group of patrons. In the evening, it filled with a cross-section of Milwaukee citizens, and they had a reputation for treating coppers well. I entered to find a group of off-duty officers from the jail. A redhead with her hair pulled back in a French braid noticed me and broke from the group. Since working the day shift, I had seen her often during my many trips with Dahmer through the lockup. She was always upbeat in our encounters.

"Well, how's the Dahmer dick?" she said, sitting down next to me. "What's he like? I see you two talking as if you're friends."

Up close, I noticed her freckles. They were scattered around her entire face.

"Yeah, you know. I have to keep rapport with the guy," I said, ordering a Coke. "Can I get you something?"

"No, I've had enough." We talked for an hour or so about the job, our families, and Dahmer until she said she had to go home. "Can you walk me to my car?" she said, tugging at my arm.

GRILLING DAHMER | 151

No one from her group noticed that we left, and once outside, she leaned against me as we walked. This was the second time a woman had cornered me for a conversation about Jeff. *Was the attention from the Dahmer case some sort of strange aphrodisiac?*

***

The following morning, I walked into the detective assembly and a clerk told me the captain wanted to see me. I saw that Murphy was not at his desk as I entered the captain's office.

"You're late," Domagalski said in his usual gruff voice.

I tried to explain that I was not used to the morning rush hour traffic and that I got caught in a jam, but he waved it off as if he weren't interested. He pointed to a stack of reports on his desk.

"These are inquiries from all over the country and some from overseas. Your boy has created quite a bit of interest. Everyone with an unsolved homicide is looking to Dahmer for clearance. You guys will have to question Dahmer about them all. I've already set up a task force to compile and answer them once you've interrogated him about each case."

I reached for the stack of reports but the captain said, "Not now. Boyle has informed me that his associate will be tied up until this afternoon. Dahmer has already requested to talk with you, but we're going to wait for Boyle's assistant counsel. Besides, I have someone that I want you to talk with this morning. Murphy is talking to him now, and you're next. Go get a cup of coffee and a hard roll. I'll let you know when he's ready for you."

I walked to the coffee bar and grabbed a roll and a cup of coffee. I sat at my desk and wondered who the captain wanted me to talk to and why. Thirty minutes or so passed, and Murphy walked through the assembly room door with a wide grin on his face. He sat down next to me.

"I've just had my head examined and you're next." He explained that the chief worried we might have trouble assimilating all that we heard and saw regarding the case. He felt some of Dahmer's insanity might rub off on us. Murphy laughed. "Hell, Kennedy, you're nuts anyway. It's too late for you." He explained there was a shrink on the seventh floor in the conference room and I should proceed there immediately. "Wait until you get a load of this guy," he said. I got up and headed for the elevator.

The conference room was wood paneled and windowless, with a large rectangular table surrounded by high-backed chairs. The chief used it for staff meetings and press events. I entered the room and saw a white man seated at the head of the table.

"Hello, Detective Kennedy. My name is Dr. Schuts. Have a seat." The doctor was small in stature, almost petite. His gray hair was combed back; he wore glasses, a brown leather sport jacket, a maroon turtleneck sweater, and beige pants. He sat with his legs crossed, perched forward in his chair. I greeted him as I sat down and asked what I could do for him.

"Well, the question is, what can I do for you?" he said in a very high-pitched voice, smiling.

He explained that the chief was concerned the investigation could cause some problems. He mentioned Gloria, and stated the chief believed it might be helpful to have a professional around in case Murphy and I or anyone else needed to talk to someone. I told him that although I had been a detective for only a year, I had been involved in many disturbing cases while in uniform. Over that time, I said, I had developed an ability to leave work-related troubles at work and I had yet to experience any difficulties. I continued that my partner, Murphy, was an experienced homicide investigator, and we talked regularly about what we experienced with Dahmer. The doctor sat back in his chair and studied me as I spoke.

GRILLING DAHMER | 153

"What about your family?" he asked. "How are they taking this whole thing?"

I told him that my children were more caught up in the excitement of all the media attention; however, my wife had some concerns.

"That's understandable," he said, handing me a stack of stapled papers. "I'm giving you a list of possible effects that can occur when people are involved in traumatic situations. Look it over and be aware of the behavior patterns." I took the papers and paged through them. "Is there anything that's on your mind now that you would like to talk about? Any trouble eating? Sleeping?"

I leaned back in my chair and shook my head no. "Not really. Doc, I've been caught up in all the excitement myself. After all, this is an excellent opportunity for my career, so I've been focused on that. Besides, I have Murphy. He's a pro. We talk about everything throughout the day, and by the time I go home, I'm pretty well exhausted. So far, so good."

The doctor spent the remaining half hour explaining how sometimes events "such as this" do not become a stumbling block for those involved until after the event. He talked about post-traumatic stress and its effects, saying that many times people under stress of this type exhibit self-destructive behaviors, such as overeating, drug and alcohol abuse, sleeplessness, sexual promiscuity, and so on. I listened patiently as the doctor finished and told him I was somewhat familiar with the disorder. I'd stay on the lookout for any trouble.

He handed me his business card and told me to call him any time—that the department handled the cost, so I shouldn't hesitate if I felt I experienced any trouble.

I thanked him and left. I took the elevator back to the detective assembly. I walked to my desk, where Murphy sat, with his legs up, drinking coffee.

"Well, did you get your head screwed on right?" he asked with a grin.

I sat down next to him. "Yeah, I think so. Man, that guy was a little weird looking, you know?"

I pulled out the list of self-destructive behaviors the doctor had given me. Murphy saw it and exclaimed, "Yeah, he gave me one of those. Hell, Pat, we already exhibit all those behaviors. I was glad to see that nothing was going to change."

We both laughed, but I did secretly wonder if I would experience any effects from the whole situation.

Captain Domagalski broke the moment's lightness. He walked over and dropped a stack of inquiries on my desk.

"Okay, fellas, these are from all over the place, including a few from Germany. I know that some of them are ridiculous, but we have to answer them all."

I picked up the stack of missing persons reports and photos. They were from just about every state in the union. Inquiries regarding body parts found in California, missing men from Illinois, and mutilated women in Germany. Murphy thought it would be easier to answer all these questions if we had a chronological timeline of Dahmer's life. This meant documenting Dahmer's whereabouts throughout his thirty-one years. We would question Dahmer about his movements and locations, and then cross-reference that with information provided by his father, mother, schools, friends, army officials, building superintendents, probation officers, employers, and neighbors. Documents such as arrest records, army records, correspondence, transcripts, and other paper trails would be useful for filling in gaps.

With this accomplished, we could then eliminate many of the inquiries; either because Dahmer never lived there or was not in the area at the time of the homicide in question. Murphy took this task, and from then on, whenever we questioned Dahmer, he meticulously recorded the chronology of his life.

The department was inundated with calls regarding Dahmer and his crimes. Anonymous callers stated that

Dahmer buried the bones of his victims throughout the city, or had plastered them into the walls of his apartment. Others said they were acquaintances of Dahmer and knew him to be involved in the occult. But the bulk of inquiries concerned missing persons. Pictures of these people and reports about them arrived from all over the country. There were even several letters addressed to Jeff Dahmer, care of Milwaukee Police. We had Dahmer open these in our presence to determine their content. The case was becoming more involved than anyone could have imagined, and I was glad that an army of detectives and police officers had been assigned to help us.

After lunch, we were informed that Wendy waited outside the assembly. We instructed an officer to show her to the interrogation room, and we took the winding maze to the jail. The large metal door opened to reveal Dahmer, standing next to a stout deputy and holding a book. I questioned him about the book.

"I got it today in the mail," he answered. "It's from the editor of *Vanity Fair* magazine. They want an interview."

I took the book from his hand and looked through it as we walked. It was titled *Killing for Company*, written by Brian Masters[4], an English author. It detailed the case of the UK's Dennis Nilsen[5], who killed people, dismembered their bodies, and disposed of them in plastic garbage bags. The incident happened several years earlier in London, and came to light when large pieces of dismembered flesh began to clog Nilsen's apartment building's plumbing. That led the police to discover several garbage bags containing body parts.

We entered the interrogation room to find Wendy waiting patiently. I handed her the book and mentioned the interview

---

4. Brian Master published the book, *The Shrine of Jeffrey Dahmer*, published in 1993. Master attended Dahmer's trial daily.

5. Dahmer read the book and, according to Wendy Patrickus, highlighted several sections of the book.

request. She looked through it quickly. "I don't know about an interview, but I'll give this to Mr. Boyle and let him decide."

We all sat down, and I pulled a fresh pack of Camels from my pocket. Dahmer nodded his thanks, opened the pack, and lit one up. Murphy held the letters addressed to Dahmer. "Jeff, it looks like you're a celebrity. I've got some fan mail for you." He set the letters down and Dahmer quizzically picked one and opened it. A photograph of a young woman with long brown hair, early thirties, posed in a rather seductive position fell to the floor.

I picked it up. "Hey, she's kind of attractive!" I said, handing it to him.

The letter was from the woman in the picture, and she wrote that she wanted to correspond with him. She had followed the case every day and found Jeff fascinating. Dahmer put the letter down and looked at us in disbelief. We read the rest of the mail; it was more of the same. Some were from people requesting an interview or asking to write his life story. Others were simply inquisitive loonies hoping to be pen pals with a serial killer. One was from an older woman in Montana who offered to help pay for his defense. Patrickus took possession of all the correspondence, noting that Boyle would determine what to do with it.

We spent the remainder of the day looking at photos of missing persons from all over the country and preparing a chronological outline of Jeff's life. He studiously viewed every picture before placing them on the desk and denying any involvement.

After a while, he spoke up. "Look, I've told you already that the only places I committed my crimes were in Bath, Ohio, Grandma's in West Allis, and in my Milwaukee apartment. I've never even been to some of these states. How could I be involved?" A pleading look of sincerity crossed his face and he turned to me for support.

"Jeff, I believe you, but if we don't do this, there will always be accusations and questions," I said, and Murphy agreed, explaining we needed to eliminate him from these inquiries as part of the investigation.

When his life timeline was complete, we could reply because we would know where he had been, and if he wanted to tell his whole story, identify the victims, and clear his conscience, this was the only way. Dahmer picked up the photos with renewed determination and continued to sort through the pile. only one cigarette left in the pack. We got up and left Dahmer in the room to finish his final smoke, and I walked Patrickus to the door.

"Well, what do you think?" I asked.

It was late afternoon and Wendy sighed, signaling that she had enough for the day. She held up the pile of letters. "These are unbelievable! What kind of people want to be pen pals with a guy like Jeff Dahmer?" She shook her head as she entered the elevator and disappeared behind the closing door. I returned to walk with Murphy and Dahmer back to lockup.

"We'll see you tomorrow, Jeff," I said, and he waved goodbye and dutifully followed the deputy back into the jail.

Murphy and I returned to our office and phoned in our reports. After reading them for accuracy, I took them to the captain and headed for the door. I noticed Murphy was still dictating and figured the chronology took some extra time. I was glad he had volunteered to compile the record of Dahmer's lifetime. Murphy was a tireless investigator and meticulous about details. He would spend many hours completing this task, and I was grateful for his patience and camaraderie. He was still calling in his reports as he acknowledged my departure.

"See you tomorrow, Pat."

Chapter 14

The house was empty. A note taped to the TV informed me that my wife had taken the three children to her folks' house for a couple of days. She was concerned about their welfare and hoped to spare them some of the media circus. Normally I enjoyed the peace and quiet of having the house to myself, which seldom occurred, but tonight the lack of family commotion was unwelcome.

I prepared a simple meal of bacon and eggs, and watched a classic John Wayne movie. I caught the late news to see the latest hyperbole about the "slaughter on 25th Street." The frenzy continued as anyone with even the slightest connection to the case had a camera pushed in their faces. The day's inquiries were fresh in my mind as I climbed into bed. Although I was exhausted, it was a fitful night's sleep.

***

I entered the detective assembly early the next morning to find it almost empty. Apparently, it had been a busy night— two people killed, and another two shot and in serious condition. Every available day shift detective had been called in to take up the slack. Jeffrey Dahmer had only added to a banner year for homicides. With his deeds included, the tally for the year eventually came to 169, the most ever for the city of Milwaukee[6]. I walked through the deserted assembly to my

---

6. The highest number of murders in one year is currently 189, according to homicide statistics released from the City of Milwaukee in 2020.

desk and found a stack of new photos. As I sorted through them, Murphy walked through the door.

"Hey, what's going on in here?" he asked, noting the empty room. I told him of the previous night's activities and why everyone was gone.

"Well, that's their problem," he said. "We've got our own case to worry about."

The phone on my desk rang, and picking it up, I was informed, "The prisoner is requesting you."

Murphy and I made our way to the lockup where we found Dahmer and Patrickus waiting for us. Murphy lifted a pack of Lucky Strikes from his shirt pocket, and Dahmer nodded his appreciation.

Once back in the interrogation room, Murphy left for coffee and rolls. I explained that today we wished to continue with the outside inquiries. There were over three hundred open homicide investigations sent to us from police departments all over the United States. Most of these included aspects of mutilation. Apparently, there were a lot of people getting away with murder. The chronological timeline of Dahmer's life was almost complete and enabled us to dismiss the vast majority since we could prove his location over his thirty-one years. Murphy returned and we settled in. The tiny room was cramped with all of us seated around the table, but by now, we were comfortable with one another and an almost workman-like relationship existed.

We started with a request from the Hollywood, Florida, Police Department. It regarded Adam Walsh[7], a six-year-

---

7. Adam Walsh disappeared July 27, 1981, almost ten years to the day that detectives questioned Jeff about his possible involvement in the South Florida cold case. Because Jeff had been in the Miami, Florida, area around the time of the abduction, many speculated for years that he must have had some involvement in the Walsh murder. Dahmer always denied the kidnap and murder of Walsh, maintaining that he had no sexual attraction toward children. In 2008, the Hollywood Police Department named serial killer Ottis Toole (d. 1996, in prison for other murders) as the likely murderer of Walsh, based on largely circumstantial evidence and a confession by the notorious false

old boy who, in 1981, had disappeared from a Sears at a local shopping mall. Adam's head was the only body part recovered and they were hot to develop Dahmer as a suspect, especially when they learned he had been in Florida around the time of Adam's disappearance. That a severed head had been connected to Jeff only increased their interest to tie him to that case. Murphy's timeline had placed him in the Miami area after his discharge from the army. John Walsh, the father of the little boy, was what made the request interesting. The work he had done connected to his son's disappearance and death turned the protection of children into his lifelong passion, which eventually led to creating the highly rated, and Walsh's best-known, first of many, TV show *America's Most Wanted*.

I placed a photo of the little boy on the table. Dahmer picked it up and sighed as soon as he saw it. "He's a kid; I wouldn't hurt a little kid."

I reminded him of the fourteen year old he met at the bus stop.

"Yeah, you told me how old he was, but at the time, I thought he was of age. Besides, I'm not attracted to children." He reiterated that he knew what he did was monstrous and selfish but that he was only attracted to men, not young or small boys. He wanted a sexually mature victim, someone who could give and receive pleasure. He seemed almost indignant at the suggestion that he was attracted to prepubescent children. I placed the photo of Adam Walsh back in its file.

***

Murphy placed some new pictures in front of him. They were a mixture of police and family photos gathered by the Dahmer Room detectives.

---

confessor, thereby officially closing the cold case of this tragic kidnap and murder.

He took a pull from his cigarette as he picked up the stack and looked deliberately at each one before discarding it in silence.

He stopped a moment and squinted. "This looks like the one I met after the bookstore guy." I quickly sorted through the pictures provided by family and found a corresponding match. I handed it to Dahmer, who studied it briefly before confirming, "Yeah, that's him."

He thought for a while before beginning. "I think it was October of 1990. I was walking on Wisconsin Avenue when I met him. I struck up a conversation and asked if he wanted to come home to my apartment for some cocktails. I also mentioned that I would pay him a hundred dollars if he let me take some nude pictures of him. He agreed, and we walked to my apartment, where we engaged in some light sex and I gave him the drink. Soon he was out, and I made love to him for about an hour or so. I decided that I would kill him, and used my hands to strangle him until he stopped breathing."

Murphy interrupted by placing the Polaroid picture found on the table in the apartment. It depicted the victim straddled on his back over the side of a bathtub. There was an incision made from the bottom of his chin to the top of his genitals. The viscera was pulled out of the body and lying, as if on display, on top of the torso. The colored Polaroid was shocking. The moist, red entrails glistened, revealing the intestines and internal organs.

"What's this all about?" Murphy said, pointing to the ghastly sight.

Dahmer picked it up and shrugged. "I wanted a picture of his insides, so I placed him in the bathroom and cut him open. I pulled the viscera from his body with my hands. The look and feel of it gave me unbelievable pleasure, and I masturbated and made love to him by placing my penis in it, like having intercourse."

He took a long, slow drag from his cigarette without looking up as the rest of us sat in silence. We had identified our sixth victim: David Thomas. Murphy, serious as ever, finally broke the silence. "How did you dispose of this one? Did you keep any of his parts?"

Dahmer answered that he became leery of placing the bones and flesh in the trash for fear of discovery. This is when he began to use the muriatic acid. He tried to save the skull by boiling it; however, he wanted to speed up the drying process and used a higher oven temperature. The increased heat popped the skull into smaller sections. Because it was ruined, he threw it into the acid. There were no remaining parts of this victim.

Lunchtime came quickly, and a deputy knocked at the door with a hot plate for their star boarder. The morning's work did not seem to diminish Dahmer's appetite, and he was already biting into his meal as we left. Wendy stated she had a hearing on another matter that afternoon that would take up the next several days. She requested we suspend questioning until then. We agreed and I showed her to the door. At the elevators, she mentioned that Boyle had requested a list of items recovered from Dahmer's apartment and wondered when it would be available.

"I know they are working on it. I'm sure it will be ready by the time you return," I explained.

My partner Mike Dubis was charged with the task of inventorying all the items taken away in the investigation. He was still assigned to the third shift, and I had not really talked with him since the night of Jeff's arrest. His job was daunting; it eventually required a one hundred and fifty-page inventory report. It contained blood samples and rotted flesh from the basement drain, along with the sledgehammer from Grandma's house, and literally everything from the Oxford Apartments location. The medical examiner inspected each item first to determine its evidentiary value. Anything thought to contain trace evidence, including all the body parts, were transported to his office.

The list was astounding. There were ten heads in all: one full head in the refrigerator, four skulls in a small floor freezer, three painted skulls in metallic colors, and two that were bone-dry white. Those that were still relatively identifiable were matched with either police or family photos. The large blue hermetically sealed industrial drum from the bedroom contained severed human flesh and four completely dismembered bodies covered in a solution of muriatic acid. There were sets of hands, a human scalp, and two well-preserved penises found in plastic pails hidden in the closet. A four-drawer metal filing cabinet from the living room contained the entire skeletal structure of a victim. The bones inside had been treated with the various solvents and were immaculately clean. There was a variety of knives. One had a large contoured black plastic handle with a six-inch serrated blade and the word Bushwacker molded into it. There was a small drill with several bits, numerous handsaws, forks, plates, and a stovetop broiler adapter, all encrusted with human bone and flesh and trace blood evidence.

The remaining items—furniture, wall hangings, clothing, personal items, and miscellaneous odds and ends—were placed in storage at the Property Control Section. The most disturbing revelation was the numerous fillets of flesh wrapped in individual plastic sandwich bags and neatly stacked in the freezer compartment of Dahmer's refrigerator. I was grateful to be working on the interrogation. The thought of locating, documenting, collecting, and transporting the gruesome assortment of evidence was more than distasteful. I could only imagine what my partner and the identification team encountered that first night as they scoured Dahmer's apartment.

I returned to find Murphy motioning me into the captain's office.

"Sit down, Pat. I want to talk to you guys a minute."

Domagalski told us the medical examiner identified the individually wrapped pieces of flesh as biceps, thighs, livers, and hearts. The utensils, plates, and broiler adapter all pointed to the conclusion that Dahmer must have been eating his victims.

Chapter 15

I looked at Murphy and his eyes widened. I felt my blood run cold. The medical examiner had found what appeared to be the markings of a tenderizing instrument on the pieces of biceps and thigh. The markings corresponded with a wooden meat tenderizer recovered from the scene. The paper-thin cuts of individually wrapped heart and liver made it look as though he was storing the "food" for later use. He wanted us to question Dahmer about this. I said that Wendy had left and would not return for several days. Boyle would certainly want her present for this type of questioning. Domagalski agreed and said it could wait until then.

"So what are you going to do with him for the remainder of the day?" the captain asked.

I answered that we still had another stack of photos for him to view, and maybe we could identify another victim. Murphy and I left the office and went to our desks to eat. I had brought an orange, a box of raisins, and a banana, which I finished quickly. I went to check on Dahmer. He had finished eating and was enjoying a smoke when I entered the room.

"Excuse me, Pat, but could I have another cup of coffee?" I grabbed his cup and returned to the coffee bar. Murphy joined me.

"So what do you think of your boy now?" Murphy asked.

I didn't know what to say. I poured a cup for myself as well, and we returned to the room. Murphy handed the new stack of photos to Dahmer, who was smoking contentedly. I couldn't stop thinking about what the captain had told us.

I must have been looking at Dahmer in a strange way because he interrupted my thoughts. "Hey, Pat, are you okay? You look kind of funny."

I told him that I must not have gotten enough sleep and I'd be fine. He again looked through the photos, and within minutes stopped and placed one on the table. "I think this is one."

Murphy quickly shuffled through the corresponding missing persons reports containing family pictures to find its match. He handed it to Dahmer, who looked at it intently. "Yeah, this is him."

I asked him what he remembered about this individual. Dahmer leaned back in his chair and gathered his thoughts.

"I'm pretty sure that I met this guy in July 1990." Murphy acknowledged that the report listed him missing on July 14. Dahmer continued. "I was at the Phoenix Tavern. I remember because he was not really my type, but he was extremely willing, so I offered him money to come home with me. He agreed and we took a cab to 25th and State. I remember that once we got to my apartment, he was all over me and we engaged in some mutual masturbation and light sex, you know, touching and kissing. He performed oral sex on me and when he was finished, I made him the drink with the Halcion. After he passed out, I made love to him by anal intercourse and then I strangled him.

"I bought a small floor freezer about a week before that to store the bodies of my victims if I was pressed for time or too tired to dispose of them right away. This was the first time I used it. I folded his body into it and kept it there for a few weeks before I cut off the flesh and placed him in the muriatic acid. I kept the head and tried to dry it out after boiling it like the other one I told you about, but the oven must have been too hot because the skull started exploding, so I had to throw it in the acid. I remember feeling the whole event was a waste of time because I couldn't keep anything of him and that was the whole point, to keep them with me."

We had identified another victim: Eddie Smith. Dahmer took a deep breath and sighed. It was almost as if the retelling brought back his deep disappointment from the event. I stretched my legs and back while Murphy restacked the photos. By now, it was time to call it quits for the day. Murphy explained that we would not be able to talk to him for the next three days because Patrickus had other legal matters.

A look of disappointment crossed Dahmer's face as he stood up. "Well, can't you guys come and get me to talk anyway?"

I told him that the department had given us time off as well, so we would all have to wait to resume the investigation. Dahmer, very likely thinking of his smoking privileges, was noticeably unhappy but resigned to the situation. He would just have to sit it out until we returned. We walked back along the secure route to county lockup and delivered him to the deputy waiting at the large metal door. Dahmer looked like a sad little boy as it closed behind him. Murphy and I returned to the assembly and called in our daily reports.

I returned to the empty house and wondered what to do with myself for the next few days. I prepared some dinner but before I could eat, the phone rang. It was a representative for *The Oprah Winfrey Show*. She wanted to know if I was interested in doing an interview. I was flabbergasted and asked how she found my unlisted phone number.

The voice on the other end of the line was polite and direct in her answer: "Well, Detective Kennedy, you know, we have investigators too. I'm not at liberty to say where we obtained your number. Just suffice it to say that we are very interested in your story and are willing to pay you in advance for an interview."

I advised her that I was under orders from the chief not to talk with anyone regarding the investigation and hung up.

I had the same conversation with two other callers over the next few days, one from *Geraldo*, and another from *Inside Edition*. The last caller said they were willing to pay as much as $30,000 for my time. I could not believe what I heard and flatly denied their requests. I thought about it though. At that time, I earned about $50,000 a year and lived comfortably, but with three kids in private Catholic school, the offer tempted me. I finished my meal in front of the television and fell asleep after the late news.

***

Back at work a few days later, the phone on my desk rang and a deputy on the other end advised me that our boy was impatiently requesting to speak with me. Just then, Murphy appeared, looking refreshed from his days off and I told him Dahmer waited for us. Together we walked and rode the elevator to the county lockup to retrieve him. During the elevator ride, I told Murphy about the phone calls I received.

"You didn't say anything to them, did you?" Murphy said, concern in his voice.

"Of course not, but what do you think about the cash offer?"

Murphy reached the same conclusion as I did about the possible career loss, and we decided right then and there that no matter what happened in the future with this case, we would confide only in each other and work in unison. The large gray metal door opened and we saw Dahmer standing next to an older turnkey with a grizzled face. Dahmer was smiling and obviously glad to see us, if for no other reason than he was dying for a cigarette.

"So, Jeff, how was it the last few days?" I asked as we rode the elevator down to the interrogation room.

Dahmer said that even though he was in isolation at county, other prisoners had to walk by his cell en route for meals and various court appearances. He told us many of the inmates knew who he was and what he had done. A few, especially the Black guys, had made threatening comments to him as they passed his cell. Dahmer wasn't worried about it, but noted many prisoners felt a great deal of hostility toward him.

When we entered the interrogation room, Patrickus was already present. She said my partner Mike had admitted her. There was a fresh pack of Camel straights in front of her on the table. Dahmer acknowledged her presence, immediately opened the smokes, and lit one up. He leaned back in his chair and relished the tobacco he had been without over the last few days.

"Do we have any coffee?" he asked, looking in my direction. I nodded and indicated I would get some. Murphy and I left Dahmer and Patrickus in the room and walked to the coffee bar.

"Well, how do you want to start it today?" Murphy asked as he poured four cups of coffee. "Do we start with the new stack of potential murder victim photos or do we hit him with the cannibalism questions?"

I walked to my desk and picked up the fresh stack of police photos and their corresponding family pictures of young men who had disappeared in Milwaukee. "Well, I'd like to get the victim from the Ambassador Hotel identified if we can. We have several good leads and family pictures that could be him. I'm not sure how he'll react to the eating bodies questions."

Murphy agreed with my suggestion, and we returned to the room to find Patrickus inquiring about Dahmer's relationship with his mother, Joyce Flint Dahmer. Joyce and Jeff had not been in communication for some time, and she was not very forthcoming with information to the defense. She lived in California and wanted nothing to do with the case. I knew Murphy tried to contact her several times to set up an interview, with negative results.

We set the pictures down in front of Dahmer, and Patrickus placed a file regarding his mother back in her briefcase. She took out her notepad and prepared for another session.

Murphy began. "Jeff, we have been trying to work on the first victim you met here in Milwaukee, the one from the hotel. According to what you told Pat, that event happened around Thanksgiving of 1987. Take a look through these police photos of people still missing from that time."

Dahmer picked up the stack of pictures and slowly looked through them. He smoked and drank his coffee. After wading through the stack, he placed them back on the table and said, "He's not in there."

I handed him a fresh stack of photos we had obtained from family members of other still-missing persons. These people had never been arrested, so no police photos were available, and tracking down the families to get a picture depicting the missing persons' likeness at the time of their disappearance was no easy task. Dahmer sorted through the photos nonchalantly. Taking a deep drag off his smoke, he stopped and exhaled slowly while holding up a faded family picture, he dropped the remaining photos.

"I think this is him." The photo depicted a white man with blue eyes and light brown hair and a pleasant expression. He was handsome and smiling. The picture was a typical family shot and showed a young man in the prime of his life. "What can you tell me about him?" Dahmer asked.

Murphy said that he was reported missing on November 20, 1987, and that he was not originally from Milwaukee, but had recently moved here from the Upper Peninsula to attend college.

Dahmer nodded as he looked at the picture.

Murphy continued, "He was last seen leaving work at the George Webb's downtown." Dahmer's eyes widened at the mention of Webb's, a local greasy spoon, quite popular in Milwaukee.

"That must be him." Dahmer nodded. He continued; in 1987, he decided to give in to his desire for gay encounters and had already used the Ambassador Hotel to engage in these activities. Because he lived with Grandma and wanted privacy, he rented a room early Friday evening before haunting the bars in search of a companion. He had already received a prescription for the Halcion and had been secretly drugging his lovers, as we knew. He figured that by the time he met this guy, he had already used the hotel and the Halcion approximately five or six times on various men with no negative repercussions.

"The mention of George Webb's rings a bell," Dahmer said. He met this guy at Club 219 and invited him back to the hotel after the bar closed. He again studied the picture. "Yeah, that's him. I'm sure of it. I remember that I met him and we hit it off right away. I didn't even have to offer him money or anything. He was a willing partner, and now I remember he mentioned that he worked at George Webb's."

Dahmer and Steven Tuomi took a cab to the hotel, and although they were both already intoxicated, Dahmer made him the rum, Coke, and Halcion drink. They took off their clothes, got into bed, and began hugging, kissing, and mutually masturbating until the guy fell asleep. Dahmer continued to drink and had anal intercourse with the guy while in his drug-induced state. Dahmer stopped and looked me in the eye.

"Pat, you remember I told you about it. I must have gotten too drunk and passed out. I don't know what happened, but I must have killed him, because when I woke up the next morning, there was blood dripping from his mouth, and his ribs and chest were sunken and looked crushed. There was blood, and marks all over his chest, and my forearms were sore, swollen, and bruised. I already told you how I went back to the mall and bought the suitcase to get him back to Grandma's. I stored him in the fruit cellar until my family left and Grandma was out of the house. I knew the cool air of the fruit cellar would slow the decomposition of the body and keep it from rotting until I could get to it," Dahmer remembered.

"After this killing, I felt that my conscience was severed. I had tried so hard to forget about the first one back in Bath, but I couldn't do it. What was the point? I remember feeling that my path was set. I made a conscious decision to give in to this overwhelming, ambiguous, and extreme compulsion. I laid him on the basement floor over the drain.

"I severed the flesh from his body with a knife and placed it in plastic garbage bags. I remember being so excited that I masturbated several times while smashing up the bones and disposing of the body. His was the first head I kept. I boiled it in a solution of water and Soilex, then I used straight bleach on it, wrapped it in a blanket, and kept it in the fruit cellar. I remember that I returned to masturbate with it about a week later and noted that the bleach had broken down the bone structure, causing it to become very brittle, so I smashed it up with the sledgehammer and threw it in the trash."

Dahmer sat there and stared into space as if he were reliving his experience.

Patrickus cleared her throat, breaking the silence. "Jeff, you said that it was an overwhelming compulsion. Did you hear voices? Was there something telling you to kill? Was it the devil?"

Murphy and I looked at each other. This was the first time the devil was mentioned and it was easy to see where Patrickus was going with this line of questioning—insanity defense. Dahmer pulled another cigarette from the pack and lit it up. It appeared as if he were formulating his answer.

"I never heard voices. It possibly could have been the devil. I don't know, but I do know that at the time I formulated my decisions to kill, thoughts of the devil never entered into it. I knew something was compelling me to act, but I figured that it was my own selfish, sick need to gratify myself in this way. I just don't know."

Patrickus wrote his answer down in her notepad as we sat in silence, watching the smoke curl above Dahmer's head. We had identified eight victims. By this time, Dahmer's lunch tray waited out in the hall. Patrickus said she would be back this afternoon and got up to leave.

I retrieved my own lunch and brought it to the room. "You don't mind if I eat here with you today, do you?"

Dahmer looked up and smiled. "Not at all, Pat. Please join me."

Murphy grabbed the photos and showed Patrickus out of the assembly.

Dahmer and I ate and talked about the quality of food served by the county to the inmates. He was unaccustomed to such starchy fare and said so.

"What do you think about Wendy's question regarding the devil?" I asked.

Dahmer put down his fork and pondered the query for a second before answering. "I wondered about that, Pat, especially during the time I spent at Grandma's, but I never heard voices or tried to invoke Satan. I remember thinking that I was just selfish. I wanted to satisfy my own sexual urges. There was no thought about the men I encountered except as to how I could convince them to come with me."

He dug back into his plate of beef, mashed potatoes, gravy, and peas. I peeled my orange while we sat in silence. After eating, I took Dahmer's tray and left him to enjoy his after-meal smoke. I walked to Murphy's desk, where he pored over the medical examiner's report on the individually wrapped body parts found in the freezer.

"Well, how are we going to handle it, Murphy?" I asked.

He put down the report. "I think we will just hit him with the medical examiner's findings, tell him what we think, and see what he says."

I nodded in agreement. He gathered up the report and we walked back to the interrogation room to find Dahmer leaning back in his chair with his feet up on the table. He looked as if he was enjoying himself. Murphy and I entered, closed the door behind us, and sat down. Dahmer sensed that the mood had changed and put his feet down and straightened his chair.

"Isn't Wendy coming back for the afternoon?" he asked.

I pulled my chair closer to him and answered, "Yeah, she'll be back later, but right now, we thought we would ask you a few questions that have been bothering us for a few days."

Dahmer nervously fidgeted in his chair as he drew another cigarette from the pack and lit it.

"You know, Jeff, we've been talking for a few days now and I thought we were getting along okay, didn't you?"

Dahmer eagerly answered, "Yeah, Pat. You guys have been great to me. I told you that before. Sometimes I don't even feel like I'm being interrogated."

I placed my hand on Dahmer's arm and continued. "Good, Jeff, because we want you to feel that you can tell us everything and not hold anything back."

Dahmer searched my face for a look of disdain. Finding none, he responded. "Pat, I haven't lied to you about anything."

"I'm not saying that you lied to us, Jeff. I just don't think that you have told us everything that we need to know."

Dahmer's eyes widened and he sat straight back in his chair. Murphy placed the medical examiner's report on the table and began. "Jeff, what I have here is a report from the medical examiner regarding the contents found in the freezer of your refrigerator." Dahmer sighed and sank in his chair with his head down as Murphy continued. "It says here, Jeff, that they found a number of items in there that need some further explanation."

Dahmer continued to look at the floor, motionless and silent. Murphy opened the report and thumbed through a few pages before continuing.

"It says, Jeff, that there were, inside your freezer, a number of individually wrapped, neatly stored body parts. Namely, some meticulously cut and trimmed biceps, thigh, liver, and heart. The biceps and thigh have very distinctive markings on them which correlate with the wooden meat tenderizing utensil found in your kitchen."

Dahmer remained motionless, his cigarette burning unattended in his hand. I reached over and touched his shoulder once more.

"Jeff, you have to believe what I told you on that first night that we were together. There is nothing that you can tell Murphy or me that will change our opinion of you. We've gotten to know and accept you, Jeff. We realize that the drinking had a big part to play in what happened and that there are possibly some other problems that might be linked to your situation; we accept and understand that, but you have got to be completely honest with us if you really want to put this thing behind you and move on with your life. Besides, if you don't tell us something and we learn about it from another source, then it leads us to believe that you have not been telling the truth all along. Don't you see, Jeff?"

Dahmer took a hard drag off his cigarette and held it in for an unusually long time before exhaling.

Murphy pulled his chair so close to Dahmer that he was damn near in his lap.

"Come on, Jeff. Tell us. You've been eating these guys, haven't you?"

Dahmer pulled back in his chair with a look of terror. He studied my face intensely as if he were a child waiting to be reprimanded. I deliberately tried to keep an air of acceptance and calm as I spoke. "Jeff, it's okay. We know. It's going to be all right. Just be honest with us and tell the truth. That's all we ask."

Dahmer leaned forward in his chair, dropped his smoke to the floor, and crushed it with his foot. With his head still lowered, he murmured a barely audible, "Yes."

Murphy didn't move and remained in Dahmer's personal space. "Jeff, what did you say? You've been eating them, haven't you?"

Dahmer leaned back. "Yes. I have. Well, I mean, not all of them. Just a few."

I again put my hand on Dahmer's shoulder. "Why didn't you tell us this before?"

He looked at me pleadingly. "I don't know. I mean, everything was going so smooth. I didn't think it mattered so much for the investigation. Besides, it seemed like you guys really liked me. I didn't know what you would think of me if I told you that. And then there is the whole thing with the press. They are going to make me out to be some kind of monster when they find out about this."

Chapter 16

Murphy pushed his chair back to give Dahmer some room. "Aw, fuck those guys, Jeff. They try to make everyone look bad. Look how they talk about the cops. I don't let them bother me and neither should you. They don't know all the circumstances like we do, so fuck 'em!"

I agreed with Murphy and stood up to announce that I was going for some more coffee. Dahmer held up his cup. "I'd like some more, if it's okay?"

I nodded, took his cup, quickly retrieved the coffee, and returned to the room. After everyone had sipped their brew, Dahmer took another smoke out and lit up.

"Okay. When did all this begin?" Murphy asked in his most nonchalant tone.

"Well, the first time I tried it was with the guy I met at Club 219. I don't think we have him identified yet. At least I haven't seen his picture. I did take a few quick Polaroid photos of him though."

I interjected. "When did you meet this guy?"

Dahmer told us that it was right after he had finished serving his time for an earlier arrest. Going through his police record, we discovered he had been arrested in September 1988 for second-degree sexual assault. He had met a young Asian boy at the Grand Avenue Mall and convinced him to accompany him home for some cocktails and nude photos.

The young lad accepted his offer and went to Jeff's first Milwaukee apartment at 808 North 24th Street. There Jeff gave him fifty dollars for posing nude, and the two drank rum and Coke. Dahmer said that the boy was kind of young and not very sexually mature, so when he was finished taking the Polaroid photos, he let him go.

Unfortunately for Dahmer, when the lad returned home and his folks saw that he was drunk, they called the police. The boy eventually led them back to Dahmer's apartment, where the police found the Polaroids and arrested him. He was subsequently sentenced to a year under the county work release program and five years probation. After his release, he moved into the Oxford Apartments at 924 North 25th Street. Dahmer said that the first time he ate human flesh was in May 1990.

Murphy handed Dahmer the stack of photos recovered from his apartment. He sifted through them and pulled out nine pictures of an African American man posed naked. He was dead. There were a few that showed the victim in various stages of dismemberment. One was the guy's head. It was freshly severed, placed on the kitchen table. The picture was disturbing. It was a lateral view with the victim's eye and mouth wide open.

"This is the guy. I remember because he had a tattoo on his chest that said Cash D."

Dahmer had met this guy at Club 219 and offered him a hundred bucks to come home with him for some pictures and light sex. He told us that he didn't think that this guy was gay but a "hustler," a guy who would do anything for money. He said that they took a cab to his apartment and once there, Dahmer tried to hug and kiss the guy, but he would only pose for pictures and allow Jeff to perform oral sex on him.

Dahmer said this victim was the most physically well-built of anyone that he had been with so far, and that he was very attracted to him. He decided to give him the rum, Coke, and Halcion drink, and soon the guy was out cold. Dahmer said that he enjoyed having sex with the man while drugged but must have spent too much time lying with him— when he tried to strangle him like the others, the guy started to wake up and struggle.

"Remember, Pat, the guy I told you about that I had to stab in the carotid artery with my knife? Well, this is him." Dahmer pointed to a Polaroid photo of the victim's head, which clearly showed a gash on the right side of his neck.

Dahmer felt it was a shame that he had to kill this guy, but he knew if he let him live, he would wake up and be angry, possibly attack him, and surely leave. Dahmer wanted to keep him. As he began to dispose of the body, he became so turned on by the long, lean, muscular build of the guy that he decided to keep his whole skeleton.

"That's the guy you found in the file cabinet," Dahmer said, and described how he had carefully filleted the flesh and separated the head and bones, boiling them in a Soilex and hot water solution. The skeleton turned out great and when Dahmer was finished, he could put the guy completely back together. The head was one of the painted skulls we found. Dahmer hesitated a moment and stared into space.

"That's when it happened. I began to feel that I needed more of a rush. I thought to myself, *I want more. I wanted to keep this one, but I wanted him in me. I wanted him to become part of me.* That's when the idea of eating part of his body occurred to me. So, I severed his biceps, which were beautiful. I also took his thigh and his heart."

Dahmer said that he ate the heart first. "It tasted spongy." He then took a bite of the thigh, but it was so tough that he could hardly chew it. He bought some meat tenderizer to use on the biceps.

I could hardly contain myself. "Meat tenderizer? How did you prepare it?"

Dahmer drew another cigarette from the pack and matter-of-factly described how he placed a little cooking oil in a skillet and lightly fried the body parts until medium rare. Sometimes he would add onions and mushrooms for flavor.

Murphy interrupted. "What did it taste like?"

Dahmer exhaled as he answered. "It tasted like a fine cut of meat, like a filet mignon."

Murphy and I sat speechless for a while, letting that sink in. Dahmer calmly smoked his cigarette. A knock on the door broke the silence. A police aide popped in and handed Murphy a stack of police photos.

Before he left, I told him, "Hey, run the name Cash D on the computer as an alias and see if we have a photo."

The aide nodded and left without a word. We handed the photos to Dahmer and he began to sort through them. He picked out a couple of possibilities, but it was hard to tell when matching them with Dahmer's own photos. Another knock at the door revealed the same police aide with a photo and runoff sheet regarding a Cash D. Murphy took the photo and handed it to Dahmer.

"That's him." Dahmer placed the police mug shot next to his own Polaroid photo. It was a perfect match. We had identified our ninth victim: Ricky Beeks.

We all sat quietly as Murphy stacked the unidentified photos. I watched Dahmer as he smoked contentedly, obviously glad that the new revelation had not changed the nature of the interrogation. There was a slight knock at the door and when it opened, there stood Patrickus with an arm full of files. "I'm sorry, guys, but I couldn't get out of court. Did I miss anything?"

Dahmer stared straight ahead, barely acknowledging her presence. Murphy looked at me with a smile. "Oh, just the usual. We did identify another victim though. Why don't you come with me and I'll fill you in?"

The two left the room, and Dahmer and I sat and looked at each other. He appeared to be searching my face for a look of disappointment. I smiled at him.

"Jeez, Jeff. Why didn't you tell me this before?"

He put out his smoke on the floor and immediately grabbed another from the pack. "I don't know. I guess I figured it wasn't all that important to the investigation. I was afraid you would be disgusted with me and call the whole thing off. I don't know, Pat. I guess I also wanted to spare my family from the gruesomeness of my acts. I suppose it doesn't matter now anyway. The press has smeared my crimes all over the place. I'll just have to live with it." He fumbled with his cigarette and sighed. I pushed my chair back from the table.

"Don't worry about it, Jeff. Besides, you heard Murphy. Fuck those guys!"

It was after four and I stood up, telling Dahmer that I was going to check on his return time with the county. I left the room and walked to the detective assembly. I saw Patrickus sitting at Murphy's desk. Her eyes were blinking almost uncontrollably as Murphy repeated Jeff's cannibalism revelation.

I walked over and sat down. "Well, what do you think?" I asked.

Patrickus shook her head. "I don't know what to think," she finally said.

We gave her the details, and she wrote the main points in her notebook. When she finished, we decided to call it a day. Patrickus said that Boyle had Dahmer scheduled for a series of interviews with two different psychiatrists the next day, and there would be no time for interrogation. She asked if we could resume on the day after. I escorted her to the door and returned to the interrogation room to find Murphy explaining to Dahmer that he would be busy with the shrink tomorrow, but that he should call for us on the following day. Dahmer acknowledged this, and we traveled the route to the county lockup.

As the large metal door opened and the deputy took Dahmer inside, Murphy said, "Good job today, Jeff. We'll see you in a day or so."

Dahmer smiled and waved as the clanking metal door closed behind him.

Murphy said, "That was a hell of an afternoon, Pat. Good job. I didn't know if he would have copped to it all like that if Patrickus had been in the room; what do you think?"

I told him how Dahmer said that he was afraid we would disown him or something if we found out.

"I wonder if there is anything else he hasn't told us," Murphy said as we entered the assembly.

I remarked that we had not yet caught him in a lie. Dahmer wasn't always forthcoming with information, but when we pressed him on something, he always told the truth and gave an explanation. We even placed pictures of known living people in the photo stacks we gave him to identify, just to see if he would pick one out and claim it as a victim. Through our investigation, we were able to substantiate that everything he had told us thus far was the truth. He may not have willingly told us everything, but when faced with pointed questions, he always answered truthfully.

We called in our day's reports and after checking them, handed them to the captain.

"Well, we're halfway there, gentlemen. Nine down, eight to go," Domagalski said, then answered his ringing phone.

I walked to my car and drove home with visions of sizzling oil and skillets rolling around in my brain. The colored Polaroids depicting severed flesh, red and glistening, did look like something from the meat section at the grocery store, and I wondered about the possibility of becoming a vegetarian after all of this.

Murphy and I spent the next day organizing our reports and meeting with the shrink. This time it was a psychiatric social worker. She was a huge woman with short, curly hair and large, rimmed glasses. She gave us more of the usual information about possible psychological problems we may experience from our involvement in this type of investigation. Murphy and I made fun of the so-called experts assigned to make sure we were all right, and wondered who was in charge of hiring these people. At any rate, we sat through their sessions and politely accepted their suggestions of expressing our feelings, exercising, eating right, and getting enough sleep. I never mentioned the cool relationship with my wife and our troubles at home. I didn't want anything to jeopardize my involvement, and feared the captain may change the routine if he were aware of any personal problems.

My evenings at home were becoming routine as well. After eating, the kids returned to summertime activities and my wife buried herself in homework or attended night classes. I retreated to the basement, where I had a barbell set and sit-up board. I worked out and watched classic movies until it was time for bed.

***

The following morning, I sat at my desk and dutifully listened to the day shift roll call. A few grizzled old detectives made comments about me sandbagging the investigation in order to get out of real police work.

The phone on Murphy's desk rang, and the voice on the other end informed us that our star witness had called. We proceeded to retrieve Dahmer and begin another day. When the door opened, Dahmer and the deputy stood silent and motionless.

We walked the hall back to the elevator and I said, "It doesn't look like you and the deputy have much to say to each other."

Dahmer shook his head. "Yeah, nobody really talks to me over there. You guys are the only ones who treat me like a normal human being."

Murphy and I looked at each other, silently grinning, before we entered the interrogation room.

Murphy began. "Well, Jeff, we want to get a few more identifications today. We've been working with the dates you have given us and have quite a few missing men for you to look at."

Dahmer sat down and relaxed himself.

I threw a pack of Kools on the table. Dahmer's eyes lit up. "Menthols, eh?" He quickly opened the pack and lit one up.

"I thought you might like a change of pace," I said, and left the room to get three cups of coffee and a new stack of photos. Patrickus had arrived when I returned to the room, and I sat down with the three of them to begin. I placed the stacks of police photos, family pictures, and Dahmer's own Polaroids on the table.

"We've been trying to gather as much as we can for July of this year, Jeff. According to the information you've given us, that was a pretty busy time for you."

Indeed, the investigation revealed that July 1991 was a watershed moment in Dahmer's heinous killing career. During that month alone, he had lured and murdered three men and propositioned five others before his last victim escaped and brought police back to the apartment.

"Things were a little hectic there at the end," Dahmer replied as he sipped his coffee.

He picked up the stack and began to look through it. Patrickus took out her notebook and prepared to write when Dahmer set down a family picture and picked up the stack of his own Polaroids. After a minute, he laid down a surreal-looking Polaroid photo of what appeared to be two headless bodies lying in a bathtub on top of each other. They were in different stages of dismemberment. The flesh was severed from the arms, legs, and trunk of the bodies, with bone peeking through the gristle. He placed it next to the family picture.

"The one on top is this guy." He pointed to the family photo and looked at me. "He's the one in the icebox."

I recalled the indescribable fear I felt on the night I opened the refrigerator door. The victim's surprised look immediately returned to my mind. The family picture was a good likeness, and I wondered why I didn't recognize him myself while viewing the photos ahead of showing them to Jeff.

Dahmer continued. "At the end, it seemed as if things were spinning out of control. I was drinking more than usual, had missed work, and was getting behind in the cleanup and disposal of my victims. At the time I met this guy, there was already a previous victim soaking in a solution of salt, formaldehyde, and water in my bathtub. I sometimes did this if I was too tired to cut up the bodies at night. This seemed to slow down the decomposition and reduced the smell, which was a constant problem."

Our investigation showed that Dahmer had been approached several times by his building superintendent, as well as neighbors, concerning the vile smells coming from his apartment.

Dahmer told us that he met this guy in the 900 block of North 27th Street at a bookstore that sold pornographic materials; it's frequented by sex workers, hustlers, and drug addicts. He mentioned that the guy was well spoken, friendly, and extremely good looking. He told Dahmer that he was a model for men's magazines and showed him some of his work. (In fact, Mike Dubis recovered a professional glossy magazine photo of the lean and muscularly built victim from Dahmer's apartment.) Dahmer offered the man a hundred dollars to come to his place and let him take a few nude pictures of him. The guy was more than willing, and brought his modeling portfolio with him. The two walked the few blocks to Dahmer's apartment, where Jeff fixed his Halcion concoction. After the victim drank the mixture, they engaged in some kissing and hugging until he passed out. Dahmer couldn't believe his luck; this guy was really attractive, and he wanted to keep him alive longer. He preferred a live partner and enjoyed lying with a warm, docile, breathing body.

"I had purchased some chloroform earlier with the idea of keeping them alive, but unconscious longer. I placed a cloth over his face and poured some chloroform on it. It didn't seem to work as well as I thought, and I had to strangle him," Dahmer recounted.

He took several Polaroid photos of this victim, both before and after dismemberment. He placed the victim's head in a box and put it in the refrigerator. As he spoke, my mind returned to the night we met, and the overwhelming rush of fear that had gripped me. It was funny that I now talked to the perpetrator of that fear as if we were old friends. Dahmer took various photos of the victim handcuffed and lying on his stomach. One depicted the victim hanging from a black strap attached to the showerhead in his bathroom. The victim's flesh had been stripped away, revealing his bony torso. This photo also revealed two other bodies lying partially dismembered and soaking in the formaldehyde solution.

"What kind of knives are these?" Murphy asked, pointing to several Polaroids that contained two large, contoured, black-handled knives.

Dahmer said that they were specially made for hunting and skinning prey. He had purchased them at a cutlery shop in the mall downtown for this reason.

He continued that he carefully removed the victim's heart and placed it in the refrigerator to eat later, but he was so enamored of him that he severed his right bicep, fried it, and ate it immediately. He said that it tasted good, and he added some onions and steak sauce to it for flavor. As he spoke, my mind returned to Dahmer's apartment. The head in the box in the refrigerator caught my attention, but now I remembered that the interior door shelves held several condiments, including steak sauce, ketchup, mustard, and mayonnaise.

Patrickus was still writing down Dahmer's narrative when Murphy said, "Well, Jeff, if this guy on the bottom was already there in the tub when you brought home this last one, you must have met him shortly before."

Dahmer took the Polaroid and studied it. "Yes, the guy on the bottom is the second guy I met in Chicago."

Murphy's eyes widened. "Good. I have a stack of pictures that arrived from the Chicago police." He left the room to retrieve the photos. The extensive work he had done on Dahmer's chronological timeline was about to pay off. The carefully detailed description of victims, along with possible times, places, and dates, was now proving invaluable. The Chicago police could reduce the number of possible victims in much the same way we did, and sent numerous police and family pictures of possible victims.

I asked Dahmer about his excursions to the Windy City. He initially went to Chicago because complaints about him possibly drugging patrons at the bathhouses in Milwaukee made him unwelcome there. He got his information about the various bars and bathhouses of Chicago by reading local gay magazines and papers. He detailed his activities, stating he had visited Chicago about ten or eleven times and always rode the bus. He usually went to Boystown, an area on Clark Street that catered to the gay population. He specifically mentioned the Country Bath Club and the Unicorn Club as favorite spots to visit. Dahmer said that the men he met in Chicago were of all different races, ethnicities, and backgrounds. He never developed personal relationships with any of them, and all the men he spent time with in Chicago were strictly one-night stands. He never left the gay area or accompanied them to personal homes or apartments, but conducted his activities in the bathhouses.

He flatly denied committing any homicides while in Chicago. On several occasions, he used his concoction to drug his pickups. One of these was a tall Black man who realized that something was wrong and accused him of putting drugs in his drink. An argument erupted and before the guy left, he punched Dahmer in the face, bloodying his nose. His victim must not have complained because bathhouse managers and Chicago police never questioned him.

Murphy returned to the room, interrupting the story. He had a handful of pictures from the Chicago PD. He set them down, and Dahmer dutifully began to sort through them. Regarding the victim on the bottom in the bathtub, Dahmer told us that he had gone to Chicago to take in the gay Pride parade. He went to Carol's Bar on Wells Street to have a drink and struck up a conversation with a mixed-race man, and the two hit it off.

"I told him I was from Milwaukee and invited him to return with me. I was surprised because I didn't offer him any money and we took the Greyhound together," Dahmer recalled.

They spent the evening making love to each other. Dahmer described this as both oral and anal sex.

"This was unusual. I'm not particularly fond of receiving anal sex. It can be painful, but this guy was so willing and eager that I let him have his way." He hesitated for a moment. "Pat, it was almost like a normal relationship. The next morning, we went out to breakfast and then spent the day walking around downtown and drinking beer. We made love again that night and I started to think that maybe this one would stay. It was wonderful."

The cigarette in Dahmer's hand was spent and he dropped it to the floor, crushing it with his foot. He sighed aloud as he pulled a fresh one from the pack.

"The next morning, he mentioned his job and that he would have to return. I remember the disappointment I felt, realizing that I could never have a normal relationship. So I made him the drink."

He separated one of the Chicago pictures and placed it on the table. "This might be him. I think he said that he was Puerto Rican and Jewish." Then he pulled several photos from the stack of Polaroids. One depicted a man's severed head lying in a bathroom sink. It was face up, and his eyes stared back with a blank expression. "Yes, I'm sure of it. That's him."

Murphy picked up the two pictures. It was easy to see that they were a match when you held them side by side for comparison. Murphy began to record the accompanying information regarding the victim's name, date of birth, and address as Dahmer continued.

"I really didn't want to kill this one, but I had to because he was going to leave and I wanted to keep him with me. I took these Polaroids of him, placed his head in the freezer, and severed the flesh from both guys in the bathtub. I threw the flesh into the trash and put their skeletons into the fifty-seven-gallon drum filled with muriatic acid."

He looked at Patrickus as he finished, but she was engrossed in writing his story and didn't notice. It was lunchtime, and Dahmer's hot plate from the county jail was waiting outside the interrogation room door. Patrickus excused herself, saying that she would return in an hour. Murphy left to contact the Chicago police and advise them that we had cleared up one of their missing persons reports. It was now a homicide.

I grabbed my lunch and returned to the interrogation room. I have a brother who lives on the Big Island of Hawaii and had recently written me a letter, sending along some organically grown and naturally dried bananas. I brought them in my lunch and as I placed the bunch of five small bananas on the table, Dahmer stopped and stared. He asked if he could have one, and I said sure.

He picked up the brown bunch and commented that they held a remarkable resemblance to a person's fingers after they had been immersed in muriatic acid for a while. He placed the banana in his mouth and chewed. "It's not bad."

We spent the remaining lunch hour eating and discussing the quality of county cuisine. We chatted like colleagues; the give and take of conversation was normal. An outside observer would detect no sinister monster engaged in evil, just a regular guy discussing food—what he liked and didn't like to eat.

Both Patrickus and Murphy returned, and we all sat around the table as Dahmer finished his after-meal smoke. We again turned our attention to the stack of photos provided by the Chicago police. As Dahmer looked through them, he recalled that the first victim he met in Chicago was about a week or two before the last victim he identified. He remembered that he had spent the evening in Boystown but was unsuccessful in finding a partner for the night. He decided to return to Milwaukee. It appeared that gay men frequented the bus terminal, and he noted one who was simply hanging around.

They started a conversation in the men's room and went to the café for coffee. Dahmer felt that the guy was willing, so he offered him money to come with him back to Milwaukee for a night of sex and possibly some nude photos. The victim agreed, and they purchased a bottle of wine to share on the ride. At this point, Dahmer picked up one of his photos. It was a photo of a Black male, naked and handcuffed behind his back. He was standing and looked like he was leaning against the wall of Dahmer's bedroom.

"Is this the guy?" Murphy asked. Dahmer nodded yes.

I asked, "Are these the poses that you would ask them to get into, or did he do this by himself?"

Dahmer took a cigarette from the pack and lit it, inhaling deeply. "No, he's already dead in that picture," he said, exhaling as he spoke.

I couldn't believe my eyes. "How did you get a dead guy into that pose?"

Dahmer explained that after returning to his apartment, he and the guy engaged in hugging and kissing while the victim drank the Halcion concoction.

After he passed out, Dahmer placed the handcuffs on him and took some bondage photos. He then used the strap shown in previous photos to hang his victims from the shower for defleshing to strangle the guy. He said that he was tired from drinking and fell asleep on top of him. He awoke several hours later to find that rigor mortis had set in and the victim was stiff as a board. "I don't know, I guess I was playing around with his body and decided to stand him up."

To his surprise, the rigor made it possible for Dahmer to lean the victim against the wall. It appeared as though he were alive and posing for the bondage picture. I picked up the Polaroid and looked at it closely. A more intense study of it revealed that the victim's eyes were closed, and his face was expressionless, yet he was standing with his arms handcuffed behind his back, leaning against the wall as though he were alive.

Dahmer again turned his attention to the stack of police and family pictures from Chicago. After a few moments, he picked out a police mug shot and corresponding family photo. He laid these two next to his own Polaroid and said, "That's him."

Murphy recorded the latest victim's personal information as Dahmer recalled severing his head and placing it in the floor freezer along with several others. His plan was to boil all the heads he kept. He placed the defleshed bodies in the blue drum to dissolve. We had now identified Victims Ten, Eleven, and Twelve: Matt Turner, Jeremiah Weinberger, and Oliver Lacy. Murphy stood up, stating that he would make the call to Chicago and inform them of the newest identification.

He remarked, "I hope those Chicago cops appreciate that we're clearing up their case load for them."

Chapter 17

Dahmer relaxed by leaning back in his chair.

I asked, "Jeff, how did you go about choosing your victims? Was it random chance, just anyone that would talk to you, or what?"

He stated that race, religion, ethnic background, or education did not matter to him. He did have an ideal body type in mind though. He explained that he was attracted to handsome young men with long, lean, muscular bodies.

"Basically, though, it all boiled down to opportunity." He described how he cruised the bars, bookstores, or the mall looking for a suitable conquest. "I watched them for a while first to see if they noticed me or not. Sometimes they did, and it was easy to strike up a conversation.

"Other times I waited to see if they were alone before I approached. When the bar was closing would usually be a good time. The bars emptied out and everyone seemed to be looking for a partner. I never tried to coerce or force anyone. They were all more than willing to come home with me. Of course, I did offer them money for their company."

As he spoke, I recalled the many nights in uniform I was charged with dispersing the crowd gathered along the gay strip at closing time. Men of every age and race mingled and conversed outside the taverns.

The area became a veritable parking lot, filled with slowly driven vehicles in hot pursuit of a pickup. Dahmer was upbeat as he described the scene.

"I really enjoyed all the campy behavior. The transvestites and drag queens gave everything a carnival-like atmosphere, and it seemed like another world." He remarked how this added to his secret and gave him a feeling of having a power of invincibility. "I was part of it, but anonymous. I came and went as I pleased. No one seemed to notice the ones that came with me, or questioned their disappearance. Each time I returned, I felt more powerful. I was in charge of my own little universe. I began to feel as if I couldn't get caught, that I had some evil power protecting me. I know it sounds weird, but there were so many times I thought I'd be found out but it didn't happen. No one knew, no one asked, no one cared."

I pressed him on this point, and he detailed a litany of times that he fooled authorities.

"The first time was in Bath. That cop had me cold, with the guy all cut up in bags resting in the back of my dad's car. Then there was my first one here in Milwaukee, the one in the suitcase. Who would believe that the cab driver helped load the guy? I ate Thanksgiving dinner with my family that day knowing the dead man's body lay in the fruit cellar. When Grandma complained of the smell coming from the basement, I appeased her with tales of a full cat litter box and poured gallons of bleach down the basement floor drain to dilute the odor. One time, as my father and stepmother were visiting, Grandma mentioned that I was throwing large garbage bags of something into her trash bins. My father investigated and found some of the bones I had pulverized. He questioned me and I told him I had decided to pursue my earlier interest in the bones of dead animals. He bought it. When I cut up the bodies, it gave off a horrendous odor and there were several times my apartment manager approached me about complaints from neighbors. I dumped my fish into a bucket and advised him that the motor on my aquarium broke down while I was in Chicago, killing all my fish. I even showed him the bucket with the dead fish. He told me to throw everything out, and from then on, I was always trying to eliminate the odor with fans, cleansers, and air fresheners.

"Then there was the judge who let me out of jail before my sentence was complete for taking pictures of that young Asian boy. My cellmate told me you could write a letter to the judge asking for leniency and explaining how you had learned your lesson. He seemed knowledgeable about such matters, so I asked him to compose one for me. It worked, and I was released early. Although my parole officer said she would make random checks of the apartment, she never did. When I met with her, I played the game and told her what she wanted to hear. I was required to meet with a psychologist because of my drinking problem. He tried to delve into my psyche, but like the parole agent, I just told him what he wanted to hear."

As he spoke, I recalled my own enforced sessions with the psychiatrist and how they tried to get me to open up about what I saw, heard, and felt. I patiently listened to them before giving the pat answer that I was okay and all was going smoothly.

"And of course, the closest one occurred when that Asian guy got away and the police were called. Even though I was drunk, I remember feeling invincible. I walked into the group of firefighters, onlookers, and police officers. I knew there was a dead man lying in my bed, but still, I invited the officers back to my apartment. I showed them his clothes, neatly folded on the couch, and the Polaroid photos he had so willingly posed for. They accepted my explanation and left. It was amazing and gave me great pleasure. I couldn't be caught."

Patrickus and I looked at each other without saying a word while Dahmer snuffed his cigarette and casually sipped his coffee. Murphy returned to the room, and announced that the Chicago detectives were ecstatic with our work and owed us all lunch. By now, it was getting late and Patrickus began to pack up her notepads. She bid Dahmer goodbye, and I showed her out. When I returned, Murphy and I walked Dahmer to the county lockup and handed him over to the waiting deputy.

Back in the detective assembly, we called in our reports, checked them for accuracy, and handed them to the captain. I drove home with the day's events lingering in my mind. I was excited about the success we were having. It looked like we were going to identify all the victims. I wanted to share the good news with someone, but was aware of the "no Dahmer" rule at home.

Dinner was finished when I arrived, and my wife advised that she had a study group to attend. She gathered her textbooks and left. School was back in session and the kids were busy with homework. I pulled a plate of leftover chicken from the refrigerator and retreated to the basement family room to eat. I periodically checked on the kids as the evening wore on, and they eventually settled into their rooms for the night. I was alone with my thoughts and felt a little agitated. The evening passed, and the kids took turns saying goodnight before turning in. I finally left the front porch light on for my wife, climbed into the empty bed, and quickly fell asleep.

***

The next morning, the detective assembly was jumping. It must have been a busy night. I was so engrossed with Dahmer that it was easy to forget that we were experiencing a banner year for homicides. But I did notice the late-shift detectives were still calling in reports and securing evidence as the morning crew listened to roll call and recorded information on the new cases.

As I walked to my desk, I noticed Murphy was talking to the same two arrogant FBI agents who had approached us before. I sat down to hear Murphy tell them that they would have to wait until we were through before they could attempt to set up an interview with Dahmer. I pretended to look through some reports as I listened to the more senior of the two agents. He told Murphy that we did not possess the expertise when it came to serial killers. They had been in contact with the parents of Adam Walsh in Florida, and now they too were convinced that Dahmer was involved. He again implied that Murphy and I were in over our heads, and we should turn the case over to the capable hands of the FBI. Murphy, who's not always the most diplomatic, patiently explained to the two that we had looked over their profile information. Dahmer did not fit into any of their so-called categories. He continued that we were gearing up and had only a few more victims to identify. After that, if they could get permission from Boyle, they could take all the time with Dahmer they wanted. I could hear the frustration in the agent's voice as he intimated that Dahmer was probably not telling us about all his victims.

I was surprised at Murphy's calm candor, and he chuckled at their suggestion. He thanked them for their offer, but again stated that we planned to continue the investigation on our own. The two agents left in disgust, knowing that the only way they could personally get involved right now was if we invited them to help us with the interview.

The phone on Murphy's desk rang, and I heard him tell whoever was on the other end that we would be right over. As we walked to the elevator and made our way over to the county lockup, Murphy exploded.

"Can you believe it? Those pricks couldn't find their asses with both hands yet they are going to help us clear this caper?"

Before I could answer, the large metal door opened and there stood Dahmer, holding a stack of letters and standing next to the same silent deputy. As we walked back to the interrogation room area, he told us that he received some additional fan mail. It was more of the same: people wanting to correspond with him, others asking for a signed photograph, and some wanted to assist in his defense.

Dahmer shook his head in disbelief. "I thought that when my deeds finally came out, I would be vilified, but these people want to be my friend. I don't get it."

We entered the room to find Patrickus already seated with a cup of coffee. I took out a pack of Camels and handed them to Dahmer, who immediately lit one up. Murphy left to retrieve coffee for us and to grab a new stack of photos. As we waited, I advised them of the medical examiner's progress; he was able to identify positively, through dental records, many of the eleven skulls we recovered. These confirmed the information Dahmer had already given us.

"Jeff, the medical examiner was wondering about a few things and we were hoping you could clear it up," I said.

Dahmer set his coffee down and looked at me quizzically. "Sure, Pat. What do you want to know?"

"Well, it appears that four of the skulls have small holes in the top of them. The medical examiner confirms that the drill bit recovered from your apartment matches the holes and contains trace evidence of human flesh and bone. I know that you stated this was done to help the boiling process and it enabled the cleaning solution to enter the brain area, making it easier for you to clean them, but if this is so, then why didn't you do this to all of the skulls?"

Dahmer pursed his lips and looked at the three of us before answering. "Well, I didn't mention this because I didn't think it was pertinent to the investigation, and I didn't want you to think I was torturing anyone, because I wasn't. Remember, I told you that I was always disappointed after I killed them? Well, this was because, as I said, I wanted to keep them with me. I really wanted a warm, living body to lie with and make love to. I was trying to come up with a way to keep them alive, but render them helpless and completely under my control. I thought if I could find a way to do this, I wouldn't have to kill anymore. So I began experimenting by drilling small holes in the top of their heads and injecting them with a syringe filled with various solutions while they were alive but still unconscious from the Halcion. I tried a boiling water mix with the Soilex. Then I tried formaldehyde and even the muriatic acid."

Dahmer explained that after he drugged the victims, he injected the various solutions into their brains. About an hour later, the victims woke up but were still out of it. "Almost zombie-like." Eventually, they all died.

With the second victim from Chicago, Dahmer was almost successful. He tried squirting some boiling water into the brain without the aid of any chemicals, and the victim was incoherent when he woke up but could be guided around the apartment and was still able to reach erections through oral and manual stimulation. Dahmer gave the victim another dose of Halcion and went to work. "I handcuffed this one to the bed before I left. I wanted to avoid another scene like that with the Asian guy."

When Dahmer returned from work, the victim was still alive, and he felt he had hit on the right solution. Dahmer gave him a shower and had sex with him that evening. "In the morning, I made him drink some water with Halcion in it before going to work and cuffed him to the bed again, but when I came home, he was dead." He described how disappointed he was. "I really hoped there would be a way to keep them warm and alive, but compliant. It just didn't work out."

Patrickus was writing furiously as he spoke. Murphy and I sat quietly and Dahmer coolly smoked his cigarette, eyes lost in a glassy stare. When Wendy finished, she looked at the letters Dahmer had brought with him and asked if they were for Boyle. Murphy told her they were similar to the previous bunch and that we had already looked through them. Patrickus gathered them up and placed them in her briefcase.

Dahmer stubbed his cigarette out in the worn plastic ashtray. He picked up the stack of photos and said, "Well, should we continue?"

We agreed, and he began to sort through the pictures. He placed a family photograph on the table.

"This looks like the deaf guy I met."

Murphy's eyes lit up. We had recovered only one piece of evidence from Dahmer's apartment that revealed the name of a possible victim. It was an identification card found in Dahmer's closet. Investigating detectives had been able to contact the mother named on the identification card, determine that he was still missing, and obtain a family photo. The interesting bit of information the mother gave us was that her son was deaf; he attended college in another town but was visiting home on the night of May 24, 1991. He went out that night with some friends and no one had seen him since.

Dahmer told the story. He was at Club 219 when they met. Tony Hughes was with a group of friends, and they were all dancing and having a good time. Dahmer said he was a "real looker" and he was attracted to him. He waited until the victim was alone at the bar and approached him. He was surprised to find out he was deaf.

"I think he could read lips though, and we communicated by writing little notes to one another in a small notebook that he had." Upon the bar's closing time, he offered the man fifty bucks to come home with him for sex and nude photos. The guy agreed, but his friends tried to talk him out of it. It took a while for Dahmer to convince the victim's friends that he was in good hands. The guy was so willing to accompany Dahmer that the friends eventually capitulated and left the bar without him.

Dahmer and the victim took a cab back to his apartment and engaged in kissing and touching while the victim drank Jeff's concoction. After he passed out, Dahmer drilled two holes in his head and used a turkey baster to inject a solution of diluted muriatic acid into his brain.

Dahmer said that the solution must have been too strong because the victim died right away. He was very disappointed and drank heavily until he passed out himself. When he woke up the next morning, he had too much to do, so he laid the victim on the floor of his bedroom and kept him there for about three days.

"As a matter of fact, this is the one who was in my bedroom the day the officers found the Asian guy in the street." Dahmer paused momentarily, took a cigarette from the pack, lit it, and continued. "I dismembered and disposed of both him and the Asian guy the same day."

Murphy recorded the new identification as I sat in disbelief. Dahmer was so good at his work that he was even able to convince a deaf man to return with him to his house of horrors.

I had seen many sides of him throughout the investigation. He had the ability to present a variety of personalities; he could be charming and childlike, sensitive and introspective, even angry and remorseful. I had even seen him cry out of fear and nearly break into a rage toward himself during our first meeting. But I couldn't help but feel as though there was an even more secret side of Jeff Dahmer that no still-living person had been privy to. I watched him as he sat, expressionless, calmly smoking his cigarette. *What was really behind those steel-blue eyes? Did he really like me as he said, or did he secretly envision me smothered in onions and steak sauce?*

Murphy broke my train of thought. He placed a stack of photos in front of Dahmer. "Speaking of the Asian guy, we think we have him identified through dental records but we would like you to confirm."

The photos contained ten Polaroids taken by Dahmer. Two were of the young Asian boy alive. These were the pictures he showed to the officers to convince them that they were lovers. They depicted the victim posing and smiling in his underwear. The remaining eight were gruesome. One was of the boy's head lying face up in the bathroom sink, a blank expression staring back at the camera. The others were of the victim in various stages of dismemberment, including a photo of him split open, sternum to genitals, with the viscera exposed. Dahmer matched his own Polaroids with the family picture and confirmed he was indeed one of the seventeen.

I looked at Murphy in disbelief: this victim was the older brother of the young Asian male that Dahmer took pictures of in 1988, leading to his arrest.

We told Dahmer that the two were brothers and asked if he was aware of that when they met. Dahmer's eyes widened with surprise. "Why, no. How could I have known? I never inquired into the personal lives of my victims. I really didn't want to know. It would have been difficult for me to carry out my plans if I had known too much about them. It would have gotten personal. I don't think I could have done it if I knew them too well."

Dahmer explained how he met fourteen-year-old Konerak Sinthasomphone at the Grand Avenue Mall, just like his brother before him. He offered him a hundred bucks to come home with him and take some nude photos. He gave him the drugged drink and performed oral sex on him while he was drugged. He diluted the muriatic acid with some water and injected it into the boy's brain after drilling two small holes in the top of his head. The victim didn't die like the other ones, and appeared to be sleeping, so Dahmer left the apartment and went up the street to a local tavern to buy some more beer. The boy apparently woke up and tried to escape because as Dahmer returned, he saw the victim standing in the street surrounded by the police and onlookers.

"I already told you how I duped the officers into believing that everything was all right. After they left, I injected another solution into his brain to render him even more helpless, but he died. I was disappointed but got busy severing the flesh from the both of them, double bagged it, and threw it in the trash. I kept both of their skulls because I wanted something to remember them by and felt it was a waste to throw everything out." I could hear the disappointment in Dahmer's voice as he spoke.

We had identified two more victims. There was a knock at the door and when opened, there stood a deputy from the county with Dahmer's lunch. We all took a break and left him alone to eat. Wendy said she couldn't attend the questioning that afternoon and asked if we would make her a copy of our findings. We assured her we would, and Murphy escorted her to the assembly door. I noticed the captain waving to me from his office, so I entered. As Murphy returned to the assembly, he saw the captain and me, joined us in the office, and we all sat down.

"How are you guys holding up?" the captain asked.

Murphy and I both said we were fine and asked what he needed. The captain said that members of our own identification division had been working closely with the medical examiner to identify the bodies found soaking in the fifty-seven-gallon drum. He told us how they had removed the outer skin from the each of the victim's fingers and placed it around their own, enabling them to produce identifiable fingerprints. With this technique, they had matched several of the victims whose fingerprints were already on file. He handed us the report, which identified Victim Three. We had already confirmed two of them with Dahmer. The third had a police record, so a mug shot was available. The medical examiner found this victim's torso in the fifty-seven-gallon drum, and his head in the floor freezer. Dahmer did not take any Polaroids of this victim, so we would have to show him both the police mug shot and the corresponding family picture.

"Let me know if you need anything," the captain said as we walked out the door and back to the interrogation room. We found Dahmer leaning back in his chair, quietly enjoying a smoke, feet up, plate empty.

"Looks like you really enjoyed your lunch, Jeff," I said, noting there wasn't a scrap of food left on his plate.

"Yeah, it was pretty good today. Not as starchy as usual." Dahmer put his feet down as he spoke.

Murphy and I sat down and placed the identification report and photos on the table in front of him. We explained the process the identification technicians used to identify the victims mentioned in the reports before him. Dahmer seemed intrigued by the method and commented on the ingenuity of the police department.

I replied, "Well, you know we're not a bunch of local yokels from some bush league department, Jeff. You're dealing with the best." Dahmer looked at me and smiled. He picked up some photos attached to the reports and studied them for a moment.

"This is the last guy I killed," Dahmer said in a noticeably somber voice. He placed the picture of Joseph Bradehoft on the table, took an exaggerated drag from his cigarette, and began. "I met him at the bus stop." He had been walking home from the Grand Avenue Mall when he encountered the man sitting at a bus stop in front of Marquette University. He had a six-pack of beer under his arm, and Dahmer sat down next to him in the bus shelter and struck up a conversation. He offered him fifty dollars to come to his apartment and pose for some nude photos, and possibly engage in some sexual activity. The victim agreed and they took the bus. Once at the apartment, Dahmer gave him the drugged drink and they began to kiss and fondle each other until the victim passed out. Dahmer placed the unconscious man on his bed and performed oral sex on him for a while before deciding to kill him. He strangled him with his hands and had anal intercourse with him.

Murphy interjected here. "Jeff, it seems that you only perform anal intercourse with your victims after they are dead. Why is that?"

Dahmer seemed really to ponder this question before answering. "I think it's because when they are dead, I have complete and total control over them. I couldn't always reach orgasm with my live lovers, but I always climaxed after they were dead. Maybe it's because there is no pressure to perform when they're dead, so I can relax and concentrate on my own satisfaction."

As I listened to him speak, I thought about the complete selfishness of his act. To pursue your own lustful passions to the point that you will kill and dismember another human being to satisfy your desires was the ultimate act of sexual selfishness.

"I remember that after I killed him, we cuddled on the bed until I fell asleep. The next morning, I wasn't up for the chore of disposing of the body, so I draped a blanket over him and left him lying on my bed for about three days," said Dahmer.

When Dahmer pulled the blanket off, maggots had begun to form on the victim's face. It had been hot that July, and the heat caused his victim to decompose quicker than usual. Dahmer severed the guy's head and placed it in the floor freezer. He filleted the flesh from him in the bathtub and placed the dismembered body parts in the industrial drum filled with muriatic acid to decompose. Another victim was in the books.

Chapter 18

Dahmer had that faraway gaze, the thousand-yard stare, that usually was on his face when he described his deeds. I broke the moment of silence. "Jeff, you told us how you disposed of your victims, but this is the first time you have referred to it as a chore. What do you mean by that?"

He sipped his coffee before beginning. "Well, it is a chore. It's a lot of work if you think about it. I know I told you that it was sexual and exciting as I did it, but there were a variety of feelings I experienced. I had to dispose of my victims to destroy the evidence. Then there was the feeling of power, knowing what I had done, and that no one else knew. I was in complete control, not only of the victims, but also of my own little world. Then there was the loss. When I placed their remains in the trash, I would experience a deep sense of remorse. Thinking about what a waste it was and how a living, breathing, fully functioning human being was now reduced to four or five bags of garbage. There were times I was almost overcome by regret for my actions, but it didn't last. Besides, I was always pretty drunk." Dahmer always drank alcohol as he did his work. "It could be a smelly, distasteful job." The drink helped him cope with the unpleasantness of the operation. His drink of choice was Budweiser, "the king of beers." He always had a supply of Bud to drink while dismembering his victims.

Murphy chuckled at this. "I guess that's where they get their slogan. I love you, man."

Dahmer winced at the remark. "I took off all my clothes, so as not to get any blood on them. Then I placed him [the victim] near a drain or in the bathtub, face up. I used a sharp knife at the top of the sternum and made a single cut down the middle of the upper torso. Once the initial cut was made, I could spread the wound and remove all the internal organs. Sometimes this would excite me to the point that I would become erect and couldn't continue until I had brought myself to orgasm by simulating intercourse with the viscera. After a while, I cut the internal organs into fist-sized pieces and placed them in a double-wrapped garbage bag."

Dahmer then cut the flesh off. He started by stripping the flesh from the arms and biceps, then the chest, and worked his way down to the feet. He sliced all the strips of flesh into small pieces and placed them into approximately three bags. He was careful not to place too much in each bag, about twenty-five pounds worth each. In the beginning, he then wrapped the skeleton in a sheet and pounded it into small parts with a sledgehammer, placing the upper torso in one bag and the lower in another. However, after he hit upon the idea of dissolving his victims in the muriatic acid, he simply dropped the dismembered skeletal remains into the industrial drum he had purchased. There, the acid would do its work. This was his usual pattern. "I normally used five double-wrapped garbage bags to dispose of a single body."

We all sat in silence, letting his last words sink in. Dahmer reached for a smoke and took one from the pack. It was now about four o'clock, and we were ready to call it a day. Murphy went to report the latest identification to the captain, and I sat with Dahmer as he finished his cigarette. By the time he was through, Murphy had returned and we rode the elevator back to the county lockup.

"We'll see you tomorrow, Jeff," I said, as he disappeared behind the clanging metal door.

Back in the assembly, Murphy and I called in our reports and waited to proofread them before handing them to the captain.

"I don't think Jeff thought your comment about the Budweiser slogan was very funny, Dennis," I said.

Murphy laughed and said, "Yeah, but it was right on, wasn't it?"

I agreed that it did bring a new meaning to the commercial and its popular tagline. I checked my reports, told Murphy I'd see him in the morning, and drove home.

I was still wound up after dinner and asked my wife if she wanted to go for a walk. She had enrolled again in college to earn her degree and struggled with a research paper. She declined, and I went for a walk alone to try to relax, but I couldn't get the day's discussion out of my mind. I returned about two hours later, took a shower, and climbed into bed.

***

I was at my desk early the next morning, already having a cup of coffee when Murphy walked through the assembly door.

"Did our boy call yet?" he asked, taking off his suit coat and sitting down next to me. "I would really like to get these last two victims identified today."

He picked up the stack of photos that had arrived for today's session and began sorting through them. The phone on my desk rang and the deputy on the other end stated that "our boy" requested to talk with us. Before we could get up to retrieve him, an officer showed up with Patrickus in tow. We told her to have a seat in the interrogation room and went over to the county lockup. By now, the task of escorting Dahmer from the county lockup had become routine. Murphy, Dahmer, and I often conversed like old friends, sometimes laughing and joking as we walked along the maze of secure tunnels, elevators, and hallways.

Other police officers, deputies, prisoners, and lawyers regularly used the route, and many were incredulous as to our demeanor with Dahmer and told us so when they caught us alone. I explained that although the content of our interrogation was deadly serious, it was important to keep Dahmer in a good mood and completely willing to cooperate with us. Most understood the idea behind it but couldn't imagine sharing their lunch, laughing, or conversing with a monster like Jeffrey Dahmer.

"How do you do it?" was the most frequently asked question.

For me, it was automatic. I realized this was the biggest case I'd ever be involved in, that I would be judged forever on its outcome, and I didn't want there to be any mistakes about how the case had been handled. My career was on the line, and so I poured all my energies into each session with him; besides, it was a high-profile case, which tends to be more exciting than the usual day-to-day police work. All the attention and the circus-like atmosphere surrounding the case had elevated my profile in a way I hadn't anticipated. It was impossible to remain anonymous in law enforcement circles, and I found myself recognized by many in the general public as I went about my daily activities. I tried not to ponder the evil and grotesque nature of Dahmer's crimes too much. Instead, I concentrated on the man himself. The most surprising thing was how very much like me and other regular people he was. In between sessions or during lunch, I pulled out the daily Milwaukee newspaper and read aloud what was being reported. Dahmer perused the latest info on the case, and we discussed other current world events. He was intelligent and articulate, pleasant and polite at all times. The give and take between us went so smoothly that anyone observing would conclude that we were friends. He displayed all the normal human emotions of love, fear, anger, and loneliness during these conversations, and it was only when we returned to his deeds that a distinct "other" personality emerged. Sitting erect and emotionless, he slipped into a trance-like monotonous state as he described the horror of his actions, his blue eyes glazed over and lifeless. Only then did I feel the chill of evil. It was extraordinary.

Patrickus patiently waited as we entered the room. She pulled a fresh pack of Lucky Strikes from her briefcase and placed them in front of Dahmer. I left to get the photos for the day and fresh coffee for everyone. Returning, I overheard Murphy and Wendy talking with Dahmer about the amazing number of wackos reported in the newspapers. Many of them stated that they had been approached by Dahmer and could have been among his victims. Others said they saw someone fitting Dahmer's description throwing garbage bags into the trash. Reports of unidentified bones found by people all over the city had to be thoroughly investigated by police, causing a tremendous strain on the already-overworked department. Of course, none of these calls proved to be true and the identification division was inundated with chicken, turkey, pork, and beef bones that had to be checked out and discarded. The captain had done a good job of plugging any further leaks to the press, so the media was compelled to speculate on the nature of Dahmer's confession, and printed many wild and unsubstantiated stories.

I sat down and placed the stack of photos in front of Dahmer. The identification division, along with the medical examiner, had already positively identified these victims through dental records; however, we still needed Dahmer to confirm and explain. He had taken seventeen photos of this victim. One showed the victim lying on his stomach with his hands cuffed behind his back.

Eight Polaroids depicted the deceased victim naked in various poses. Another showed an incision from the base of his neck to his pubic area, with the skin spread apart and his internal organs exposed. Still others showed the beheaded victim lying in the bathtub, stripped of his flesh. The strangest of all were the numerous photos of the man's severed head, hands, and genitals. They were placed in the kitchen sink with ice to keep them fresh and lifelike. It was almost as though he were playing with these body parts, posing them in various positions. Dahmer picked up the stack and began to look through them. He smoked deliberately as he did so. Finally, he set down the pictures.

"I think I met this guy in February of 1991. I remember because it was cold and I went to the bus stop to catch a ride downtown. He was already there, and I sat down and struck up a conversation as we waited. He seemed interested, so I offered him money to come home with me and watch a video. I also intimated that we would have something to drink and possibly engage in sexual activity. He was willing, so we walked back to my place. I put a video in and gave him the rum and Halcion concoction. Soon he was out cold, so I performed oral sex on him and rubbed and cuddled him for a while. I was low on Halcion tablets and was afraid he would wake up, so I used the strap to strangle him right away."

Dahmer had taken the Polaroids both before and after death, and defleshed the body right away as well, but decided to keep his hands, head, and genitals. He wanted to preserve the genitals for future oral sex, so he soaked them in formaldehyde for about two weeks in his refrigerator and let them air-dry on a towel. I remembered Dubis telling me about his ghastly discoveries on the night of the arrest. He was amazed that the severed penis and scrotum were pliable and lifelike, and he wondered how this could be. I now could tell him the secret of their preservation.

Dahmer successfully boiled this victim's head; it was one of the bleached, unpainted skulls. Murphy and I recorded the identification of Curtis Straughter, and I placed the last remaining pictures in front of Dahmer. He picked them up and began to sort through them.

"I'm pretty sure I met this guy in early spring. It was either late March or early April. I think it was early April."

Again, he was able to remember correctly the dates and times of each pickup. Information received from the victim's mother confirmed that she last saw her son, Errol Lindsey, the first week of April while on his way to the store. Dahmer met him on 27th Street, not too far from the twenty-four-hour news and bookstore. It was the same come-on: money for sex and possible photos. The victim accepted and followed Dahmer to his apartment. Dahmer gave him the drink and soon he was rendered helpless. Dahmer kissed and hugged him as they lay together, and he masturbated several times before strangling him.

Dahmer placed the family photo and his six matching Polaroids on the table. "That's him."

Two of the Polaroids depicted the victim in identical positions, lying face up, stretched out, and naked. In the second photo, his hands were severed and he had been completely skinned. It was unbelievable. It looked just like an anatomy poster of a man you might see in a health class or doctor's office. The cartilage, ligaments, and fleshy muscular areas were intact, but all the skin and hair on his face and body were gone. I had never seen anything like it in my life.

Murphy blurted out, "What the hell is this all about, Jeff?"

Dahmer sat straight up in his chair, obviously troubled by the outburst, and stammered a bit. "Well, I guess I was experimenting a little. I wanted to see if I could take off all his skin and save it."

"Yeah, but how did you do it?" I broke in.

Dahmer, again composed, lit another cigarette before he answered. "It did take a long time, about two hours. I used a small, very sharp paring knife. I think I saw it in one of the Polaroids. Anyway, I started by making an incision from the top of his head down the back of his neck. Then I carefully cut along the skull. It was a little tricky around the ears and nose."

I picked up the photo. It was shocking and compelling at the same time.

"Yeah, Jeff, but how did you get the skin to come off so completely?"

He shrugged his shoulders. "It was really no big deal. The skin is detachable, just like pulling the skin off a chicken you are about to cook."

Dahmer explained that human skin peeled off easily if he made the correct incision. He was very careful to detach the victim's facial skin in one piece. "I wrapped it around my own face and looked through his eye holes. It was like wearing a mask."

At this point, Patrickus, Murphy, and I looked at each other in disbelief.

I had to ask. "Jeff, why did you wear this guy's face?"

Dahmer continued to smoke as he answered. "Pat, I already told you that I wanted to keep these guys with me. I didn't want them to leave. I loved them. That's why I killed them. That's why I saved their body parts. That's why I ate them—so they could become one with me. I thought if I could preserve this guy's skin, I could wrap myself in him. His outer shell would surround me. I would actually be in him. We would be one."

The room fell silent. Patrickus wrote in her notepad, and Murphy and I sat without a word, letting Dahmer's heartfelt explanation sink in.

He had attempted to preserve the skin like a hide, placing it in a solution of water and salt for about a week. He concluded that he must have used too much salt, because the skin broke into pieces and he had to throw it out. "It was very disappointing."

Patrickus had been writing nonstop since Dahmer began his explanation. There was a knock at the door and when a deputy with a hot tray declared, "Lunchtime," I was glad. I needed a break.

Patrickus said that she had brought her lunch along and asked if she could remain. "I just want to make sure I get this down. I'm sure Boyle will want to hear all of it."

Murphy and I left them alone in the room and walked into the assembly.

"Do you believe that freak?" Murphy said, rubbing his neck as if to remove a kink.

All I could do was shake my head. I sat down at my desk and pulled out my bag lunch. Murphy said he was going to inform the captain that all seventeen victims had been positively identified. I could hardly believe it myself. The past several weeks had gone by so quickly, almost like a dream. Now that the task was complete, I wondered how much longer I'd be kept assigned to the day shift. The explosion of crack cocaine was a little slow to find its way into our fair city, but its arrival brought with it a dramatic increase in violent crime. Although I was completely engrossed with Dahmer, it was impossible to miss the work done by the men and women of the Criminal Investigation Bureau. The detective assembly constantly hummed with activity. My colleagues occasionally asked me for tidbits of information about Dahmer, but most were too busy with their own investigations to take up much of my time.

Murphy interrupted my train of thought as he returned and sat down next to me. "Well, Pat, we did it." He bit into an apple as he spoke. "One thing, though. The captain says that he's had several calls from that prick in the FBI, saying that we may not have gotten a full confession from Dahmer. They think he is responsible for a lot more homicides. The same shit about being too close."

Murphy's painstaking task chronicling Dahmer's life eventually dispelled these accusations. But more importantly, I had no doubt he told me the truth. I had spent time with him, touching him, dining with him, discussing life and death with him. I had been witness to his fear, rage, anger, sorrow, love, and remorse. I looked into those blue eyes before they began to take on a trance-like state, and saw another human being, like myself.

I believe Dahmer felt he had found a kindred spirit in me. I know it sounds strange, but we had connected on some level. He trusted me and felt I accepted him. Hell, I did accept him. At the same time, the FBI's questions lingered in my head. My years in law enforcement gave me a skeptical nature and I learned not to be too sure of anything. I finished my lunch, grabbed a few more cups of coffee, and went back to the interrogation room. I found Dahmer sitting alone, smoking contently.

He answered my look. "Wendy went to the bathroom. She said she would be right back." I placed the coffee down in front of him and he grabbed it immediately, sipping it in combination with his cigarette.

I said, "You looked like you were lost in thought when I came in. Is everything okay?"

Dahmer took a long drag off his smoke and downed his remaining coffee before exhaling. "It's hard for me to believe a human being could do what I've done, Pat, but I know that I did it. I want you to know that when we discussed Satan and the devil, it was not to defuse my guilt or blame for what I've done, because I realize what I've done, and know it was wrong. But I have to question whether or not there is an evil influence or force that I may have tapped into or been consumed by. I'm not sure if there is a God, or devil, but I know that I've been doing a lot of thinking lately about both, and I have to wonder what influenced my life so destructively." Dahmer dropped his cigarette and butted it with his foot.

"Oh, there is a God; you can bank on that, Jeff," I said, pulling my chair close to him.

"I wish I could be as sure of that as you are, Pat." Dahmer took another smoke from the pack.

"Jeff, there is something that's been bugging me. It's not so much me as it is questions from outside agencies," I told him. He looked at me quizzically. "The questions we keep getting from these people are: Is he telling the truth? Is he telling you everything, all of his deeds? You see, Jeff, they think you're involved in many more homicides. They feel that you and I have become too close, and that you are afraid that if you tell me all of your crimes, that I won't like you, or I'll be disgusted with you or something like that."

Dahmer shook his head in the negative as he leaned forward in his chair. "Pat, what good would it do to admit just half of my crimes? Why would I admit to you the horrible things I did and leave others out? I know in the end that it will be me that has to stand before God. He will know if I was truthful and if I truly helped clear this matter up. I'm telling you the truth now because I want to clear my conscience. All that I've told you is the truth, and I've left nothing out."

The door opened and Murphy entered, sat down, and placed some reports on the table. I realized how close I was to Dahmer and pushed my chair back to give everyone a little room. Murphy put his hand over the reports and began.

"Jeff, I have here a report from your employer at the chocolate factory. It says that they gave you notice of termination. They were also wondering if you placed anything other than the prescribed ingredients into the batches of confections you were mixing."

Dahmer sat back quickly in surprise. "What do you mean? They think I put some body parts into the candy? What kind of monster do they think I am?"

We sat silently. Neither of us wanted to comment on Dahmer's statement.

"No," he said emphatically. "No, I didn't put anything into the candy."

He shook his head in disgust. I decided not to tell him about the many jokes circulating about the possibility of his adding real fingers to the Butterfinger bars.

"What about the job, Jeff?" Murphy asked again.

Dahmer composed himself. "Yes, I knew I was being fired. They gave me two weeks' notice."

Chapter 19

Dahmer explained that many times he drank too much on Sunday night and passed out. In the morning, he was too hungover for work and had to call in sick. He knew he was out of sick time, but the drinking got the better of him.

Dahmer told us, "The termination notice meant no money and eventually no apartment. I had to come up with a plan. It would have worked too, if only I hadn't gotten so drunk."

He intended to destroy all the evidence of his crimes. He planned to place the torsos, skulls, heads, bones, hands, and penises into the large blue industrial drum and cover it all with the muriatic acid. After it became slushy enough, he could flush it down the toilet. When his rent came due, he planned to check in to the Milwaukee Rescue Mission for a month or so until he obtained another job and found a suitable apartment.

"In a way, I felt this could be a new beginning, a chance to start over and stop the nightmare I had been living," Dahmer said.

I questioned him as to whether he truly believed that by destroying all the evidence and starting over again, he would be able to stop. Dahmer paused and contemplated the question before answering.

"If I am to be honest with myself, I would have to say no. I have to admit that if I set up in another apartment, had access to money, and was presented with the opportunity, I would kill again. It's like I have a driving compulsion to commit these acts. Even now, when I'm lying in my cell, I think about it. Over at the county jail, they play the radio for the inmates at night. They alternate stations to suit everyone's tastes. One night it's country western, the next it's rock, and then soul or dance music. Listening to the dance music takes my mind back to the gay club scene, and I enjoy fantasizing about the many long, lean, muscular men that go there to dance. Yes, I'm sure I would have started again." Dahmer looked into my eyes and said, "Obviously a higher power than myself was fed up with my deeds and decided it was time for me to be stopped."

I continued to hold Dahmer's gaze and nodded my acknowledgement to his reference of our first night's discussion. There was a knock at the door and Patrickus entered.

"I just talked to Boyle, and he wants Jeff to talk with the psychiatrist again tomorrow before the trial."

Murphy interrupted. "Just one more question, Jeff. The medical examiner says he noticed flesh had been severed from the feet of the victims found in the blue drum. What about it?"

Dahmer knowingly nodded. "Well, the flesh on the bottom of the feet is extremely tough. I found that by cutting off the sole and heel, it was easier for the muriatic acid to work on the bones of the foot."

"Makes sense to me," Murphy said as he stood up.

Dahmer took a long last drag on his cigarette before dropping it on the floor. Patrickus said the psychiatrist was waiting for Jeff at the county lockup.

"I can let myself out. I'll see you all tomorrow in court." She had obviously become comfortable with the setup of the bureau and confidently strolled down the hall.

We took Dahmer back to the county jail and told him we would see him in court as the large metal door closed behind him. On the way back, Murphy told me that Captain Domagalski planned to take all our reports to the district attorney that afternoon to draft a criminal complaint. I never heard of a captain performing this menial task and said so.

"Yeah, I know, but I think we're going to see a lot of firsts in this case," Murphy said as we entered the detective assembly.

I called in my day's reports and waited to proofread them before handing them to the captain.

Domagalski told me, "You did a fine job, Pat. I'm meeting with DA McCann and his associates this afternoon. I've decided to keep you on days a little longer, in case some more questions come up. Now go home and get some rest."

The trial was scheduled to be in Judge Gram's court the next day. The case had been assigned to him, but he was on vacation. The relief magistrate felt that if he took the preliminary hearing, he should handle the entire case. According to the press, a little battle was developing between the two judges over who would preside in the upcoming trial. This caused the chief justice to step in and settle the matter. Judge Gram, although on vacation, would preside over any future court proceedings. It seemed that even the judges wanted to be a part of the biggest case ever to occur in Wisconsin.

***

The next day, the courtroom buzzed with TV cameras, reporters, victims' families, and the select few who grabbed the remaining public seats. A line started as soon as the Safety Building opened that morning, and the halls were filled with people queued up in hopes of admittance. Extra deputies had to be brought in to keep order as people jockeyed for position. I knew that I would not be testifying and was relaxed and at ease. I enjoyed watching the spectacle as everyone scurried about.

Finally, the bailiff called out, "All rise."

The courtroom fell silent as the judge entered and took his seat. The door to the right of the bench opened, revealing Boyle and his entourage, followed by Dahmer, who was wearing a new blue suit that looked a little too big for him. Two large deputy sheriffs flanked him as he entered and took a seat at the defense table. The gallery was silent as camera operators worked the tools of their trade, zooming in on Dahmer's face. District Attorney McCann, accompanied by several assistant DAs, took his place at the prosecution table as the charges and case number were read aloud.

The entire hearing took only ten minutes as Boyle waived Dahmer's right to a preliminary trial and stipulated there was more than enough evidence to proceed. After several motions by McCann, a court date was set, and Dahmer was led back to the county lockup. Murphy and I returned to the detective assembly and compiled a list of questions for the final interviews.

I spent the rest of the day hanging around, fielding questions from my colleagues anxious for insider information on this celebrated homicide investigation. I tried to keep a humble attitude, but I knew that I had cracked him, and nobody could dispute that. I felt proud of my accomplishment and secure in the knowledge that I had become a good detective. Still, it was a strange but heady experience, and I could tell people recognized me as I went about my normal, routine business.

I retired to bed after catching the latest Dahmer revelations on the late news.

***

I drove to work the next morning feeling great, without a care in the world. I knew the pressure was off now that all the victims were identified. From now on, it was simply a matter of clearing up a few loose ends in the investigation.

I entered the detective assembly and saw Dubis. He was working on a new homicide from the night before.

"Hey, big man, when are you coming back to the late shift to do some real police work?" he said to me.

I smiled and sat down at my desk. We were understaffed at the bureau, and every detective was loaded with work. Surprisingly enough, the unit was clearing approximately ninety percent of their caseload, an impressive number, and a credit to the men and women working there. I was proud to be a part of it and knew that my seventeen homicides, all cleared by confession, had added to the high clearance rate. If you committed murder in Milwaukee during this time, there was a ninety percent chance that you'd be caught and brought to trial.

I chatted for a while with Dubis until Murphy arrived with a stack of reports containing questions we needed to finalize with Dahmer. I told Dubis that I didn't know when they'd ship me back to late shift, but it would be soon, as this was probably my last interview with Dahmer.

The phone on Murphy's desk rang with the news that Dahmer wanted to talk with us. We traveled to the county lockup where he waited.

"Well, Jeff, how do you feel today?" I asked.

Dahmer took note of my chipper attitude, stating, "I feel fine, Pat. You seem in a very good mood today."

I didn't want to tell him that the reason for my upbeat mood was that I probably wouldn't have to see him for so many hours each day anymore.

"Yeah, I feel great. Let's go get some coffee."

Dahmer smiled and nodded his head. "Sounds good to me."

We walked to the interrogation room, and Murphy pulled a pack of Camel straights. Dahmer lit one up right away.

I went to retrieve some coffee, and on the way back, the captain informed me that Patrickus called, stating she would not be in today. Returning to the room, I told Murphy about Patrickus and sat down.

I began. "Jeff, there are a few things we would like to clear up. We found a number of devices related to security in your apartment, namely alarms and a video camera. Did you videotape any of your encounters?"

Dahmer coolly answered, "No, no video. It was mainly for show. I was afraid of a break in."

Indeed, investigation revealed that his apartment contained door and window alarms. There was a small camera attached to the ceiling and positioned to capture anyone entering his unit. The wires for the camera disappeared into the wall but were not connected to any electrical outlet.

Dahmer said that as his killing progressed, he was aware of how his apartment held enough evidence to lock him away for life, so he decided to safeguard it. The alarms on the windows and door screeched if tripped by an intruder. "I suppose you already know the camera wasn't connected to anything. I placed it where you couldn't miss it. That was the whole idea. I took great pains to show the security system to the guys that I let go. I bought all that stuff at the Radio Shack in the mall downtown."

As I wrote down his statement, Murphy took out a police photo and placed it in front of him.

"You know that we have been getting a lot of bogus information from people about your supposed activities, Jeff. Almost all of it we were able to disprove with the timeline, but this guy says you tried to kill him with a hammer, and he gives a pretty detailed description of your apartment. How would he get that kind of information?"

Dahmer picked up the photo and studied it. "Yeah, I know this guy. I met him at the Phoenix Tavern. I was actually with him a couple times. I asked him the first night if he would be willing to come home with me for some nude pictures and cocktails. I did offer money, but he was more than willing without the financial incentive."

Dahmer said that once at his apartment, they engaged in normal sexual activity and talked about meeting again at the same bar the next night. "This was a new experience for me, and I wanted to see if he would be there. When he left, I made no attempt to stop him."

The following night, Dahmer went to the same tavern and again met the man. They returned to his apartment and drank heavily.

"I decided that I would keep him." Dahmer chuckled a little before continuing. "I knew I was out of Halcion, so in preparation for the evening I went to the hardware store and purchased a medium-sized rubber mallet-type hammer."

Still looking at the photo, Dahmer recalled his plan to have him pose in a bondage picture with his hands cuffed behind his back. He thought that once the victim was in this position, he would be able to render him helpless by striking him on the head with the mallet. Once the victim was out, "it would only be a matter of strangling him to finish the job." Dahmer lit another cigarette and took an extremely slow drag.

"Well, Jeff, go on." I said.

He continued matter of factly. "Well, I didn't have him cuffed behind his back, but he was drunk and posing on his stomach." He took another slow drag on his cigarette. "Pat, do you know what happens when you hit someone on the head with a rubber mallet?"

I shook my head no, and prodded him to go on.

"Well, they get mad at you," he said with a smile. He struck the guy as hard as he could, but he didn't pass out. He only got angry and the two got involved in a fight. Dahmer said that they fought on the floor of his apartment for about fifteen minutes, until they were both exhausted. He screamed at Dahmer as to why he hit him.

"I tried to calm him down by explaining that I was afraid he was going to rob me after I fell asleep." He said that the two talked for quite a while. "We didn't engage in any more sexual activity, but just talked all night. It's funny, because as we talked, I began to sober up. I know that my plan was to kill him, but after I got to know him personally, I lost my desire to do so."

He said that he ran into him several more times, on the street and at the mall. "One time, he even introduced a friend to me. I don't know why, Pat, but after that, I was not attracted to him and just said hi when we met. I never invited him back to my apartment again." Dahmer sat back in his chair, smoking, staring straight ahead as if lost in thought.

Murphy placed the photo back in the pile as I pulled out several newspaper articles.

"Jeff, there has been a lot of speculation in the press concerning your activities."

Dahmer butted his cigarette and retrieved another. "How do you mean?" he asked.

I continued. "Well, everyone is trying to figure out why you did these things. I know you said that you approached the ones you found the most attractive, but many are saying you were acting out of some kind of personal vendetta or hatred."

Dahmer looked at me quizzically. "Hatred? Hatred of who?"

I showed him the news clippings that suggested he had a deep-seated hatred of gays, that this was the real reason behind the killings and why he dismembered the bodies. The term "gay overkill" was used to describe the deaths.

"What do they mean, 'gay overkill'?"

I tried to explain by giving him details of several murders I previously investigated. The method of operation was the same. In each case, the suspect, who did not identify as gay, smoked crack with the openly gay victim for several hours, which eventually led to sexual activity. After completing the act, and fully realizing what had occurred, the suspect became so distraught and disgusted with their behavior that they turned on the victim in a most vicious manner.

In their drug-crazed rage, the suspects not only killed their victims, but also mutilated their bodies in a bizarre manner. This led to the term *overkill*, as the victim would be strangled and shot, or stabbed numerous times, then run over by a vehicle or set on fire. In one case, after strangling and killing the victim, the suspect spent hours dropping a large piece of concrete on the victim's face, until it was unrecognizable. The experts claimed the suspect was psychologically so ashamed of his sexual actions and decisions that he wanted to obliterate any evidence or witness to the act.

"I think it's really a sexist term, Jeff, because in my experience, heterosexuals have committed similar heinous acts of depravity," I told him.

Dahmer looked surprised. "But, Pat, that's not me. I told you, I loved these guys. I'm not ashamed for being gay. I don't hate gays. I didn't mutilate their bodies. I was careful and precise when I cut into them because I wanted to keep parts of them with me. Mutilation had nothing to do with it. I simply needed a way to dispose of the remains when I was finished."

Dahmer seemed upset by the supposition that he harbored hatred toward anyone, especially gays.

I laid another newspaper article in front of him with the headline "Slayings of Minorities Disturb Black Leaders." It described how these leaders were particularly distressed that so many of his victims were Black. A professor of community studies at the University of Wisconsin-Milwaukee stated that it was clear Dahmer had a hatred for Black men and purposely targeted that population.

Dahmer read the short clipping before putting it down on the table. "This is preposterous. I don't hate Black people."

I reminded him that ten of his seventeen victims were Black men.

"That may be, but I didn't target Blacks. I told you, I picked the ones I found most attractive. I had a physical profile; I wanted young, long, lean, smooth-skinned, muscular men. Color did not enter into it. If they fit the description and were nice looking, I would approach them."

It was easy to see how his killings could be misconstrued. The death tally was three Caucasian, two Latino, one Asian, one Native American, and ten African American men. He had proven to be a multicultural killer[8].

Murphy recorded his answer and asked, "Yeah, Jeff, but how did you decide which ones you were going to kill and which ones you would just have sex with?"

Dahmer said that his decision to kill was based on a variety of factors. "Usually I knew when I went out if I was looking to keep someone. Before leaving the apartment, I crushed five to seven Halcion tablets in a glass and left it on the kitchen sink."

He said while in the tavern, he drank by himself and observed the different people in the establishment. He noticed one, maybe two or three, who fit his profile and who he found attractive. He looked for men who were alone, or at least not with a tight-knit group. After detecting a suitable victim, he waited until closing time, as the patrons were filing out of the tavern, to approach. Sometimes the victims returned his glances and indicated their willingness to converse. Then he asked if they wanted to come home with him for pictures, sexual contact, and cocktails.

Dahmer noted, "Of course, I always offered them money for their company. Normally between fifty and a hundred dollars."

This was the pattern, except when he met his victims on the street, in the mall, or in front of the bookstore.

"During these times, I tried to strike up a conversation. I could usually tell pretty quickly if they were interested before I made any offers. When I first started, I shopped around until I found someone who was really attractive, but

---

8. Statistics show that serial killers tend to kill within their own race although that is not always the case.

toward the end, it seems like the compulsion took over and I just wanted a live and willing body."

Murphy looked up from his notepad. "Jeff, I know we talked about this but it seems that the head was the most important part of the body for you. Kind of like a big-game hunter. Did you consider these trophies?"

Dahmer seemed to wince at Murphy's bluntness. "No, I didn't consider them trophies, but I did want to keep their heads. To me, the skull represents the true essence of the man. I felt that by keeping the heads, their death would not be a total loss. The skulls were most valuable. They would always remain with me."

Dahmer's plan was eventually to boil all the heads and paint them in the same fashion as the three we found, but he never got around to it.

I told him we were flooded with calls from numerous people in Milwaukee, Ohio, and other locations where he had lived. They claimed to be good friends with him and some gave interviews to the press. These reports detailed conversations or time spent in the company of Dahmer; however, he steadfastly maintained that he was a loner and had no close friends in Milwaukee or anywhere else. The truth was that throughout the investigation we were unable to produce anyone who could give inside information regarding Dahmer or his crimes.

He was truly a loner; in fact, phone company records showed that during the entire time he lived at the Oxford Apartments address, not a single phone call was placed to his residence. The more time I spent with him chronicling the facts around his activities, the more I felt sorry for him. He was a pathetically lonely and inept human being. He was unable to make a real connection with anyone and was totally self-absorbed. His lifestyle was a continuous hedonistic pursuit of pleasure. All his time, effort, energy, and money went to his overwhelming desire for a warm, compliant human body, with alcohol fueling his every move.

Alcohol was a big part of the investigation. Dahmer was completely intoxicated on the night of his arrest, and subsequent interviews centered on his use and abuse of alcohol. That first night, I shared some painful experiences of my own with the demon rum, and it was this insight and honesty that led Dahmer to trust me and begin our conversation. I had developed a routine to control my alcohol addiction, which included morning meditations, AA meetings, and Sunday mass, yet it was still a daily struggle to remain sober. I wondered if Dahmer experienced any mental or physical withdrawals from the drink since being in custody, so I asked.

"No. Not really. I was a little shaky those first few days but the coffee, cigarettes, and conversations we had really helped. I do miss the drinking though, especially at night when the guards play the music."

Murphy interrupted. "Are you having any trouble sleeping? Do you miss the Halcion tablets?"

Dahmer shook his head no. "I think I may have only taken them a couple of times. They worked great, but I mainly used them to drug my victims."

The investigation showed that he received twenty-seven prescriptions of sixty pills each from five different doctors after he was first given the prescription. He told us how he changed doctors every so often, bluffing them with his story about being a third-shift worker unable to sleep. Murphy finished logging his answer and looked at me for more questions.

"That's it for me," I said. "I have nothing else. What about you?"

Murphy shook his head no, and picked up his notepad. "I'm pretty sure that's it, but I'll go check with the captain." He got up and left the room.

Dahmer looked over at me in a panic. "What does he mean, that's it? Are you saying we're done?"

I explained, "Well, yeah, Jeff. Now that all the victims are identified, unless there is something else of importance you want to discuss, we're finished."

His face looked fearful. "Does this mean I won't see you anymore?"

I searched his face as he spoke. He didn't look like a murderer at all—just a scared, confused, lonely guy, trying to make a connection.

"Oh sure, Jeff. In a few months, the trial will begin, and I'll see you then."

He continued in a tone that betrayed his anxiety. "Well, what's going to happen to me?"

I explained that he still had to work with his lawyers to prepare his defense. "I'm sure they will take good care of you."

Dahmer shook his head slowly. "I know, Pat, but I was getting used to our little talks, and I enjoy being with you."

Murphy interrupted the moment by opening the door. "I already called the jail and told them to hold his lunch. Come on, Jeff, we'll take you back over."

I was slightly perplexed at the sudden and emotional reaction Dahmer had once he realized this part of the investigation was winding down. The three of us made our way, for the last time, through the maze of secure areas leading to the county jail. A deputy waiting for us took custody of Dahmer, and as he handcuffed him, I said as casually and light as I could, "I'll see you later, Jeff."

Dahmer looked at the floor, not saying a word as the door closed behind him. As we walked back to the elevator, I mentioned to Murphy that Dahmer really seemed to like us and that he said he would miss our interviews. Murphy laughed hysterically and slapped me on the back.

"Maybe you, big fella, but I get the feeling he'd like you a little more if you were smothered in barbeque sauce." He said that he didn't believe a word of it. "That guy is a cold-blooded killer, Pat. The only thing he's going to miss is the time out of his cell and the smokes we gave him."

He was probably right, but as weird as it sounds, I felt that Dahmer and I had made a connection. During the weeks of interviews, I had developed feelings for him. I felt sorry for the guy. He was so pitiful and alone, and in a strange way, I kind of liked him. It gnawed at me that I could be "friends" with him, and I wondered if there was something wrong with me. *How could I feel sorry for this serial predator and murderer?* I wondered about Murphy's cut-and-dry attitude about the investigation. *Was his grizzled old detective personality a veneer to protect him? Why couldn't I feel that way?*

We entered the assembly and called in our final reports. After checking them over, I walked into the captain's office and handed them to Domagalski, who was reading the daily felony summaries.

"Well, Kennedy, all finished, eh? You did a good job, kid. I've scheduled you to report back to the late shift the day after tomorrow. Why don't you take the rest of the day off?"

The day off went by quickly. School was starting again and the family was busy preparing. Before I knew it, I was walking into the assembly for late-shift roll call.

"Well, who's the stranger?" Lieutenant Harrell quipped. "Welcome back to where the real police work gets done." He took the podium and began to read the night's list of wanted felons. As I approached my desk, I noticed my old partner from uniform.

"Welcome back, big man," he said, extending his hand and pulling me into his massive chest.

"P-Mo!" I exclaimed. "When did you get made?" I was so caught up with the Dahmer investigation that I forgot he was next on the detectives' promotion list. "Congratulations, my good brother!" I said, returning the embrace.

Percy Moore was as big as a bear. We worked an inner-city squad while in uniform for several years before I made detective. As a matter of fact, Percy was the reason I took the promotional exam. He was the best copper I ever worked with. He was a powerfully strong man with a low, velvety voice that evoked visions of Barry White and the Love Unlimited Orchestra. His deep melodic tone, coupled with his huge physique, had convinced many a hardened criminal to come along peacefully. This was not lost on all the officers who worked with him, who called him Sweet Daddy.

He told me he had been assigned to the homicide unit and that while Dubis was on vacation, he would be teamed up with me. I was glad. Percy was a good friend, with a quick wit and a sly sense of humor. He would make the transition back to late shift a lot easier. There wasn't much time for small talk; a shooting came in, and we were back at it. A man was lying dead in the street with a gunshot wound to the head.

Harrell interrupted roll call with a bellow. "Kennedy and Moore, meet squad 73. They got one on 26th and Vienna."

Chapter 20

The pace was relentless for the next few months. During a one-week spurt, Percy and I cleared five murders on our own: two by arrest and three through interrogation and confession. It was so busy I hardly gave Dahmer a thought, except for the occasional ribbing I got from the old day shift detectives in the morning. They loved to see me engaged in the mundane activities of detective work and often exclaimed, "From a hero to a zero!"

I logged 1,300 hours of overtime that year, but I don't remember getting tired. I loved being a detective and enjoyed cracking open a case. The bureau was a haven from the rest of the department. Detectives were given deferential treatment from the uniforms, and the close-knit homicide unit was in a league of its own. This didn't spare me from the tempest created by the Dahmer investigation.

Revelations brought to light regarding Dahmer's brush with the police who had originally come to the aid of the young Asian boy found wandering in the street caused a tremendous uproar in the entire city. Criticism of perceived police attitudes toward minorities and gays grew louder and angrier. The press interviewed witnesses who claimed that the victim was found running from Dahmer, bleeding from every orifice, and badly beaten. The officers involved were vilified for failure to investigate fully before returning the young man to Dahmer's apartment.

Many opined that four lives could have been spared if they had done due diligence. They became scapegoats for all that was wrong with the Milwaukee Police Department. The chief placed them on suspension with pay while an internal review concluded they should be dismissed from the department.

I couldn't help but feel responsible; after all, I was the one to start the ball rolling when I contacted the veteran officer on the night of Dahmer's arrest. I was brought up in a police family and well aware of the thin blue line's supposed "code of silence." I was uncomfortable about revealing my findings because I knew these officers would be in for a rough time. In the intense scrutiny of the situation, I found myself summoned to Internal Affairs. It seems some felt my report concerning that night was purposely structured to provide cover for their actions. I was grilled on what I "left out" of Dahmer's statement that night and why I called the officers involved instead of going directly to my supervisor with my findings. It was suggested that I purposely did so to give them time to get their stories together.

There was some truth to that. However, I maintained that the fluid nature of the interrogation demanded I stay with the suspect, and I had only Dahmer's word that the incident had taken place. I ordered the officers in to confirm the validity of the story. I advised their district commander of the situation and then filed detailed supplements of their actions from that night. My report of the incident was taken directly from Dahmer and I recorded it verbatim. I refused to change it.

On the other hand, I felt some officers thought I had broken the code by revealing the story in the first place. I was not a snitch and took pride in the fraternal order to which I belonged. No one said anything to me concerning this, but the uneasy feeling haunted me. The police union president, angered by the suspensions of the two officers who responded to Dahmer's apartment that night, called for a vote of "no confidence" in the chief's handling of the situation, and ninety-three percent of those voting called for his resignation. I was torn about the whole thing. I knew the officers involved and they were good men. I also knew the inside information regarding Dahmer's ability and history of fooling authority figures.

There was no doubt that a mistake was made that night, a deadly one, and a mistake that cost a young man his life. It was later revealed that a citizen from the neighborhood had called 911 after the police had left Konerak Sinthasomphone with Dahmer, who immediately killed the young boy once left alone with him. The 911 call was released to the media and made public, which added to the anger and frustration of the larger community, who felt that their voices were neither heard nor believed by law enforcement.

To dump everything on the shoulders of these two men was ridiculous and unfair. It was easy to speculate on what could have been done after the fact. I didn't vote "no confidence" because I felt the chief was right about looking into the incident for a determination of what went wrong. The previous chief would have blamed the victims and their lifestyle for their demise.

Chief Arreola was openly meeting with leaders and members of both the Black and gay communities. These meetings concerning the sensitivity of the Milwaukee Police Department were widely reported in the press. He was adamant about changing the attitude of his officers, and called for increased education and training of the entire department in cultural diversity. Many in the department were angry about this and mocked the chief, claiming he was more interested in appeasing members of certain communities than backing his own force. The press reported on the open feud between the chief and the police union.

Adding to the discourse was Lenny Wells, the president of the League of Martin. The league was an organization of Black police officers named for Martin Luther King Jr. I worked with Lenny at District Five. He was a good cop and a fiery speaker, calling for wholesale change in training and oversight in the department. He was quoted in the press, stating that racism and homophobia were rampant in the ranks and that this attitude reveals itself in police interactions with people of color and gays; honestly and unfortunately, I could not disagree with him.

Religious and civic leaders in the Black community held protests in front of Dahmer's apartment and called for a federal investigation into police education and training. The gay community also clamored for recognition of any current police practices and intimated that police failed to investigate these crimes properly because they didn't care if a few Blacks and/or gays went missing. TV and newspaper reporters flooded the gay area of town, randomly interviewing patrons about the situation, and often showing clips inside these nightclubs, featuring men in drag, and dancing and having fun. Fake bomb threats to these areas added fuel to the frenzy, and daily snippets of anything gay related dotted the local section of the newspaper.

In early December, I received the much-anticipated subpoena. I was listening to roll call when Harrell dropped it on my desk. *The State of Wisconsin v. Jeffrey Lionel Dahmer*. The date was set. The trial was set to begin January 13, 1992. Harrell told me that I was to report to the day shift on the twelfth. Apparently, the district attorney wanted me available to shuffle papers, run errands, and prepare for testimony. I would be assigned days for the length of the trial. Generally, the nights went by quickly and I again began to think about all my conversations with Jeff.

***

I had the next day off, but decided to get up early with a cup of coffee and peruse the daily paper for available apartments for myself. The time had come in my marriage that I needed to be on my own and in my own space—as difficult as it would be to be away from my kids. There was one in the downtown area, close to the lake, and it was open at noon. I showed up early and parked the squad car in front. It was a classic old Milwaukee Cream City brick, three-story walk-up. A tiny older woman stood in front. She was a bit startled as I approached.

"Is there a problem, officer? You are the police, aren't you?"

"Yes, ma'am," I responded, extending my hand. "No, there is no problem; I am looking for an apartment."

She seemed relieved and walked to the left side basement door. "It's an efficiency one bedroom," she said, opening the door to permit entry. Two rooms and a bath with a tiny kitchen was the extent of it.

"I'll take it. Can I move in today?" I asked.

She was caught off guard at the certainty of my response. "Well, I was going to have the carpet cleaned, and repaint first," she said, looking at me inquisitively. "Well, it's okay with me. The rent is four hundred a month with heat. Since you're the police, I guess we can forget about the first and last months' security deposit."

I thanked her for her kindness and understanding as she handed me the key.

***

The next day, I walked into the detective assembly to find Murphy sitting at his desk. "Welcome back to the day shift."

I smiled in answer as I grabbed a cup of coffee and sat next to him. "So, what's on the agenda?"

We were to go to the district attorney's office for further instructions. We rode the elevator to the ground floor and walked toward the Safety Building. The entire street was packed with media trucks and trailers, vans, autos, reporters, and technicians sporting the logos of various news organizations. The hype had died down a bit since Dahmer's arrest last summer, but now they were back in full swing; it was a veritable feeding frenzy. Every news outlet in the state and from all over the world was in attendance. I saw crews from Japan, Australia, Europe, and Canada. A media center was set up on the second floor of the Safety Building, and there were cables crisscrossing the street. They converged at a basement entryway and snaked through the halls, creating an obstacle course for pedestrians.

Murphy and I entered the district attorney's office to find McCann and his staff preparing for the case. They were huddled around a large desk covered with boxes of reports. A young court assistant took us aside and informed us that until it was time to testify, we were to escort and prepare witnesses, along with helping locate and ready reports and evidentiary items. He handed each of us a large black three-ring binder. I opened mine to find it contained the chronological order of supplements I filed after each session with Dahmer. It was bulky and contained hundreds of pages. I knew the weeks I spent with him produced numerous reports, but feeling the heft of the binder brought back the intensity and breadth of my interrogation.

I perused the first few pages, starting with my original arrest report and confession. It was simplistic yet covered all seventeen homicides.

Looking through it transported me back to that first grueling night, and an image of the head in the box appeared in my mind. It had been a while since this occurred and the fear of that memory was still with me. I remembered how all that changed as I became his close confidant and "friend." I thought about how I eventually began to feel sorry for him and the mental turmoil I experienced because I actually liked the guy. My brief trip down memory lane was interrupted by Murphy.

"Come on, Pat, let's go check out the courtroom."

We took the stairs to the fifth floor and walked into a hallway of pandemonium. It was packed with people. News technicians and reporters congregated near the courtroom door, where two brawny deputy sheriffs tried to maintain order. A line of citizens queued up to claim the seats available for spectators. As we approached, one of the deputies recognized us from our many trips back and forth with Dahmer.

"Good luck, fellas" he said, parting the sea of humanity and opening the door to permit entrance.

We walked into the large, beautifully wood-carved courtroom. It had been altered in preparation for the trial. An eight-foot high barrier of bulletproof glass and steel now separated the gallery from the courtroom proper. There were one hundred seats available: twenty-three for reporters, thirty-four for families of the victims, and forty-three seats for the general public. It had been swept for explosives and everyone entering was subject to a pat down search. It was a madhouse. I walked into the holding area in the back of the judge's chambers.

There, in an isolated cell, was Dahmer. He was clad in a blaze-orange county jail jumpsuit, white socks, and blue tennis shoes. A deputy with a face withered from years of service sat outside. Dahmer noticed me and stood up immediately. "Hi, Pat."

I walked over to him and shook his hand through the bars. "Long time no see, eh?" I motioned for the deputy to open the cell so I could enter. "How have they been treating you?" I asked as we sat down.

He looked clean and refreshed and I said so. He answered that it must be the three squares a day and all the time he spent with Boyle and his cadre of psychiatrists. I was a bit surprised that I was glad to see him. The time separating our last interview was so crammed with additional homicide investigations, and being back and forth between the family home to see the kids and my new apartment that I had almost forgotten our camaraderie.

"So, did they get your head screwed on right?" I said, loosening my tie and opening my shirt.

"Yeah, I guess so." He chuckled.

"What about your mom and dad?"

His face lit up with a smile. He said his fears of being disowned by his family never materialized. Indeed, Lionel Dahmer (and stepmother, Shari) had embraced his son, forgiven him, and granted interviews—making several appearances on TV magazine shows decrying his crimes and criminal behavior, refusing to give up on his son and maintaining his love and support of Jeff. Although initially Jeff's mother Joyce did not want to have anything to do with the investigation and remained largely behind the scenes, she eventually came to accept Jeff back into her life once he was incarcerated.

Two gallery seats were assigned for Lionel and Shari and they were quietly present for every court appearance despite an obviously hostile public both in and out of the courthouse. Dahmer said the sessions with the various psychiatrists and psychologists were interesting and informative.

"Pat, I thought I was just an evil, selfish, lustful monster. But after talking with everyone, I'm beginning to think that there is something psychologically wrong with me. You were right about the alcohol though. It fueled my desires and kept me from feeling guilty. I haven't felt this healthy or alert in a long time. I'm actually looking forward to the future sessions they have scheduled to figure me out."

I told him I was glad to hear about his family, and felt his desire to understand his actions would help him cope with incarceration. "It's going to get hectic over the next few weeks, and I don't know if we will be able to chat, but I will see you around." I got up and walked to the tiny cell door, which the deputy opened. I shook Jeff's hand as I walked out and the grey metal bars clanged behind me.

The rear door of the judge's chamber opened, and Boyle and his entourage entered carrying boxes of files. McCann and a host of assistants followed closely behind. Boyle and McCann were two Irish Catholics with a shared history.

In the mid-sixties, the two worked together in the district attorney's office as deputy and assistant prosecutors. When the vacancy came up for district attorney in 1968, the two men faced each other in the election for the job. McCann won and had held the office ever since. The fact that Murphy and I were also Irish and Catholic was not lost on the press or insiders, who regularly referred to the lot of us as the Irish Mafia.

The two groups exchanged pleasantries before everyone filtered through the doorway leading to the courtroom. McCann and his crew entered first and made their way to the prosecution table amid the noisy chatter of the gallery. A hush fell over the courtroom as Dahmer entered, flanked by Boyle and Patrickus. The many cameras, set up with their lens pushed against the thick glass barrier, buzzed away as their operators zoomed in on Dahmer.

Within minutes, the bailiff bellowed, "All rise," and the courtroom came to order.

Presiding was Circuit Judge Laurence Gram, a jurist known for his good judicial temperament, fondness for Tyrolean hats, participation in Bavarian vocal groups, and skill at cooking pork roast and spaetzle. There had been some grousing and ennui among civic leaders regarding the trial and its center-stage position in the press. They feared their "Great City on a Great Lake" risked association in the world's collective mind with the horrifying deeds of Jeffrey Dahmer. City image-makers even flirted with the idea of a media campaign to counter imagined damage that the trial, with all its gory details, might cause. They were glad to have a calm and respected jurist at the helm.

Boyle began. He was a silver-haired man of some girth, and approached the courtroom as if it were a good friend's living room. He moved about slowly, speaking in clear tones, with a measured cadence and a Wisconsin accent. His face seldom betrayed emotion other than congeniality. He was popular with his clients, and Milwaukee juries seemed to like him. He announced that his client intended to plead "guilty but insane" for the fifteen Milwaukee County murders. Dahmer was charged here with only fifteen counts because the first slaying took place in Bath, Ohio, and McCann didn't feel he had enough evidence to prosecute in the first Milwaukee death at the Ambassador Hotel. Dahmer had been charged in Ohio and was set to stand trial there after his sentencing in Wisconsin.

Boyle stated, "I want to emphasize that the decision to plead guilty is Mr. Dahmer's."

Judge Gram then asked Dahmer if he understood what the plea meant, to which he answered, "Yes, Your Honor."

McCann had a more combative style. His voice rose in a tone approaching indignation when he sought to expose a weakness in the testimony of defense witnesses. He was well known to Milwaukeeans for his anti-abortion and anti-capital punishment positions. An intense man, he communicated an image as the people's prosecutor and had been reelected to that office for the last twenty-four years. He made no objections to Dahmer's guilty plea; however, Boyle's motion to pick the jury from outside Milwaukee County was vigorously objected to, and upheld by Judge Gram.

In making his decision, the judge stated, "Quite frankly, no other county is anxious to see us come. Pretrial publicity doesn't make a difference as to where we pick the jury. Publicity has not only been extensive, but pervasive, not just throughout this state or throughout this country, but throughout the entire world."

By pleading guilty, Dahmer avoided the initial phase of the trial, held to determine guilt, and moved directly to the sanity phase, which under Wisconsin law focused solely on his mental state at the time of the killings. If judged sane, he would receive a mandatory sentence of life in prison; however, if the jury found he suffered from a mental disease and did not realize his conduct was wrong or could not stop himself from committing the crimes, he could be sentenced to an institution for the criminally insane. There, his possibilities for release hinged upon whether he was believed to be a danger to society.

Boyle dropped a motion to suppress Jeff's initial confession to me along with the evidence taken from Dahmer's apartment on the night of his arrest, which conceded that Dahmer's rights had not been violated. Judge Gram picked January 27 as the start date for jury selection, with the trial to commence immediately afterward. The entire proceeding lasted about thirty minutes. The courtroom erupted with noise after Gram and Dahmer's defense team exited through the back-chamber door. Reporters scurried to interview victims' family members for their reaction to the insanity plea.

"Jeffrey Dahmer knows what he's doing," a sister of one of the victims cried into the camera. "He's insulting our intelligence by saying he was insane. All of us want him to go to prison and take his punishment like a man."

Many in the press wondered if the guilty plea would hold back details of the slayings, but an assistant DA reported that the defense had to persuade the jury that this crime was so bizarre and so pathological that Dahmer couldn't be held responsible.

"I don't see how they can do that and avoid the details of the crimes."

Murphy and I gathered at the prosecution table, where busy assistants packed files and discussed the proceedings. A young assistant DA declined our offer to help transport the boxes back to his office and said that McCann's instructions were for us to familiarize ourselves with the hundreds of pages of interviews we recorded with Dahmer and to remain on call for witness preparation and transport.

He struggled with the large white box of files, and before walking away, he said, "I don't have to remind you not to talk with the press."

With all the publicity, it appeared that McCann was taking no chances with further media leaks by keeping access to possible trial information in the hands of his staff.

Murphy laughed to himself at the reprimand from the young assistant. "Well, Pat, it looks like we have a free ride." He had been on call for other big cases in the past, and explained that all we had to do was report in every day and stay in radio contact with the bureau and the DA's office. "We are pretty much on our own, Pat. Just make sure you answer your radio and stay close in case they call."

At my apartment, I prepared a light supper and ate it in front of the secondhand TV I had picked up at the Salvation Army earlier in the week, browsing the various local channels for their take on the day's proceedings. Each tried to outdo the other with catchy tag lines like the "Milwaukee Massacres," "Slaughter on 25th Street," and "Horror in Milwaukee."

I was relatively inactive for the next two weeks except for the occasional witness pickup at the airport or meetings with assistant DAs to pin down certain aspects of the confession. The daily papers were filled with interviews of the victims' families, along with rumors and innuendos regarding Dahmer's activities. People came out of the woodwork. Anyone who had ever known, lived next to, went to school with, or worked with Jeffrey Dahmer was sought for interviews to fill news space until the trial started.

Every day the newsstands carried another twist in the story. *Newsweek, Time, People,* and numerous weekly magazines pasted large color photos of Dahmer wearing my son's striped shirt on the cover, blasting headlines like "The Secret Life of Jeffrey Dahmer," "Inside the Murderous Mind," and "Horrors in Apartment 213." Some of the trashy tabloid publications took to reporting pure fiction. One led with the headline "Jeffrey Dahmer Eats Cellmate While Awaiting Trial."

A tiny publishing company named Boneyard Press released a comic book, *Jeffery ⁹Dahmer: An Unauthorized Biography of a Serial Killer*, by Hart D. Fisher. It illustrated Dahmer's life and times, recounting already-published police accounts of the killings. The local section of the press continuously bombarded the Milwaukee Police Department. Reports on the antagonism between the union and the chief, the call for a federal investigation into the incident with the young Asian boy, and other police miscues were the norm. There were numerous articles and pictures of protests from various groups that gathered in front of the now-infamous Oxford Apartments, City Hall, and the police administration building, calling for improved education and training of the police.

The whole city was saturated with Jeffrey Dahmer. Another article, "Chicago Cop Lauds the Locals," provided an interview with a serial killer "expert" from the Chicago police. He had been involved in several Chicago cases, including John Wayne Gacy. He gushed with praise over my initial interrogation and concluded that Murphy and I were as good as or better than ninety-nine percent of all the detectives in any department. He emphasized our relationship with the suspect and our ability to keep him cooperative. This, he noted, was unusual for serial killers, as few had done so in the past. It was flattering and a bit overwhelming. Not to mention the ribbing we endured from our peers when the articles hit the newsstand. "From a zero back to a hero" was a constant refrain from the older detectives in the homicide department, who noted that I wasn't doing much of anything lately but basking in all the good press and slacking off on the job.

***

---

9. Fisher misspelt it.

I was up early the day jury selection began. I ate a breakfast of toast, coffee, and orange juice while watching the local early morning news. Every station had an expert trial lawyer commenting on the process. They were almost giddy as they explained the possibility for horrific and cadaverous details to emerge. I was a bit restless and left early for work.

I entered the detective assembly and found Murphy already there. He had been in communication with the DA's office and said that we were on standby if needed to shuffle potential jurors back and forth in the Safety Building.

We walked to the courtroom and entered from the judge's chambers. There were Dahmer and his legal entourage, headed by Boyle. Dahmer seemed relaxed, and he looked up to greet me. He was dressed in a tieless white shirt, brown sports coat, pants, and black shoes. He appeared emotionless as they conversed, but not in the way I had become accustomed to while he robotically described his deeds. This was a more detached look, and I wondered if they had him on sedatives to keep him calm and passive during voir dire[10].

About one hundred and fifty potential jurors reported to the courthouse, and from this group, seventy were chosen for the jury pool. During questioning, twenty-five said they could not serve on a jury that would be sequestered for an expected three-week trial. They were taken one by one into the judge's chambers with the lawyers, Dahmer, and a pool of three members from the media to explain why. All twenty-five were excused, including one woman, a bird breeder, who said that her birds would die if she were unable to hand-feed them daily. Others cited financial or family reasons, saying they couldn't be away from home or work for three weeks.

"Judge, I just don't have the stomach for it," explained another woman.

---

10. A term derived from Old French and Latin, *verum dicere*: to say what is true. Voir dire is the questioning of prospective jurors by a judge and attorneys in court. The voir dire process determines if any juror is biased and/or cannot deal with the issues fairly, or if there is cause not to allow a juror to serve.

The remaining group of forty-five was retained for questioning about their feelings on serving at a trial expected to include details of necrophilia, cannibalism, and crude lobotomies.

Boyle began. "There are going to be graphic descriptions, verbal statements relative to what happened in Mr. Dahmer's apartment and other places. Are any of you, sitting here, queasy about your ability to handle this type of thing?"

Four women and two men said such evidence may prove overwhelming to them, and were excused. During explanations to the remaining jury pool, Boyle contended that Dahmer's murderous impulses were those of an insane man unable to control his actions. In contrast, McCann said Dahmer's demons were of his own cunning, and he deserved to live his life in prison.

McCann bellowed, "This is not a prosecution for having sex with a dead body. This prosecution is about responsibility—responsibility for the murders."

Boyle countered that there was an underlying fear that if found insane, Dahmer could eventually be released. He made it clear that he wanted Dahmer to spend the rest of his life in a state mental institution. "His possible eventual release is a phantom fear—a phantom fear," he stressed. He asked any potential juror who harbored that fear to disclose it. None did.

Over the next three days, fourteen people were chosen: twelve jurors and two alternates. Seven men and seven women; thirteen Caucasians and one African American. They were immediately sequestered.

A relative of one of the victims was upset about the makeup of the jury. "It's not fair," she said. "Picking a jury with only one Black when the majority of the people killed were Black. How can they do that?"

Boyle answered in the press. "I am a little offended that anyone might like to turn my conduct into anything racist...

It wouldn't have mattered to me if half the jury were Black. In my opinion, this is not a racial issue."

McCann came to his aid, stating that there were only five or six Blacks, and no Hispanics, Asians, or Native Americans among the pool interviewed for the jury. He was satisfied with those who would serve.

Both sides disclosed their lists of potential witnesses. Boyle's included Dahmer's father and stepmother, Lionel and Shari Dahmer; his brother David Dahmer; and his mother, Joyce Flint Dahmer. The prosecution said it planned to call nearly one hundred witnesses, including Tracy Edwards, who had escaped in handcuffs and flagged down police. There was only one brief disruption during the jury selection process, when a sister of one of the victims was removed from the courtroom for making an obscene gesture. She raised her middle finger at Dahmer when he seemed to look her way. The press in the hallway immediately surrounded her, where she said, "If it were possible, I would put a hole in his head. If I can get close to him, I will. If they figure he can do all this killing, why can't I?"

McCann said that he would meet with victims' relatives before testimony began. "If they feel it [an outburst] coming on and they can't contain themselves, I've asked them to leave the courtroom. If they are escorted out, they won't be allowed to return."

The trial was to begin the next day. Murphy and I walked back to the detective assembly to punch out. Before I could do so, I was called into the captain's office. Domagalski sat with the young day shift lieutenant who tried to switch Murphy and me during the initial interrogation.

"Pat," Domagalski said almost apologetically, "we've been talking it over and decided that because Dahmer has already pleaded guilty, there is no need for both you and Murphy to take the stand. Some people are worried that because of your lack of tenure in the bureau, testifying might be tricky. I am not saying you're a loose cannon—you've done a wonderful job—but it's been decided that Murphy, as the more senior homicide detective, will testify. He will read from the supplemental reports filed by both of you. You'll still be on days, though, for the rest of the trial."

When I heard the decision, I was floored and then angry. I was the one Dahmer trusted. I was the one who established the rapport that cracked him and eventually got him talking. I was the one who spent the grueling initial hours conning and cajoling Dahmer to trust me and divulge his crimes. I took his initial confession, and now I was being shut out. I was already a little shaky because of the marital separation and impending divorce; now it seemed my job had abandoned me too. I tried not to let my facial expression betray my true feelings, but secretly I thought that there were some in the bureau who didn't believe that a rookie deserved this kind of credit and felt threatened by my success. I believed the decision smacked of departmental politics, and I was pissed. But I kept my thoughts to myself.

"Okay, sir, I understand." I glanced at the young lieutenant and made a quick exit.

***

I awoke the next morning well rested, and prepared for work while watching the early morning news. The director of the Milwaukee County Mental Health Association was talking with a reporter.

"This isn't something that's in the textbooks," she said. "We've already seen the effects here in Milwaukee, including more calls to the crisis line and longer appointment times at counseling clinics." She advised limited exposure to the case, concluding, "The gory details may bother the sensitive."

I decided to stop and pick up a paper on my way to the bureau. I figured I would need some reading material since I wouldn't be testifying and wouldn't have to spend any more time reviewing the enormous file. The local page screamed, "Dahmer-Watching May Be Unhealthy." It quoted experts who felt that listening to the details of Dahmer's gruesome crimes could injure mental health. They cautioned Milwaukee school officials not to let children watch the trial, which would be covered by Court TV on cable.

I could see the hubbub around the Safety Building as I crossed the street from the parking lot. A line of people stood around the block waiting for the doors to open. Besides the adults vying for one of the coveted public seats, there were many high school students hoping to get a glimpse of Jeffrey Dahmer. Reporters were shoving their microphones into anyone's face who appeared to have something to say.

"We just want to see him," squealed one sixteen-year-old girl from Beloit, who had skipped school with her friends. "We want to get his autograph, if they will let us. That would be cool to have Jeffrey Dahmer's autograph because he's a killer."

The circus had begun.

Chapter 21

The assembly was a flurry of activity. The Dahmer trial had little effect on the growing violent crime rate in Milwaukee, and the late shift stayed busy filing reports and packaging evidence. Murphy was dressed in his best blue suit and sitting at his desk with a large black ring binder containing our hundreds of pages of interviews with Dahmer. "Well, kid, are you ready?"

I nodded and we proceeded to the courthouse.

"Don't worry, Pat." Murphy knew that it was unusual for the lead detective not to testify, and I could tell he felt badly for me about the sudden decision to have just one detective conduct the testimony of a multiple-murder case.

The cavernous courtroom was empty, and we entered to find both Boyle and McCann huddling with their respective staff. Murphy and I took our seats at the prosecution table. Everyone was busy shuffling papers and sifting through files. A young assistant sat down next to Murphy and asked if he was ready to go, as he would be the first prosecution witness called after opening arguments. I listened intently, even though I knew he wasn't talking to me. I decided not to be upset. I knew what I had done and was proud of it. My peers and colleagues were aware of my accomplishments, and that would have to be enough.

The courtroom came alive as the deputies opened the doors. Family members of Dahmer's numerous victims, reporters with their camera crews, and members of the general public claimed their seats. Some were dour and sullen, and others appeared almost jubilant as they scurried for the front-row seats. I turned to watch the gallery and its activity when I noticed Boyle walking toward the prosecution table.

"Detective Kennedy," he announced. "You will be my first witness. Are you prepared to testify?"

I looked up in shock, but before I could answer, the young lieutenant abruptly stood up and interjected. "Excuse me, sir, but we have decided that Detective Kennedy is not to testify."

Boyle looked at him in disdain. "You don't decide who I'm going to call on, Lieutenant."

The brash young lieutenant's face turned beet red as he looked around. He eventually sat back down.

I didn't have time to think about the turn of events. The bailiff entered and said, "All rise."

The courtroom came to order and Judge Gram took the bench. As opening arguments were delivered, Murphy asked if I wanted my supplemental reports from his binder.

"No," I said under my breath. "I don't want to look disorganized with all these people watching." I had spent many hours in previous weeks going over my interviews and felt confident I could give a good accounting of my work. Time seemed to stand still as I tried to organize my thoughts. I was jolted back to reality as Boyle stood to address the Court. "I call Detective Patrick Kennedy to the stand."

I could feel my face flush as I walked to the witness chair. I said a silent prayer asking for calm and strength as I raised my hand and swore to tell the truth. I sat erectly with my hands in my lap and surveyed the packed courtroom. It was deathly silent except for the whizzing and whirling of news cameras and the technicians operating them. Everyone, it seemed, focused on me.

I spent the next hour and a half recounting the events of the first night I met Dahmer. I tried to be matter of fact with my answers and maintain a cool demeanor. Boyle took me through my entire confession report, which brought intermittent gasps from the gallery. I never looked directly at the spectators or news cameras, but concentrated on Boyle for the questions and the jury with my answers. As the testimony continued, I became more comfortable. It was obvious that Boyle believed that my take on Dahmer and the emotions he displayed that first night could bolster his case for insanity.

"That's all I have for this witness," Boyle said when he was finished. There was no cross-examination from McCann, and I stepped down from the stand. I noted that my undershirt was completely soaked with perspiration as I took my seat next to Murphy at the prosecution table.

"Good job, Pat," Murphy whispered from the side of his mouth. I sat in my chair and stared straight ahead, still a bit shocked by the immediacy of what had just happened. I returned to reality when the judge declared a break for lunch.

"All rise," the bailiff demanded.

As soon as the judge made his exit, the gallery burst into a tumult of chatter and activity. News personalities cornered family members for their reaction to the morning's revelations, and I could feel their camera lenses concentrating on me as I stood listening to McCann detail the afternoon strategy to his crew.

Murphy broke the huddle and shook my hand with a smile. "Excellent work, Pat. You sounded like a wily old veteran up there." We walked through the judge's chambers and exited into the hallway. A number of reporters waited there. When they noticed me, they scrambled to block my exit.

"Detective Kennedy, do you think Dahmer is insane? What was it like to look into the eyes of evil? Are you having any trouble dealing with this case?" The questions peppered me rapid fire, and I used my extended arm to part the crowd.

"Excuse me... no comment."

Murphy and I ducked into the stairwell and returned to the detective assembly. There we found a crowd of day shift detectives, command officers, and support staff sitting around a television set. They had ceased all work and were watching coverage of the trial. When they saw us enter, a cheer went up.

"From a zero back to hero!" a voice shouted from the back of the room.

I blushed uncontrollably as I sat at my desk. I tried to eat the lunch I brought in between the congratulatory back slaps and words of praise from my peers. I felt buzzed, but satisfied. The rush of testifying was still with me, and it took a while before I came back down to Earth. The afternoon was a breeze. I was excused from the prosecution table and watched Murphy begin the tedious task of reading all the supplemental reports we had prepared during our interviews with Dahmer. I had a ringside seat back in the judge's chambers, where I could observe the proceedings out of sight of the gallery or TV cameras. It was exciting—now that my part was over, I could concentrate on the trial and all the drama that went along with it.

When the day's hearing was complete, the bailiff returned Dahmer to the holding cell in the judge's chambers. He stood looking at me through the grey bars.

"Well, Jeff, how are you holding up?"

"Okay, I guess," he answered.

I pulled my chair next to the cell and we both sat down. Dahmer spoke again. "Listening to your testimony brought back the hazy horror of that night. It seems like a dream now. I was so drunk and out of it, I almost forgot everything we talked about. I still can't believe you stuck with me, Pat."

"Come on, Jeff. We've been through all that. It's my job. Besides, there is a reason we were put together, remember? We were just a couple of drunks trying to work it out."

He smiled sheepishly at my statement, and I stood up to shake his hand.

"I'll see you tomorrow, Jeff."

I navigated the activity-filled halls, and took the stairway back to the assembly to punch out.

The sun was setting as I drove toward my apartment, and I dreaded the thought of being alone in the little efficiency space. I decided to stop on Water Street in an area filled with mostly upscale taverns. I entered Rosie's, a popular after-work watering hole. The patrons of the bustling tavern were glued to several TV monitors, all set to coverage of the trial. I found an opening in the middle of the long mahogany bar and stepped into it. The bartender was busy mixing cocktails and chatting with customers. As I waited to summon her, I felt the stare of a man standing next to me. It was uncomfortable and I turned toward him.

"Hi, pal, how's it going?"

His eyes widened as he compared me with the TV monitor, which was showing my taped testimony.

"Hey! You're the Dahmer detective." He turned to address the crowd. "Hey, everybody, look! It's the Dahmer dude." He grabbed my hand and shook it vigorously. "Good job, man."

I looked around and noted that the entire establishment was staring at me. A spontaneous round of applause erupted, and several patrons crowded about slapping me on the back and grabbing for my hand.

"Way to go, dude."

"Nice work, man."

"Hey, let me buy you a drink."

The young barkeep joined the others. "What'll you have? It's on me," she said.

The sudden celebrity caught me off guard and I stammered, "Oh, I guess I'll have a Coke." I began to feel trapped. I decided that going home might not be such a bad idea. I maneuvered through the high-fiving crowd without touching my drink.

The phone rang as I walked toward my front door. Quickly fumbling with the new key, I answered the phone and heard my wife's voice.

"Why didn't you tell me you would be testifying today?" she started. "I would have taped it for the kids."

I tried to explain that I had no idea I was to take the stand until minutes before it happened. She didn't buy my explanation, believing that I purposely kept the information to myself to spite her. She hung up the phone in disgust. I couldn't believe it. She wouldn't allow me to discuss the case around the kids or share my feelings with her while I was home, and now she was angry about missing my televised testimony. Apparently, the Dahmer celebrity had infected her as well.

There were three more telephone calls in a row. They were from friends and acquaintances who had caught my act on TV and wondered if I wanted to get together. I begged off on their offers and unplugged the phone. I guess I wasn't ready for all the attention and not really sure how I felt about it. I undressed to my underwear and turned on the TV. A John Wayne movie played after dinner. The Duke took me into the nightly news, but I was too tired to watch. I tumbled into bed and fell asleep fast.

***

The next morning, I walked into the detective bureau to find a copy of the *Milwaukee Sentinel Journal* on my desk. The headline screamed, "Dahmer Knew Right from Wrong; Detective Cites [Dahmer's] Cover-Up Efforts." The entire main section of the paper was Dahmer-related. The inside had pictures of Murphy and me, and quoted the more troubling aspects of his confession. The latest edition of the newspaper featured a large color photograph on the front page of me testifying. Wouldn't you know the press chose the most uncomplimentary picture of me to display? It was nasty, and I looked as if I had just bitten into something sour. Taped to the side of my desk was a mimeographed copy of the newspaper photo, superimposed with a picture of Dahmer. The words in a balloon floating above it read *"He's like a brother to me."* This would be the first of many such articles gleaned from the press and put together by my colleagues. For the remainder of the trial, I would find a new one, equally distasteful, on my desk every morning.

I was assigned the duty of preparing reports for Murphy to read on the stand. I was glad my part of the trial was over—and to think I was upset initially that I wouldn't be given a chance to testify. Because of the newspaper, I was more popular than ever. Walking the halls between the Safety Building and the bureau, I was accosted by officers, deputies, clerks, and defense lawyers who all had something to say about my front-page coverage. I could feel the eyes of citizens and heard their whispers as I went about my duties. "That's him, the detective who caught Dahmer."

I knew it was bullshit and wanted to stop and tell them the truth—a potential victim had gotten away, flagged down two uniformed police who eventually uncovered Dahmer's morbid world, and I had simply shown up for work and caught the call—but it continued despite my explanations. Several young men, flamboyantly attired and clutching a copy of the *Wisconsin State Journal* congregated near the DA's office when they saw me.

"Hey, officer?" they squealed, and rushed over to surround me. "Thank you for stopping him. Will you please autograph my paper?"

I pulled a pen from my shirt pocket and scribbled my name across the front page. "Look, fellas, I just questioned him. He was already arrested when I got there."

They didn't seem to care. "Oh, thank you," they said, smiling, looking at my signature as if it were a prized possession. It was clear that everyone had their own take on the case and the hard facts were irrelevant.

It was Friday afternoon and when court adjourned, I found myself wondering what to do over the weekend. I decided to get away from Milwaukee and all the media attention, so I hopped on the freeway and headed north to Fond du Lac. I still had many friends there and thought it would be a haven from the trial. My close friend, Mike Soffa, owned a successful music business there and I was godfather to one of his triplet boys. I entered the store and Mike greeted me, holding a copy of the *Fond du Lac Reporter*—the local news rag. On the cover was an even bigger color photo of that terrible picture of me with the headline, "Ex-Fond du Lac Resident is Dahmer Detective." The article explained that I had gone to Marian College, where I played basketball, worked for UPS, and started a family. It had interviews with some of my old teammates and coaches.

Mike was beaming. "Hey, buddy, look. You're a celebrity."

I was flabbergasted. There didn't seem to be anywhere that was not infected with the Dahmer drama.

***

When Monday morning rolled around, I was refreshed and ready. I continued to assist Murphy with files and picked up several witnesses from the airport but other than that, I was free to observe the proceedings from my prime spot in the judge's chambers. It took the entire week for Murphy to testify. McCann had him read selected excerpts of our interviews with Dahmer, and his deadpan, unemotional style juxtaposed grimly with the anguished look on the faces of victims' families as they listened to the monstrous deeds performed by Dahmer on their loved ones.

My father was following the trial at home on Court TV, but had come to town for a quick visit. Now that he was in Milwaukee, he wanted a ringside seat. Monday morning, I took him with me to work where he was a hit in the bureau, and I was proud to introduce him as a retired Detroit police officer. Many of the old timers spent time chatting with him, and several captains regaled him with amusing anecdotes about his son. I could tell he was pleased with my accomplishments within the police department and glad that I had successfully followed in his footsteps. I told Murphy I was heading to court early that day in attempt to get my father one of the few public seats.

"Good luck," he said. "The line is already around the block."

On the short trip to the Safety Building, we waded past the army of news trucks, satellite dishes, and technicians. We took the stairway to the courtroom to avoid the crowds and entered through the judge's back chambers. I introduced him to the two brawny deputies charged with admittance to the gallery. I told them about his service as a longtime Detroit police officer and asked if he could take a seat before the doors opened. This was no easy task. Since the trial started, people had lined up every night for the chance of admittance. It was strictly on a first-come, first-served basis, and several disruptions had occurred as people jockeyed for position.

The deputies were gracious and shook my father's hand but stated they could do nothing to help me get him into the gallery. Family seats were assigned and they were afraid that any perceived favoritism regarding the remaining public chairs would land them in hot water with their department, or even worse, a negative story in the press.

I continued pleading my case, and Dad tugged at my arm. "Pat, who is this guy? I think I know him."

I looked up and saw the district attorney, E. Michael McCann, walking toward us. "No, Dad, I don't think so. That's the DA. You don't know him."

I returned to my efforts with the deputies but my father persisted. "Gee, I'm sure I know that guy."

GRILLING DAHMER | 259

I was exasperated with my attempts to convince the deputies, and then McCann approached us. He stopped short of entering the courtroom and stared at my father.

"Pat? Pat Kennedy?" he said. I was dumbfounded. A knowing look passed between the two.

"Mike McCann. I thought that was you," my father said as the two shook hands.

McCann then looked in my direction. "I never made the connection. So, this is your son."

It turned out that McCann and my father attended college together at the University of Detroit. After some small talk, Dad explained that he wanted to sit in on the proceedings for that day, if it was all right. McCann waved off the deputies, who were as surprised as I was. He then escorted my dad to a seat inside the Plexiglas barrier directly behind the prosecution table. It was within fifteen feet of the chair where Dahmer himself sat. The two again shook hands and McCann disappeared into the judge's back chambers. My father sat contentedly, waiting for the day's events to begin. He later often recounted to his grandchildren or anyone else who listened how he sat close enough to touch Jeffrey Dahmer and how he had looked into his cold, blue eyes and seen evil there.

The several days my father stayed with me were tremendous. Spending time together, going out to eat after a day in court, and talking about my current marital situation and life in general gave me great comfort and strength. The night he returned to Michigan, I took him to the airport. He embraced me in a huge bear hug.

"Keep the faith, big guy," he said before boarding. I waited until his plane left the runway and returned to my empty apartment filled with both gratitude and sadness. The tiny efficiency seemed to engulf me and I sat for a while alone in the dark until my eyes grew heavy.

***

The next few days of the trial, I passed the time in the judge's chambers listening to testimony and talking with the various deputies, lawyers, and witnesses who passed through the area. Under Wisconsin law, the burden of proving insanity lies with the defense. To be proven insane, a defendant must show that they suffered from a mental disease, and that the disease kept them from knowing right from wrong or made them unable to stop themselves from committing the crimes. Boyle's claim was that Dahmer suffered from a sexual disorder, a paraphilia that compelled him into actions that were beyond his control.

Of all the experts Boyle put on the stand, Dr. Frederick S. Berlin was the most credible. In technical terms, his diagnosis was that Dahmer was an antisocial, schizoid, and schizotypal personality. He was a chronic alcoholic who suffered from three distinct paraphilias: necrophilia, the desire to have intercourse with a dead body; frotteurism, the uncontrollable urge to rub or grind one's self on another person or thing, including masturbation; and splanchnophilia or partialism, the extreme urge to cut open a body and look in to it. Both Boyle and Berlin hammered home the fact that Dahmer suffered from a biological or psychological predisposition that rendered him unable to control himself, therefore making him a victim of these sexual diseases, and rendering him legally insane.

On the other hand, McCann characterized Dahmer as a clever master of deception and deceit, who knew very well what he was doing, and who could turn his urges on and off. To this end, he paraded his own set of shrinks to drive home his point, in particular Dr. Park Dietz. Dietz had gained notoriety as a prosecution witness in the trial of John Hinckley Jr., who was acquitted by reason of insanity in 1982 for shooting President Reagan. Dietz had interviewed Dahmer for about eighteen hours over three days and agreed that Dahmer did exhibit some of the symptoms described by Dr. Berlin; however, he concluded that they were not beyond his control.

Dietz stated, "In my opinion, at the time of each of the charged homicides, Mr. Dahmer had substantial capacity to appreciate the wrongfulness of his conduct. The evidence on which this opinion is based includes but is not limited to: (a) Mr. Dahmer told me that at the time he killed each of these victims, he appreciated that it was wrong to kill them; (b) Mr. Dahmer took steps to reduce the chances he would be identified as the last person seen with a victim; (c) the fact that Mr. Dahmer in each instance committed the charged offense in a private setting, hidden from the view of others; (d) the fact that Mr. Dahmer found it necessary to drink alcohol to overcome his inhibitions against killing the victims; (e) the fact that Mr. Dahmer feared being caught in the act of killing a victim or in the presence of a drugged, comatose, dead, or dismembered victim; and (f) the fact that Mr. Dahmer took elaborate steps to destroy evidence of his crimes or to hold it secure against discovery by others by decreasing odors, securing his apartment, and painting skulls that he retained so that they would appear artificial."

His answer sounded quite a bit like my confession report and I wondered if he had read it. It was obvious to me that Jeff knew the wrongfulness of his deeds. The bigger question was whether he was predisposed beyond his control. Did he have the capacity to conform his conduct to the requirements of law? Could he control himself? Both sides pressed on this point.

Dietz responded to this query. "In my opinion, Mr. Dahmer had substantial capacity to conform his conduct. The evidence on which this opinion is based includes but is not limited to: (a) the fact that Mr. Dahmer told me that at the time he killed each of these victims, he would have refrained from doing so had the victim agreed to remain with him voluntarily for a few weeks; (b) the fact that Mr. Dahmer told me that at the time he killed each of these victims, he would have refrained from doing so had a witness entered the room; (c) the fact that Mr. Dahmer was able to suppress his sexual behavior other than occasional masturbation for a prolonged period around 1983 or 1984, when he immersed himself in religion; (d) the fact that Mr. Dahmer was able to satisfy his sexual desires with masturbation at all times; (e) the fact that Mr. Dahmer did satisfy himself exclusively with masturbation from about 1973 until the murder of the first victim in 1978, from that time until his entry into the gay subculture of pornographic bookstores, bathhouses, and gay bars in the early 1980s, and at various times thereafter; (f) the fact that Mr. Dahmer prepared himself for some of these murders by clearing space in his apartment for victim storage, by powderizing tablets before going out to find a victim, by drinking, by viewing pornography, by watching the movies that allowed him to identify with evil and powerful characters, or by a combination of these methods; (g) the fact that Mr. Dahmer generally limited his murders to weekends when he could have sufficient time to enjoy and initiate disposal of the victim before returning to work; (h) the fact that Mr. Dahmer did not kill any of the men he was attracted to while in bars, on the street, at the mall, in the peep show booths of pornographic bookstores, or in bathhouses after discovering how hard it was to remove a corpse from a downtown hotel, but rather controlled himself unless and until the circumstances were more opportune for promoting privacy and evading detection; (i) the fact that Mr. Dahmer did not kill those men whom he found attractive and had rendered unconscious even after lowering his inhibitions through drinking where the bathhouse setting would not preclude readily escaping detection; (j) the fact that Mr. Dahmer did not kill men he drugged unless he continued to find them sufficiently attractive to warrant further steps; (k) the fact that Mr. Dahmer reported that after rendering each of his victims unconscious, he voluntarily drank additional alcohol for the purpose of overcoming his natural inhibitions against killing them, and (l) the fact that Mr. Dahmer did in each instance wait until the victim was in his place of residence, under his control, and behind closed doors before killing the victim."

The doctor's unemotional and lengthy response was met with a hush from the gallery. His methodical delivery, erect posture, and monotonous style were reminiscent of the deliberate, almost robot-like tone Dahmer slipped into as he recalled his deeds for me. I couldn't help thinking that the two were physically alike in many ways. Both were understated, tall, well built, blond, bespectacled, and pleasant looking. I wondered what their interviews had been like. *Did Jeff show emotion? Did he cry or get angry? Was he allowed to pace the room? Was there any levity or humor?* I looked at Jeff, sitting statuesque with no affect, staring straight ahead, almost trance-like.

McCann was content to let the doctor's words sink in and took a long pause before excusing him from the witness stand. Boyle stood to deliver his closing argument.

"Jeffrey Dahmer is an insane, steamrolling, killing machine who had sex with dead corpses and ate his victims' flesh," he thundered. "He couldn't stop killing because of a sickness he discovered, not chose. He had to do what he did because he couldn't stop. This isn't a matter of choice, but an overwhelming and uncontrollable compulsion to murder."

Finally, turning toward the jury, Boyle hung his head and said, "No human being on the face of the earth could do anything worse than what he did. Nobody could be more reprehensible than this man. The devil would be a tie. But if he is sick, then he isn't the devil."

In rebuttal, McCann portrayed Dahmer as a cool, calculating killer who cleverly covered his tracks. "He's fooled a lot of people. He sacrificed others for his sexual pleasure, drugged young men to make it easier to kill them, and now merely seeks to escape responsibility. This is not the case of a psychotic man who didn't know the difference between right and wrong. Please, please do not let this murderous killer fool you with this special defense."

One by one, McCann theatrically displayed 8x10 color photographs of each of Dahmer's victims, many of them smiling, to the jurors.

"I don't want you to forget who they are," he said, causing several relatives of the victims to break into tears. A minister, flanked by counselors, helped escort them from the courtroom with TV cameras catching it all.

The jury, who had endured twenty-one days of court proceedings, and listened to twenty-eight witnesses testify over the last twelve days, was given final instructions from Judge Gram. They began deliberations late that afternoon and retired to their hotel rooms for the evening. A court official reported that if they reached a decision, it would be announced the next day.

I returned to the assembly to punch out and noticed some postal letters on my desk. They were from the parents of several victims and addressed to me personally. They contained short but heartfelt thanks for my work on the case and for bringing closure to their torment. I sat quietly for a while, letting their words sink in. I had received letters of commendation for exemplary actions on the job in the past, but this was the first time murder victims' families took time to write and express their thanks. The letters left me numb. I had worked so hard to control my own emotions that I couldn't feel anything. Although I had used the families' uncertainty regarding their loved ones as leverage with Dahmer, it was only a detective's trick. The reality of that technique became clear to me for the first time. I tucked the letters into my suit coat pocket and trudged toward the parking lot. It was Friday night and the city was jumping with activity.

As I drove past Water Street, I noticed the bright lights and the after-work crowd milling about from tavern to tavern. I thought about joining them but continued to my tiny efficiency apartment. I entered and undressed. The phone rang, and I hesitated about picking up the receiver. I let it ring. I didn't want to talk to anybody. I didn't know how I felt or what to do. I checked the fridge: a quart of milk and a chunk of cheese were the meager offerings. From the cupboard, I produced a can of bean with bacon soup and some crackers. It would have to do. The phone rang several more times throughout the evening, but I wanted to be alone without any interruptions. I didn't answer. I spent a restless night unable to achieve a deep sleep and was glad when the alarm clock signaled the new day.

***

Saturday mornings in the bureau were quiet, as the day shift maintained a skeleton crew. Murphy and I sat around reading the morning paper, drinking coffee, and eating fresh pastries until court was to begin. The paper was filled with speculation by court watchers as to what the jury would decide. Their deliberations would determine whether Jeff went to prison for the remainder of his life or to a mental institution from which he could petition for release every six months. If there were a split verdict, insane on some counts, sane on others, he could likely be sent to a mental institution and if ever eligible for release there, would be sent to prison.

As I read, I thought about my time with Jeff. *Was he crazy?* To do what he did, one would have to be insane. On the other hand, in normal conversation, he displayed no oddness that may lead anyone to question his sanity. Through the weeks of interviews, we had become intimate acquaintances and in the depth of our conversations, I often wondered if I was confronting darkness. *Was it evil that I walked into that night?* Still, I couldn't help but feel sorry for the guy. He was a pathetic human being, unable or unwilling to connect. *Could it be that all his horrific acts were simply his undisciplined pursuit of wanton sexual pleasure and selfishness?* There was no mistake about his ruthless deeds, but somehow, I didn't see him as a cold-blooded killer. *He must be insane.*

My thoughts were interrupted by Murphy. "Court resumes this afternoon."

I made my way to my listening post in the judge's chambers. The courtroom was packed and filled with activity before coming to order. The jury had reached a decision.

Judge Gram quickly perused the document before announcing in a strong and steady voice the jury's 10–2 decision followed by a grim roll call of the victims. "Sane on all counts."

"Praise Jesus!" a woman cried from the gallery, while others shouted in pain. Some family members rocked with sobs.

I looked at Jeff; he showed no emotion and sat staring straight ahead, as if transfixed. Gram set his sentencing for ten o'clock the following Monday. The jury was dismissed, and the courtroom broke into pandemonium as soon as Gram left the bench. Two huge deputies hustled Jeff past me and placed him in the holding cell. People were shouting and crying. The Plexiglas door separating the gallery opened, and dozens of family members rushed McCann to hug and thank him for his efforts. "God bless you, my brother," one relative said as he reached out to touch him. Another deputy ushered Jeff's father and stepmother into the judge's chambers. They cried and embraced Jeff through the grey bars. It was agonizing and painful to watch. The jury met with two psychiatrists hired by the court to counsel them because of their exposure to the grisly details. Hordes of hungry reporters waited impatiently outside the door for a chance interview. Most jurors declined to meet with reporters, but several did.

"I think he was a real con artist," said one, a retired autoworker who spoke with a thick German accent. "He could even fool police and get away with it."

Boyle, who was holding an impromptu news conference in the corner of the hall, stated, "I knew the odds for insanity were bad. He was sick and just didn't realize what was wrong with him. I just hope that now he can live in whatever way he can without suicide."

The scene was like a political convention, with jurors, lawyers, spectators, news reporters, and their technicians all scurrying about, clustered in camps and talking at the same time.

I decided I'd had enough and slipped out the judge's back door and down the stairwell. No one noticed or approached me en route to the detective assembly, where I punched out and returned to my apartment. My mind raced and I felt unsettled. I decided to change and go for a walk along the lakeshore.

The icy winds off Lake Michigan slashed at my face, and the tingling felt good as I increased my pace to keep warm. The lakefront was desolate in February and matched my mood. I couldn't control my thoughts as scene after scene of my interviews with Jeff in that little interrogation room presented themselves in my mind. The startling look of death on the face of the victim's severed head in the refrigerator was there too, and I walked all the harder to dismiss it.

Upon returning, I soaked in a hot bath. The turn-of-the-century tub was more than adequate for my size, and I stayed until the hot water ran out. TCM featured Clint Eastwood as Dirty Harry. I ordered pizza and settled in for the evening. For some reason, I again refused to answer my phone. I was too tired to talk to anyone. It rang on and off throughout the night.

Chapter 22

Sunday morning's paper was loaded with coverage. "Dahmer Sane" said it all. I awoke to a cold and dreary Monday. I shaved, showered, and decided on my best blue suit for the sentencing. The detective bureau was in its usual hubbub as I sipped coffee and read the paper. Captain Domagalski stopped by my desk.

"Well, Kennedy, this is it, eh?"

"Yes, sir, the last day," I said, coming to attention in my seat.

He continued, "When it's over, you can knock off. Take a personal day before you head back to the late shift."

"Thank you, sir," I said. "That sounds like a good idea."

It was close to ten o'clock and I strolled to court, taking my spot in the judge's chambers. A cohort of deputies entered with Jeff, who was no longer wearing his new brown suit but a county orange jumpsuit, white socks, and flip-flops.

We acknowledged each other with head nods as he was unshackled and escorted to the defense table.

The thick pane of Plexiglas could not contain the anticipation and energy in the majestic wood-paneled gallery. The emotion was palpable, as survivors were permitted to make victim impact statements before sentencing. For the next half hour, relatives relived what Jeff's crimes had done to them and their families. One mother read a poem dedicated to her son.

Another woman sobbed, "That was my baby boy you took from me."

Someone's brother cried, "I hate you. I hope you go to hell."

A young woman spoke in Spanish, calling him *diablo, puro diablo*. Then, the grief exploded as a young woman wearing a t-shirt with bold letters that read 100% Black stepped to the podium.

"Jeffrey Dahmer, I hate you, you motherfucker! This is how you react when you're out of control," she screamed, lunging toward him with outstretched arms, hands balled into fists. Four deputies quickly jumped up to restrain her. "Satan! I hate you, Satan!" she continued as they struggled to return her to her seat. Jeff did not flinch. He remained motionless, staring straight ahead with no facial expression. The judge recessed the court for a few minutes, leaving the bench, allowing things to calm down before proceeding.

After the last of the family members had their say, Boyle rose to address the Court. Although he had not allowed Jeff to take the witness stand during the trial, he announced, "Mr. Dahmer would like to address the Court before sentence is passed."

A stony silence enveloped the cavernous room as Jeff stepped up to the podium to make his first public remarks since his arrest in July the previous summer. His only sign of emotion was the deep breath he took before reading a statement he had prepared. He spoke in earnest, flat tones, his body trembling slightly.

"Your Honor, it is over now. This has never been a case of trying to get free. I didn't ever want freedom. Frankly, I wanted death for myself. This was a case to tell the world that I did what I did not for reasons of hate; I hated no one. I knew I was sick or evil or both. Now, I believe I was sick. The doctors have told me about my sickness, and now I have some peace. I know how much harm I have caused. I tried to do the best I could after the arrest to make amends, but no matter what I did, I could not undo the terrible harm I have caused. I feel so bad for what I did to those poor families, and I understand their rightful hate.

"I decided to go through with this trial for a number of reasons. One of the reasons was to let the world know that these were not hate crimes. I wanted the world and Milwaukee, which I deeply hurt, to know the truth of what I did. I didn't want unanswered questions. All the questions have now been answered. I wanted to find out just what it was that caused me to be so bad and evil. But most of all, Mr. Boyle and I decided that maybe there was a way for us to tell the world that if there are people out there with these disorders, maybe they can get some help before they end up being hurt or hurting someone. I think the trial did that. I should have stayed with God. I tried and failed, and created a holocaust. Thank God there will be no more harm that I can do. I take all the blame for what I did. I hurt so many people and I am sorry. In closing, I just want to say that I hope God has forgiven me. I know society will never be able to forgive me. I ask for no consideration."

He stoically returned to the defense table and sat erect, staring straight ahead. McCann had recommended the maximum sentence possible for each count and Judge Gram obliged, factoring in an additional one hundred and fifty years for being a habitual criminal. Jeff received a sentence of 936 years. He would not be eligible for parole until the year 2928. It was a ridiculous sentence, but the gallery burst into spontaneous applause and shouts of joy as court was adjourned.

Two deputies flanked Jeff and returned him to the holding cell. I walked over to him, standing alone, locked inside. As I approached, he moved closer to the bars of his cell. I reached through and took his outstretched hand.

"Pat, I want to thank you for everything you did for me," he said.

Shaking his hand for what I believed would be the last time, I said, "Good luck, Jeff. Take care of yourself." Then I turned and walked away.

The celebration had started. The courtroom spilled into the hallways and people were everywhere. Reporters, followed by camera operators, scurried to net an interview with McCann, Boyle, jurors, survivors, anyone who had something to say. The cheering, crying, and hugging were infectious and seemed to spread throughout the crowd.

I didn't want any part of it. I slipped down the back stairwell and returned to the detective bureau to punch out unnoticed. It was biting cold, and I could feel that the temperature had dropped as I crossed the parking lot to my car. The winter sun was going down as I drove the short distance to my apartment. Upon entering, I turned up the heat, put away my revolver and cuffs, and disrobed to my underwear and socks. I sat in my own small and barely lit efficiency apartment. I looked around at the few belongings that now made up my life. Through the dimness, I focused on the calendar hanging on the wall before me. I could barely make out the date: Monday, February 17, 1992.

It was my thirty-eighth birthday and I was alone, again.

******

Chapter 23

November 1992

The Oxford Plaza Apartments building, located at 924 North 25th Street in Milwaukee, Wisconsin, was torn down. All the former residents had to find new homes.

1994

Jeffrey Dahmer, Multiple Killer, Is Bludgeoned to Death in Prison

November 29, 1994 | by Don Terry | Reuters

CHICAGO—Jeffrey L. Dahmer, whose gruesome exploits of murder, necrophilia and dismemberment shocked the world in 1991, was attacked and killed on Monday in a Wisconsin prison, where he was serving 15 consecutive life terms.

Mr. Dahmer was 34, older than any of his victims, who ranged in age from 14 to 33. He died of massive head injuries, suffered sometime between 7:50 and 8:10 A.M., when he was found in a pool of blood in a toilet area next to the prison's gym, said Michael Sullivan, secretary of the Wisconsin Department of Corrections. He was pronounced dead shortly after 9 A.M.

2013

Jeffrey Dahmer's crimes against his victims were not about instilling fear, sadistic torture, or abuse. Dahmer killed because he had insatiable urges: lust, power, and complete sexual control over a passive male partner.

He took many chances, but ultimately, he was a coward. Sometimes mild mannered and soft-spoken, he was also dangerous and depraved. He needed alcohol to do what he did, he was honest with police about his crimes, and he lived an empty, go-nowhere existence all his adult life. He craved completely compatible and utterly compliant sexual partners. He had odd habits, many strange compulsions, and a vast sexual appetite. He made fatally bad choices that cost many people their lives.

He didn't boast about his crimes or attempt to play games once caught by authorities. Described as sensitive, Dahmer seemed to have a genuine and earnest interest in learning more about why he was the way he was and presented a more human side when interviewed—first by police, and then doctors, and later, FBI specialists. Dahmer first killed at a young age, but was able to go on living a reasonably normal life for nine years before truly beginning the serial killer period of his life.

As difficult as it might be for most to believe or understand, many psychiatric and legal professionals who interviewed Dahmer after he and all his crimes were uncovered found that he actually had a nice way about him. Dahmer understood and even accepted and agreed that he deserved any and all hatred felt by anyone.

***

It was the story of the shirt—the short-sleeved white shirt with blue stripes in the now-infamous photograph that appeared on the cover of *People* magazine with Dahmer looking pale and unshaven—that initially drew me to contact Detective Patrick Kennedy. He described how Dahmer asked about his first court appearance. Dahmer felt that he should dress appropriately and more formally. While most officers might have uttered "tough" to this admitted serial killer, Kennedy agreed to find something for him to wear to court, and ended up bringing in clothes from his then fifteen-year-old son, Pat Jr.'s, closet—a shirt given as a Christmas gift by Kennedy and loathed by his son—and a newer pair of black jeans[11]. This act of kindness, coming during a horrific case of multiple murders—as well as other comments Kennedy made in various interviews about the human side of Dahmer in various profiles and specials on serial killers, indicated to me that Kennedy (who was asked to become the Milwaukee Police Department's go-to guy on the subject of Dahmer) might be able to shed some light on questions I had had about Jeffrey Dahmer, the person.

After a few months of corresponding via email, Kennedy and I agreed to meet in April 2013 in Madison, Wisconsin, when he would be there to help promote the film *The Jeffrey Dahmer Files*. The film had come full circle, first premiering in Milwaukee in early 2012. Since its debut, it and Kennedy, along with the film's director and fellow Milwaukeean, Christopher James Thompson, faithfully participated in media interviews, panels, radio profiles, and call-ins all over the country. Now that the majority of the publicity had started to wind down, the film was back in Wisconsin, premiering in Madison.

At six feet, seven inches, Kennedy's long, solid, tree branch-like arms completely enveloped me in a warm, welcoming Midwestern bear hug. I was interested to find

---

11. The clothing became part of Dahmer's estate upon his death, which is now the legal property of the families of the victims. The families wanted to auction off some 312 items, including a 55-gallon vat he used to decompose the bodies; the refrigerator where he stored body parts; a saw; a hammer; and his toothbrush.

out what Kennedy, fifty-nine, thought about Dahmer in comparison to other notorious killers, what he was like during and in between interviews, and either to confirm or dissuade my idea that Dahmer was unique because he didn't kill out of a place of rage, but rather to keep his victims with him. Like Britain's Dennis Nilsen, who was convicted in 1983 of killing many young men, Dahmer ultimately killed for sexually available company who would never be able to leave him. As Kennedy explained, after Dahmer was in custody, *Vanity Fair* magazine invited Dahmer to review a book about Nilsen, as there were many similarities between the two killers.

The parallels between Nilsen and Dahmer included necrophilia, the preference for strangling most of their male victims, dismemberment, and the idea of killing to keep the corpses as company. They also kept the corpses and shared the fact that neighbors around them complained about nefarious and unpleasant odors coming from their respective residences. Nilsen and Dahmer were both loners with largely uneventful younger lives, and profound interests and fascination with dead bodies. In Nilsen's case, his interest developed after his grandfather's death, when he presumably saw his first dead body. Both men were compulsive, alcohol dependent, and chronic smokers.

Nilsen revealed to police that he killed people "because they would have left." Nilsen confessed to police that he killed sixteen people (he was later convicted of six counts of murder and two counts of attempted murder); Dahmer confessed to seventeen murders in Wisconsin, but was ultimately charged with sixteen killings[12]. In a 1993 interview, Nilsen said that "it was the combination of his

---

12. Dahmer confessed to seventeen murders but was charged and convicted of sixteen murders in the state of Wisconsin as there wasn't enough evidence to charge him with Tuomi's murder. He also pleaded guilty to the murder of his first victim, Steven Hicks, in Ohio, ultimately bringing his total convictions to seventeen.

own power and his victim's passivity that he found so arousing."

Like Nilsen, Dahmer was not a sadistic killer, but rather one whose desires were dark, perverse, and depraved. As time went on, he began to cannibalize his victims (although not something Nilsen is known, or admitted, to have done) due to a pathological need to be with his murder victims. Dahmer preferred to drug his victims to unconsciousness and then strangle them, unlike Nilsen, who, for the most part, strangled his victims from behind while they were asleep or awake.

Some might wonder why it even matters. Dahmer is long dead and it has been so many years since his crimes—what could this case still teach us? He was a monster, not even fit to be called human, as far as some people believe. However, simply referring to him as *evil* or *wicked* seems too simple an explanation. Perhaps there was more to Dahmer than originally thought and presented, primarily based on what we were told about him shortly after his crimes were discovered, then revisited at the time of his death in 1994.

Had he survived, it is almost certain that he would have continued to talk; not about his crimes specifically—he had already told detectives, his lawyers, his family, and eventually the world what he had done. I do believe we could have learned more about what created the individual who could commit such crimes. How does one allow his sexual fantasy life to overwhelm his real life? Why it was so important for him to have so much control, physically and mentally, over men whom he was attracted to? Why didn't he want an interactive and engaging relationship? Why did he fear abandonment so much? What was it that he experienced as a child, observing his parents' relationship or any marital relationships around him such as neighbors or other family members, that made him incapable of wanting a normal, healthy, compromising relationship as an adult? What was it about his personality—or lack of—that made the act of communicating with others so difficult? Later in life, he claimed not to understand why people got married, as it seemed to him that "married people fight all the time."

Had he ever considered confessing to his first murder in Ohio in the hours or days after it occurred? At the time, it was conceivable that he could have explained that it was an unjustified murder that unfortunately happened spontaneously between two bored teens who had been drinking and wrestling. He would have been punished and sent to prison, but then once released, he could have moved on with his life with the knowledge that he had taken responsibility for the homicide. The parents of the young man would not have had to wait thirteen years to learn what had happened to their son, who left one day for a music festival, never to be seen or heard from again.

Because Dahmer was killed so early in his prison sentence, Kennedy was one of only a handful who had sat face to face with a sober Dahmer over an extended period of time and spent a great deal of time asking questions and discussing various topics during the course of the investigation. It seems Kennedy was able to bring out other sides of Dahmer during those interviews, and it is those thoughts and memories that are worth preserving.

***

Among the legions of narcissistic, cruel, and sadistic serial killers, I believed there was something slightly more human, and therefore possibly more redemptive, about Dahmer that deserved some additional thought. He was a desperately lonely and introverted man whose killing was not *the end* but rather a means to an end. For Dahmer, it was about obtaining attractive male bodies for sex and then having the company of their corpses.

Dahmer was also noted for taking responsibility for his crimes, unusual among killers who often hold back information in an effort to frustrate and confuse investigators, or in an attempt to hold on to some power over authorities by playing games. There are also the publicity-seeking narcissistic serial killers who write letters to the press before they are caught, such as Dennis Rader (the BTK Killer), and David Berkowitz (the Son of Sam), or who leave manifestos behind if they plan to kill themselves, be killed, or get away. If anything, Dahmer did all he could to avoid drawing attention to himself, obviously in order to avoid detection, but also because he was ultimately not one who really craved fame and attention. Like Ted Bundy, most serial killers blame others, maintain their innocence, and try to minimize their culpability at every opportunity.

Dahmer told an *Inside Edition* interviewer in January 1993, "The person to blame is the person sitting across from you. Not parents, not society, not pornography. Those are just excuses."

Most retired detectives are incredible storytellers, so I was anxious to read Kennedy's manuscript, Dahmer: My Life with Jeff, which comprehensively detailed the intense six-week period that he spent interviewing and questioning Dahmer. A day-by-day recording of the events as they unfolded, it included the chronological interviews with Dahmer once he had been caught and brought into police custody, the effects the case had on Patrick personally and on the entire city of Milwaukee, as well as the devastation of his crimes and their immediate aftermath.

"I wrote it all out immediately afterward just to get it out of me and then put it away for years. Eventually, over time, I began to review it and work on it as it became clear that I was probably always going to be known for this case for the rest of my career, so I wanted to make sure it was as complete a record as possible. After meeting Chris and participating in the film, I was encouraged to see if there would be interest in this story from my point of view inside the interrogation room," said Kennedy.

While the film and subsequent interviews, Q&As, and articles were somewhat cathartic, it also stirred up memories of the nightmare the whole situation had been back in 1991, and his feelings about Jeff Dahmer, the serial killer. Now after two decades, as Patrick approached his sixtieth year, he looked tired from so much travel in the past year.

It was an opportunity to have it available in one publication—all his thoughts, ideas, and feelings about the case permanently recorded in one place. Also, a possible chance to come to terms with the frightening image of the decapitated head staring back at him from the inside of Dahmer's refrigerator. The image of the head was forever seared into his brain, along with the psychological trauma and horror he had felt wash over him, that he could relive at any time, so many years later. When a person witnesses something so horrible, it is impossible to forget it.

It seemed that each time Kennedy told the story of visiting Dahmer's apartment, he felt it all—mentally, psychologically, emotionally, physically—and it made sense that he write the story down because, for better or worse, the case was part of his professional and personal legacy, and an achievement given the work he did in the years following the Dahmer case. Most important to Kennedy, though, was taking lessons learned from the experience in order to bring about much-needed change to the relationship between police and the diverse communities that they serve.

Finally, he needed the opportunity to speak about Dahmer as completely as possible, with less focus on the gore and repulsive aspects of the case. The focus of which had infuriated him with some earlier documentaries and programs done on the story, and, most disturbing, the fact that photographs of the victims found in Dahmer's apartment had been made public over time and, thanks to the Internet, could be found easily.

Kennedy preferred to focus more on Dahmer himself and his impressions of Dahmer at the time of the arrest. To use the benefit of time, more recent history, and his own and other efforts made on the part of the Milwaukee Police Department and the education system that administered criminal justice programs to improve the efforts of people going into law enforcement by beginning to focus on community work much earlier. To focus more closely on the candidates wanting to go into law enforcement much earlier in the process of recruiting and teaching such as during the screening and training processes. He wanted to concentrate more on the importance of building better relationships between people and law enforcement and those who commit crimes. Basing law enforcement on the principal objective of basic human rights, respect, realistic inner reflection, and a more sensitive reverence for the individual experience, and personal and familial history and heritage, in addition to being more culturally aware, knowledgeable, receptive, and responsive when working with the communities that the police protect, serve, and represent. This includes everything from race/ethnicity, gender, religion, sexuality, dis/ability, and socioeconomic class. His manuscript was created from notes that he wrote about the interrogations, media scrutiny, and the police and legal politics that ensued immediately after his first introduction to Jeffrey Dahmer in 1991, and then it remained in the drawer of a desk at home for years after.

It was only much later—at the end of his career as a homicide detective in Milwaukee, when he decided to continue his education and earned a PhD in criminology—that he began to work solely on the main professional focus of his life. He worked with others in law enforcement to identify and create new practices, procedures, and policies identified as major problem areas during the Dahmer investigation regarding his previous police and parole encounters. His passion was always for the work in the areas of policing and diversity, and acknowledging and recognizing the ingrained tensions between cops and community.

***

I think Patrick quickly realized by my questions that I, too, could see the something in Dahmer that he had recognized, which ultimately allowed him to connect to this man the media labeled the "Monster of Milwaukee" in the days after Dahmer was revealed as a serial killer. That once you stripped him down to the man sitting across an interrogation table—he was a human being in need.

"People always say that I must have seen evil in his eyes as I sat down face to face with him during our interrogations, and I have to honestly tell them that I didn't. I saw a very normal, ordinary guy who—when we talked about things other than his crimes—seemed very much like me, like you, like anybody you would meet," said Kennedy.

Despite Dahmer's crimes, Kennedy describes an odd kind of kinship that developed as he genuinely began accepting Dahmer's remorse for his numerous murders, and therefore experienced some grief when Dahmer was beaten to death a few years later. Kennedy quickly adds that he didn't befriend Dahmer at all during the time they spent meeting, and never considered him as anything other than a murder suspect. He did not continue to correspond with him and, in fact, never saw him again after Dahmer was led off to serve his sentence.

I asked Kennedy whether Dahmer complained about being bullied as a young person. Kennedy said that Dahmer never used the word *bully* specifically in their conversations, although he knows that Dahmer did tell others that he had been victimized as an adolescent. Others, who knew him as a teenager, claim that Dahmer was the target of bullies on occasion, and was once badly beaten up by a group of older teenage boys.

Others in law enforcement and forensic psychology who interviewed Dahmer after his arrest also seem to find him more pathetic than psychotic; sad rather than sadistic; more desperate than demented. According to retired FBI agent Robert Ressler in his book *I Have Lived in the Monster*, "His intent was to kill the intellect of the victim and to keep their bodies alive and compliant. This action seemed to me the ultimate expression of Dahmer's inability to relate in any normal way to another human being."

"Wherever people become alienated from society, wherever neighbors hardly know one another, wherever families do not keep in very close touch, wherever runaway teenagers roam dangerous streets, wherever violence is made to seem a viable response to troubles, an upsurge in serial murder will be one troubling response. ... The big city gives rise to alienation, anonymity, and anger, all of which are elemental components of serial killings."

Home movies of Dahmer as a boy show a fairly carefree, shy, curious, and physical youngster. While either cycling around the woods in his Bath, Ohio, neighborhood or swimming in the family's above-ground pool, Dahmer appears to have been normal in most ways. His parents expressed some concern at times, as he grew into preadolescence, about his obvious inwardness and introverted behavior, but often chalked it up to being similar to his father at the same age.

Lionel Dahmer has been quoted in interviews as saying that when he was young, he found it difficult to make friends, interact, and connect with members of his peer group at school and the kids in his neighborhood. Lionel, it seemed, grew out of this as he matured and, though awkward at first, managed to learn the art of making conversation by asking questions, finding common ground, and eventually gravitating to people with whom he had similar interests. I think that Dahmer's parents believed that Jeff, too, would outgrow the insular world he had started to create and inhabit, which was apparently supported by his teachers when Dahmer's parents expressed their concerns about his lack of social development and reserved nature.

To help combat a loneliness that they feared might further separate him from his peer group, they bought him a dog, Frisky, hoping that it would encourage him to be outside playing and other kids in the neighborhood might join in. They also encouraged Dahmer to participate when their second son was born, allowing him to name his baby brother (David), and to assist his mother with the care of a younger sibling, as many parents do in order to help children feel included, along with the responsibility of being an older brother or sister. Both parents have said that Dahmer liked holding his brother, helping his mom with collecting clothing or diapers from the nursery, and entertaining his younger brother as he grew.

As a child, Dahmer is not known to have tortured or killed animals, which is common in the childhoods of notorious killers. However, Dahmer is known to have collected, inspected, and dissected the corpses of dead animals he found in the woods or road kill from the streets near his family's Ohio home. While escaping his parents' fighting at home, young Dahmer rode around the slightly isolated neighborhood on his bike or hiked the woods behind his house. Dahmer was fascinated by animal corpses, the innards, the bones, and the decaying flesh. He found a bag or box, and using a stick, picked up dead animals. Once alone, he picked at the dead animal, examining its insides, removing the organs, and extracting the bones. He asked his father about using chemicals to burn away fur and flesh, thereby leaving the bones completely cleaned.

His father, a chemist, believed he had a prodigy with an interest in chemistry in his midst, and so encouraged him. His dad showed him how to clean the bones using acid rather than questioning his interest in this unusual and perhaps unhealthy pursuit. While other parents may have questioned their child about this particular kind of pastime, Lionel felt that he should encourage Jeff in something that he seemed to have an interest in. It is believed that at this time, when

Dahmer was alone with these animal carcasses, that strange ideas and thoughts began to enter his psyche. To reiterate, Dahmer is not known to have tortured or shown cruelty to animal, nor did he feel the need to exert control over another living being by inflicting pain and suffering or torture at this time.

According to Lionel Dahmer, who wrote in his book *A Father's Story* about driving with his eldest son, "As for Jeff, he sat in the backseat, rather blank, neither excited nor particularly frightened as if his emotional range [at age seven] had begun to narrow. He seemed more passive, his attitude taking on the strange resignation that would soon become a central feature of his character."

Despite efforts to try to engage Dahmer, his parents found he preferred to keep to himself rather than to be surrounded by friends or schoolmates.

As he became a teenager, there is strong evidence that he began to drink alcohol on a regular basis. It was not at all unusual for Dahmer to show up to school with a paper cup of alcohol taken from his parents' house that he sipped from before school started for the day. This could explain some of Dahmer's lack of motivation and the desire to be left alone, as well as his low ambitions as far as deciding what he wanted to do with his life. Dahmer drank to ease the pain of his loneliness, and perhaps to make it easier to be around other teens, to ease or lessen the anxiety. It was also likely a distraction from the problems that were going on at home when his parents fought.

Although painfully shy, Dahmer is described as someone with a quiet charm and odd sense of humor about him. A story that demonstrates Dahmer's abilities is often told by some of his peers. One year, a group of students, including Dahmer, traveled to Washington, DC, to see the sites and visit important landmarks. While on this trip, someone dared Dahmer to make a crank call. He contacted the offices of then Vice President Walter Mondale and managed to charm his way into an invitation for Dahmer and his fellow high school classmates from Ohio to meet the VP.

But it is also at this time in Dahmer's life that he complained bitterly about the relationship between his parents. Although from all accounts it seems that the marriage was rocky from the start, there were several factors that apparently caused stresses in the marriage and eventually led to a permanent end to his parents' relationship. It was also a time when Dahmer struggled with the realization that he was attracted to men, worried that his family would find out he was gay, and admitted to having more frequent dark and violent fantasies about the bodies of men.

Dahmer began to engage in a dangerous fantasy life that ultimately became his real life. Dahmer repressed his sexuality because of how he thought it might affect people who knew him. He maintained a double life—the young man people saw, and the Dahmer who had a secret sexual fantasy life. He had a difficult time making and keeping friends, and he was often described as weird, or invisible in a crowd. He could appear normal when he needed to be and was an expert liar. Was it Dahmer's depression and alienation, and/or possible guilt over the 1978 murder, that added to his alcohol-fueled dark fantasies? Perhaps he used alcohol to unleash his dangerous thoughts about sex, power, control, and domination over sexual partners to move from simple fantasy into behavior and violent action.

***

Dahmer was a sensitive, shy, and immature young man. He lacked motivation, passion, and ambition—that perhaps can be blamed in part on his habitual drinking problem. There doesn't seem to be any evidence that he attempted to equip himself for a more productive life, and he always allowed alcohol to take over and ruin any progress he did make.

Eventually, his crimes, once embarked upon, would become the focus of his entire world.

From interviews with Lionel Dahmer, and others who studied Dahmer and his upbringing, there were significant areas of potential problems that manifested themselves after the dissolution of Dahmer's parents' marriage. One was the fact that Joyce Dahmer suffered from depression and anxiety. While not unusual now, in this day and age, there is still a stigma about mental illness, and mental health professionals and social agencies try to combat those issues through awareness, information, and education campaigns. In the late fifties and early sixties, however, most laypeople were unaware of how to handle or treat individuals suffering from anxiety and/or depression. Joyce was hospitalized several times during Dahmer's early years. When at home, while trying to function as best as she could with the resources available to her, she was often in bed sick, or simply asleep, and unable to be a strong and stable presence in the early years of her eldest son's life. Almost certainly because of his mother's mental illness, the feelings of abandonment Dahmer was prone to seemed to have taken root early on.

Dahmer's childhood was also lonely due to his father's drive to succeed in his profession. An incredibly intelligent man, Lionel was a man of science who often spent long hours away from home working—not only to support his family, but to obtain further professional achievement, advanced degrees, and success. Again, due to a lack of general understanding at the time of the corrosive nature of improperly treated mental illness, it is difficult to know how well equipped Lionel was at managing a mentally ill wife and co-parenting his two young sons, while putting in the kind of hours, mental energy, and focus required for a burgeoning career in chemistry. Dahmer has recalled this time as one of great tension at home, with his parents constantly fighting with each other, and he struggled to understand why they couldn't get along.

At this pivotal time in his life, upset family dynamics may have been what led Dahmer to start experimenting with alcohol and disappearing on his own for long periods of time in search of escape. However these activities may have started, they were a part of who he became as he matured. He was occasionally bullied for being strange, friendless, gay, odd, and a weird prankster with a dark sense of humor. He was marginalized and behaved strangely; Dahmer spent a lot of time alone, craving companionship, and he found that darker and darker thoughts were taking over, allowing increasingly darker and darker thoughts to take over. He became focused and obsessed with death and dead things, and allowed his fantasies to take hold. He spent lots of time on his own, with few friends to involve him or engage him in other interests.

Forensic psychiatrists have often pointed to this period in Dahmer's development—a time when adolescent boys start to sort out their sexuality and what is attractive to them—as when Dahmer began to confuse and combine his feelings of attraction with his interest in the insides of animals. While experimenting with deceased animals, this became intermingled with his sexual development. He may have known at a young age that he was gay, but for fear of upsetting his family, he did his best to repress those feelings. Dahmer may have also realized from an early age that his sexual interests involving viscera were deviant, and that what stimulated him was unusual and likely not what others around him found arousing. At an age when young men are stimulated by sexually graphic photographs or films, dating, and developing an early-stage sex life, Dahmer was dismembering road kill, watching horror movies, and fantasizing about sex with incapacitated men.

His severe drinking habits followed him to college, where he was intoxicated most of the time before being kicked out in his first year. He then joined the army after some gentle persuasion from his father and stepmother Shari. Dahmer initially managed to keep his drinking under wraps and seemed to thrive in the early months of army life. Photos from this time show him as a buff, short-haired, mustached, smiling young man seemingly proud of his new fit physique and success in military life in Germany. But before long, the call of bars and alcoholic drinks beckoned, and he was often drunk. After a discharge from the army, Dahmer found himself back in the United States, in Miami, Florida, where he worked a series of menial jobs. Often short of money, he resorted to sleeping on the beach. Most of the money he earned went toward alcohol, and before long, he called Ohio looking for a way to come home. His father, instead of sending money, offered to send him a plane ticket and when he went to pick up Dahmer at the airport in Cleveland, he was disappointed and distressed to find him once again intoxicated.

It is fair to say that alcohol was an escape for Dahmer, who by this time must have wondered where his life was going. Whether his lack of continued education, or his inability to make a plan for his future concerned him is unknown, but it does seem to mark a time when, as his father and stepmother put it, he was running out of options. Alcohol was likely also an escape from the pain he still felt over his parents' marital breakdown, the division of his family unit, and his feelings about his sexuality. It also provided him with the means of a vivid, if very strange, fantasy life. Alcohol fueled his hidden desires to have sex with men. He flipped through magazines and books and found photos of men in advertisements that had the kind of physique he found most attractive, and decorated his various living spaces with items and objects he liked. Alcohol also provided him with an outlet to fantasize about the kind of relationship he wanted in terms of having a companion he could completely dominate and control. Dahmer told police he found some sex acts more appealing than others, and he wanted a fully compliant partner who would not demand or even ask for sex in ways that Dahmer found uncomfortable, painful, or not arousing.

※※※

Dahmer was later diagnosed with borderline personality disorder (sometimes and more recently known as emotionally unstable personality disorder), but if you analyze the definition, many of the behaviors and symptoms have also been used to describe his mother Joyce, including sometimes irrational fears of abandonment, low self-esteem, unexplained anxiety, and depression, which must have affected him in childhood and as he grew up.

While Dahmer was in custody, and suddenly cut off from alcohol, Kennedy describes that during their down periods discussing things other than Dahmer's murders and sexual activities, he demonstrated great ability to show a caring, empathetic, and even loving nature toward others. For those who wonder if Dahmer was psychopathic, he did seem capable of having great feelings of love and affection toward his father, mother, brother, stepmother, and grandmother despite seeming to have no conscience about killing so many people. It seems that Dahmer spent a great deal of time alone and loathing himself, fantasizing, and escaping his existence through alcohol.

I think of Dahmer as the reticent, polite, and sensitive young man who first appeared looking blank and pale in court and in interviews where he and his father Lionel tried to answer the questions so many people had as to why these crimes occurred. Dahmer was pathetic and incredibly selfish as he began the process of trying to find sexual pleasure and companionate happiness with another man, only to discover that what he really wanted was a completely incapacitated and compliant sexual partner who fit the very specific body type that he deemed perfect.

Dahmer experimented on some of his drugged victims by drilling holes into their heads and pouring acid or boiling water into the wound. He hoped to create living, breathing zombie boyfriends whom he could control sexually, but his plan inevitably failed when his victims died. He then performed necrophilic and cannibalistic acts on the corpses and tried to dispose of the bodies without arousing unwanted suspicion or attention.

Dahmer's preferences, when it came to the male physique, were slender and lean, yet athletic and slightly but not overtly muscular young men. Because so many of Dahmer's victims were African American or, for the most part, men of color, it was at first presumed that Dahmer hated non-Caucasians. Dahmer denied that any of the murders were racially motivated, and said that what led him to approach the men he did was whether or not he was attracted to them; but, even more importantly, that they met the physical requirements that stimulated him the most. Investigating detectives found no indications that Dahmer had problems with people of color. Dahmer emerged as truthful as far as the detectives determined, yet not necessarily always immediately forthcoming.

"Jeff would never volunteer information. We would pose questions to him about some aspect of what we were discovering on an hourly, then daily, basis, and he would confirm or deny it, and it always checked out. I am convinced that everything Jeff told us was the truth, as we were able to confirm almost everything. That said, he wouldn't talk about anything related to his crimes unless we brought it up or asked first," said Kennedy. For example, Dahmer initially did not bring up the fact he had cannibalized some of his victims.

Kennedy tended to believe that Dahmer's less than forthcoming nature was more about who he had been all his life, because when they discussed innocuous subjects in between interviews, he still occasionally needed to pull information out of Dahmer.

"Jeff was secretive. No question. He obviously found it difficult to share information and because of his crimes, he was always careful about what he said. He was a consummate liar and manipulator. Initially, he lied to almost everyone about his sexual orientation, the extent of his drinking problems, and obviously all of his criminal activity. But it seemed, even at that time, engaging in conversational exchange also seemed difficult for him, as it seemed to take a lot for him to relate and ask questions, even though he seemed naturally curious about other people," Kennedy said.

Some, of course, would say that Dahmer willingly confessed because he was essentially caught red-handed with body parts all over his apartment, but one has to be reminded of the arrogance and irrational claims of John Wayne Gacy in Chicago, who—despite the fact that police pulled twenty-nine bodies out of his basement crawlspace (he was ultimately convicted of thirty-three murders, and more bodies have been found that are linked to him)—maintained right up to his execution that he didn't know about the bodies or that his young, male employees must have committed the murders because they had access to his house and crawlspace.

Deferential and unassuming, Dahmer never abducted anyone off the street. He managed to charm and converse well enough with most young men that, unfortunately, all his victims went with him willingly. He lured his victims back to his home—he didn't attack them in public or break into homes to find victims. Many have described Dahmer as quiet, reserved, and even boring and bland, and didn't necessarily see the appeal that he must have had in order to encourage each of these young men—all complete strangers—to accompany him back to his apartment. In some cases, the lure may have been free alcohol and/or drugs, or the chance to make some money by posing for photographs, and possibly sex, but there must have also been something else. Ultimately, though, Dahmer knew that these men needed to leave at some point. They had to return home to families or to work, so he killed them in order to keep them.

Kennedy came to know Dahmer the human being, which was difficult for most, who found it easier and more palatable to label him an evil monster. Kennedy and I seem to be part of a small group that distinguish between the evil and monstrousness of Dahmer's behavior and actions without necessarily seeing Dahmer as evil and monstrous. I felt that what drove me to talk to Kennedy was that he believed that Dahmer was a human being; admittedly, a man with many problems, personality disorders, and serious flaws, but a man who ultimately wanted and looked for someone to be with in a way that only appeals to a very small segment of the population: necrophilia.

Kennedy wouldn't refer to his relationship with Dahmer as a friendship. He had too much respect and reverence for the relatives and friends of Dahmer's victims. Even calling it a relationship made Kennedy uncomfortable, although ultimately it was usually how he described it: a fateful situation that brought the detective to Dahmer's door.

Over time, Kennedy began to know Dahmer, and without saying directly that he liked him, went so far as to say that he didn't dislike him. He often commented in interviews that he felt odd or guilty for admitting that he felt something for the pathetic and lonely man who traveled down a dark and disturbing path only to end up with a wildly alarming and disconcerting fantasy life. When fantasy proved not enough to satisfy, his reality turned into meeting attractive men he was able to con just long enough to return to his home and accept a drugged drink.

I asked Kennedy about remorse and whether he felt that any of Dahmer's claims of being sorry for what he had done felt genuine, and he did. He believed that in the end, Dahmer seemed regretful and contrite, had feelings of guilt, and claimed to be sorry for what he had done. Usually killers do not express guilt or remorse because so many lack empathy and human emotion and often feel completely justified in committing murder.

"It may be easy to say you're sorry after you are caught, because if you're really sorry, you wouldn't have done it in the first place. Dahmer couldn't stop himself, but once he was caught and sobered up, he did say he felt sorry for the pain that he caused so many people. Most killers don't," said Kennedy.

Dahmer seemed incapable of participating in a stable relationship, so instead chose to pick up partners for casual encounters, or, in most cases, offered his victims money to pose for photographs at his apartment. Not surprisingly, the inability to maintain healthy relationships is common amongst many serial killers. As Ressler writes, "... young men who were loners as children... turned to fantasy as a result of physical and mental abuse during childhood, and were mentally unstable to participate in normal, consensual sexual relationships as young adults."

Dahmer was well into his killing addiction by the time he was stopped by police. Among those who study serial killers—particularly sexually motivated, predatory killers—there's the belief that they'll never stop on their own. While this addiction obviously hurt the people around him, there doesn't seem to be that much difference between Dahmer the alcoholic[13] who couldn't stop drinking, and Dahmer the serial killer. The definition of addiction is a condition that results when a person ingests a substance (e.g., alcohol,

---

13. When Dahmer served his work release sentence for the 1988 molestation of a thirteen-year-old boy, Lionel Dahmer wrote a letter to the judge urging that Jeff receive psychological therapy or treatment for his chronic alcohol abuse. "I have tremendous reservations regarding Jeff's chance when he hits the street. [An alcohol addiction program] may be our last chance to institute something lasting," his father wrote. Dahmer was released two months early from his twelve-month sentence (at Jeff's written request to the judge) and just prior to the receipt of his father's letter.

cocaine, nicotine) or engages in an activity (e.g., gambling, sex, shopping) that can be pleasurable, but the continued use/act of which becomes compulsive and interferes with ordinary life responsibilities such as work, relationships, or health. Users may not be aware that their behavior is out of control and causing problems for themselves and others.

Once he was caught, Dahmer had time to dry out and to consider all the lives that he had destroyed. It's possible he felt remorse for all the destruction caused by his own hands; perhaps he was also sorry for the damage to his own family, but he expressed his sorrow to the many families and friends of his victims in court. His family, who spoke with him after he was forced to stop drinking, observed emotions that were void for so much of his teen and adult life.

Most perpetrators of homicidal crime won't even admit to committing the crimes they are charged with and vow to overturn convictions, even when overwhelming evidence points to them as the guilty party. Some admit to what they have done while very few will appear remorseful and express their regrets. Dahmer's delivery sounded emotionless as he read from a prepared statement in front of the judge and the families of his victims, but his apologies in court didn't ring hollow. This was typical of Dahmer, according to Kennedy, who eventually came to realize that he was just not an emotional speaker.

It is easy to write Dahmer off as another twentieth-century serial killer who was jailed and ultimately murdered at the hands of a fellow prisoner. That said, it is important to possess a better understanding of how loneliness, isolation, and internal dysfunction can dramatically affect a vulnerable person, perhaps to curb the almost inevitable slide into sometimes dangerous and violent fantasy that is at the root of mass shootings and spree killings. Dark fantasies can overtake the life of a young person needing to fill a void, and it isn't long before the fantasies are not enough. Thoughts then may turn to planning and strategizing, and ultimately deciding whether to cross the line into criminal activity. It is very common among serial killers such as Dahmer, but also, as we see more and more in this century, in public mass killers. We know how bullying can lead to abandonment/rejection, withdrawal, and alienation, which can become violent fantasy leading to antisocial behavior and eventually, a desire finally to act out violence against an innocent victim or multiple victims.

After the case, Kennedy believed that police needed to be involved more with the communities they served, and that more training about engaging and communicating with neighborhood leaders and longtime residents needed to be implemented in efforts to work together more closely. He also stressed how the police in the Konerak Sinthasomphone case had been told differing stories by Dahmer's neighbors and others on the scene, including the slurred Laotian words of the victim, but in the end, the police believed the polite Caucasian man who sounded and looked like them, and unfortunately that decision cost the child his life. This aspect of the case is one that always haunted Kennedy and was almost always included as part of the training he developed for his students when he became a professor of criminal justice. The story of law enforcement's reaction to Dahmer should be framed in the historical context that existed at that time in terms of society's view of anonymous gay male encounters. Training in the areas of sensitivity, compassion, and respect toward gays in Milwaukee was unfortunately nonexistent at that time, according to Kennedy, but that was generally the case everywhere in the United States in the late eighties and early nineties. Sadly, though, there is much work to be done between police and the communities they serve and protect as tensions of all kinds continue to divide communities.

In many ways, Dahmer's confession answered a lot of questions specific to his criminal activities and his victims. Other, larger issues arose, though, and Kennedy felt that the investigation revealed some of the long-standing racial oppression and institutionally supported prejudices still held by some authorities. It became apparent to many after the Dahmer case that relationships between several communities had to be developed to build better communication, understanding, and societal representation.

***

A critical time in Dahmer's life often mentioned by family, high school acquaintances, and others who studied his upbringing was when his parents split up and divorced. Kennedy explained that when Dahmer was eighteen and living at the house in Bath, his father had moved out and already lived with his girlfriend, who later became his wife and Dahmer's stepmother. His mother decided to leave Ohio and took Dahmer's younger brother David with her. Because relations between Dahmer's parents were strained, it seemed that each came and went without notifying the other of their plans. Dahmer was still completing his final year of high school, so he remained in Ohio. Dahmer was left in the family home alone for an extended period of time, and during this time, he committed his first murder.

Much has been made of this period of so-called abandonment when Dahmer was on his own, but Kennedy said he never really bought it. "He was eighteen years old, for heaven's sake. It wasn't like he was a little kid unable to fend for himself."

I asked if it was possible Dahmer may have even orchestrated it to some extent—perhaps Dahmer had been told by his mother upon her departure that he get in touch with his father to let him know that she and their other son had vacated the house. As an eighteen-year-old man used to spending time on his own, drinking to excess, indulging in slightly unusual pastimes, might he not crave the run of the house as relations between his newly separated parents simmered down? Kennedy believed that it was feasible, especially because of Dahmer's secretive nature, well-practiced ability to omit crucial details, and his skill as a liar. It wasn't until Lionel Dahmer returned to the house, found Dahmer alone, and confronted him that he learned that his former wife and other son had left Ohio for Wisconsin. Many reported that the abandonment was a significant period in Dahmer's life because the arrangement left Dahmer with no money, food, or a working refrigerator in the house. Depending on how resourceful Dahmer was at this time of his life, it may have indeed been a time where he felt utterly alone in the world and began to fear abandonment by anyone who chose to leave him in the future.

Dahmer began to retreat from any kind of an emotional world at a young age, and lived a rather lonely existence that became more pronounced as he got older. He was left with a void, capable of creating his own definition of love and relationships through fantasies that became very dark early on. Eventually, he was unwilling to be left alone by anyone he found attractive and wanted to be with once he met him. This led to Dahmer's first murder, which went undetected for thirteen years until he confessed to that murder and ultimately so many more. There was much made about the possibility of studying Dahmer's brain[14] after his death in order to find out if it was impaired in some way, or if damage had caused him to behave the way he did. It would have also been interesting to know what the state of Dahmer's liver and kidneys were at the time of his death because of the amount of alcohol he had consumed in his short life.

One must realize the effects of long-term alcohol abuse on the body and mind. The effects of alcohol on the brain, especially chronic drinking, are fairly well documented—

---

14. It was later released that after his death, Dahmer's brain was examined at the request of his parents. Nothing abnormal was found. Later, Lionel and Joyce Dahmer fought a court battle over the brain, with Lionel coming out the victor. The brain was cremated along with the rest of Dahmer's remains.

it can affect mood, personality, motivation, and ambition, which explains some of Dahmer's inability to pursue education or training in any meaningful way. Chronic substance abuse can also affect one's ability to empathize or sympathize with others; it made Dahmer uninterested in the world around him. It suppressed his curiosity about life, people, and events, and any emotion or sensation he had was stifled under the weight of alcohol. It can also make a person less inhibited, so that when he approached young men, police, or his neighbors, Dahmer could come across as more interesting and engaged in the world, but it was a false reality.

Once Dahmer began to murder more frequently, he often discussed his anxiety and depression with his probation officer, and related it to his sexuality, his solitary lifestyle, his dependence on alcohol, and his financial difficulties (he spent most of his money on alcohol and supplies needed to conceal and dispose of bodies). He occasionally admitted to harboring suicidal thoughts.

Kennedy recalls observing Dahmer in custody as he slowly came down from the high of the alcohol he had consumed that day, recognizing the signs from his own days as a drinker. Initially, Kennedy believes, Dahmer may have even had a sense that despite the police discovery of the Polaroid photos and the severed head in the refrigerator, he could somehow say the right combination of words that would make the whole situation go away, and that he may even be allowed to go home that night. Part of him must have known that this was it, he was in serious trouble, that all the killing and deviant sex were now over. At the same time, Dahmer had always had an uncanny ability to talk his way out of tense situations. According to Kennedy, it was only when he mentioned that police and crime scene investigators had descended on his apartment and were going through everything room by room that Dahmer sat up straight. "The police are in my apartment right now?"

It actually hit him then that there was nothing he could say to explain any of this without being charged with several serious crimes, and then he asked Kennedy for his gun.

It is a fairly common technique that many detectives employ with varying degrees of success: befriend the perpetrator, make him your buddy, and get him talking. In this case, however, considering what Kennedy had seen only an hour or so before, it is quite remarkable he was able to keep his composure and mental focus as he spoke coolly with Dahmer and listened to details while casually extricating himself from the interrogation room to confer with his supervisor to hear the latest gruesome atrocity discovered in Dahmer's apartment. Kennedy maintained Dahmer's trust, and he fortified the rapport and the bond he built with Dahmer, all while under the glare of media spotlights camped out at the apartment building and police station, as the speculation of double-digit number of bodies and dismembered body parts began to circulate among the corps of neighbors standing in astonished horror in the lights of police cars, crime scene trucks, and media cameras.

The story outside the interrogation room was getting more bizarre and depraved by the minute as Kennedy calmly conferred with his colleagues several times before returning again and again to the cramped room with Jeffrey Dahmer and his strange story.

One needs to remember: police hadn't been hunting a killer—much less a serial killer—because until that night, no bodies or body parts had been discovered. There were missing persons reports on some of the victims, but there was no reason to believe these men were deceased, or any reason to believe that one person was responsible for killing any of the apparently happy and healthy men who had disappeared.

Dahmer was unlike other serial killers, who leave their victims to be found, thus alerting everyone that someone among them is killing people. Serial killers usually choose vulnerable victim types, such as senior citizens, children, women, or people who live high-risk lifestyles. Dahmer's victims were different. These were healthy, physically fit young men who only became vulnerable through intoxication and drugging. These men were young, athletic, social, and, in some cases, gay or bisexual, but not people normally perceived as physically vulnerable, and who didn't perceive Dahmer as a threat. He incapacitated these otherwise capable men by drugging them until they passed out, therefore always creating a completely vulnerable victim.

In a time long before CCTV, cell phones, and social media, family members must have been worried and fearful as they reported their family member missing. Dahmer concealed and usually destroyed the bodies of his victims so there was no evidence that anything violent had happened, or that anything like serial murder was occurring in the city of Milwaukee.

During Dahmer's entire crime career, there were no bodies, no evidence, and no crime scenes. Almost all the crimes occurred in his apartment, which no one except Dahmer accessed until the night of his capture. As far as anyone knew, these men were alive but missing. Family and friends of the missing want to believe that their loved one is alive and that they will see them again. In the Dahmer case, there was no reason for the victims' families to give up hope that their missing family member would eventually come home safely.

Kennedy's manuscript wraps up on the day he last saw and spoke with Dahmer. It was the day the jury returned with the verdicts and Dahmer was sentenced at the courthouse. Pat recalled the scene at the courthouse as chaotic—family members of Dahmer's victims, the media, members of the police force, and members of the general public all felt the need to be present as this horrific case reached its conclusion. Despite it all, Kennedy remembers feeling a kind of hollowness—he knew Dahmer was going away forever, and that he needed to be put away without any chance of getting out. He knew that public anger toward the police had been building steadily regarding Dahmer's ability to kill so many young men without detection. When the public learned that there had been more than a few chances to stop him—odd and curious smells in the apartment that went ignored for months; a victim who had managed to escape only to be brought back to the waiting arms of his killer; and the seemingly general lack of interest in all the missing young men suddenly gone with no explanation—no one was able to provide answers.

Kennedy knew that because of the size and scrutiny of this case, Dahmer and his crimes would never be forgotten, and that somehow all of this would become a cautionary tale of a twentieth-century serial killer. There was something else, though. He knew that the chances he would ever see Dahmer again were slim to none. He did not consider Dahmer a friend nor did he have any desire or drive to continue communicating with him. In fact, Kennedy knew it was inappropriate to consider Dahmer anything more than a killer serving his time. Dahmer actually seemed to like police and law enforcement, which is rare among criminals, especially when caught and punished.

Kennedy had interrogated suspects for far less serious crimes who were much worse to deal with than Dahmer, who seemed resigned to his fate and prepared to pay for his crimes. Unlike most suspects, Dahmer was polite, answered their questions, and was respectful of the police guarding and escorting him from his jail cell to the police station and back.

Due to Dahmer's notoriety, he was placed in solitary confinement for twenty-three hours a day in a cell, with one hour outside for physical activity. For a lonely man who craved companionship, this must have been nearly impossible to bear, and within a short period of time, he requested to be placed with the general population. He knew that it was a certain death given his infamy.

Prison also reawakened Dahmer's reliance upon and interest in religion, as he once again tried to "get his life right" as he put it, as he had when he lived with his grandmother and attended church regularly.

He had always believed in a Christian God, as he explained to his family before and during his crimes, and to police and his lawyers once he was caught. He remarked in court that once he had committed his first murder, he believed his life and soul were doomed. He felt that what he had done could never be forgiven and he was destined to go to hell, so it didn't matter if he killed more people. Throughout his early and mid-twenties, he sought solace in alcohol, which essentially wrecked everything that could have helped him to turn his life around and lead a normal life.

Instead, at eighteen, he felt his life was over for what he had done (his first murder), and that he didn't deserve to be happy or successful. So alcohol, which he had already established as his escape, and he began to go through the motions of life until his dark fantasies took over. He always believed that a turning point in his life happened while in the haze of a lonely, alcoholic, sexless, emotionally bankrupt life. The simple act of an anonymous man at the public library—who tossed Dahmer a note offering to give him a blow job in the bathroom—caused him, at that moment, to decide to abandon the legitimate life he had created and instead pursue sex, and finally achieve love and physical relationships on his terms. He didn't follow the man, but it seemed to have triggered a crisis of conscience in Dahmer, so deep that he finally admitted to himself that he was and always had been attracted to men, and in turn, that some men were attracted to him. He decided to live a lie no longer, and knew that he "wasn't fooling anybody." Further, the incident seemed to reawaken his lustful desire to engage with unconscious or dead bodies—to do whatever he wanted with the corpses of men.

A few years later, Dennis Murphy, Kennedy's partner on the Dahmer case, had been to the prison on another matter and had seen Jeff, which he reported to Pat. According to Murphy, Dahmer had requested the transfer to the general population; he remembers many of the officers around him predicting that he wouldn't survive a year.

Dahmer was a marked man from the day he entered the penitentiary. His murder in prison was inevitable, and Dahmer would have been told this prior to being moved out of solitary. His desire to be around other people must have outweighed his fear of being killed, or he simply didn't care anymore.

***

Before Dahmer's 1991 arrest, he did nothing to draw attention to himself. He wanted to fly under the radar. He wasn't looking to give himself a name to identify his serial murders. He didn't write and send anonymous letters to the print press or television media. Even when captured, he never sought out the cameras as he came in and out of court. He was interviewed after he was sentenced, but it seemed much less about self-promotion and more about a sense of duty to answer questions about his crimes.

However, toward the end of Dahmer's life, rumors started filtering to police that Dahmer had changed in other ways too. Because of the pervasive publicity around him and the attention he received when someone pointed him out, he always acknowledged who he was. Some might believe that this ultimately proves he was really a scumbag who actually did crave attention—even negative and unhealthy attention—and that this certainly negated any redeeming qualities he may have had.

Perhaps, though, it makes him even more human. After years of trying to downplay media-created labels, Dahmer found himself in prison with no place to hide. He didn't revel in what he had done nor did he try to minimize it. He didn't attempt to make money from his crimes or exploit his victims (at least any further than what he had done to them originally), and he genuinely took responsibility for what he'd done and tried to find the cause of why he had committed these crimes.

Killing his first victim was a horrible occurrence in his mind and he was wracked with guilt, but that turned to a kind of invincibility that he found strange but powerful. He lived in fear of being found out, so he began to go to great lengths to seek out his sexual desires without hurting anyone else. He stole a mannequin that he kept in the closet of his bedroom at his grandmother's house so he could lie with it and use it as a masturbation aid. Dahmer began to think of himself as omnipotent, with supreme control over his victims—men he wanted, but who ultimately left him or tried to leave. Because he didn't want to fight every victim, he began to drug his casualties. Once on his own, he visited bathhouses where he drugged other men's drinks until someone complained, and he was asked to leave and not return. Even his early attempts to incapacitate his victims by drilling holes in their skulls and filling the wounds with acid or hot water, though crude and misguided, show that he tried everything he could think of to seek out and satisfy his necrophilic urges. Finally, his cannibalism appeared, by his admission, to be a part of some sort of romantic notion and bizarre attempt to keep his lovers with him forever.

***

On November 28, 1994, Dahmer was sent with two other prisoners to clean a bathroom at the Columbia Correctional Institute in Portage, Wisconsin. Inmate Christopher Scarver first beat Jesse Anderson, the other prisoner, in front of Dahmer before turning his weapon, a grip from a barbell weight, on Dahmer, who put up no resistance. Coincidentally, it was the very same kind of weapon Dahmer used against his first murder victim at age eighteen.

During the autopsy, the pathologist did not find any marks or bruises on Dahmer's arms, which are normally found if the victim attempted to defend himself. It's troubling, as it is human instinct to defend one's self against physical harm, but Dahmer knew he was a marked man; furthermore, he'd expressed his wish to die on numerous occasions. He saw a man die in front of him before the killer turned his sights on Dahmer. Dahmer allowed himself to be killed.

Dahmer was a target for several reasons. Because the majority of his victims were African American, prisoners who were also African American likely wanted him dead as payback. Another reason was Dahmer's infamy. For better or worse, cottage industries of comics, collector cards, and everything in between seem to spring up whenever an infamous serial killer is caught. Dahmer apparently received a lot of mail and attention because of who he was. When he walked through the prison, people whispered and pointed him out, or called out to him. He may have been invisible to some extent in the outside world before he and his crimes were discovered, but once incarcerated, he was considered a famous prisoner amongst low-level killers, rapists, pedophiles, etc.

After killing Dahmer, Christopher Scarver claimed that he believed he (Scarver) was Christ and that he had to punish Dahmer for his sins. Twenty-one years later, while still in jail but trying to sell his unpublished manuscript, he claimed that Dahmer's dark sense of humor and proclivity for tasteless and inappropriate jokes were the reasons he decided to beat Dahmer to death.

Photos of Dahmer taken at his arrest show a young man with trim hair and a fit and lean frame. During his incarceration, he gained weight (approximately thirty pounds), most likely due to a combination of the typical high-starch diet that seems prevalent in penitentiaries, a general lack of physical activity during his confinement, and high levels of antipsychotic medications. A photo of him taken shortly before his death show a much older man than his thirty-four years, with slightly longer hair and an ashen, grey-colored appearance. Dahmer is paunchier, bloated, and uncomfortable with the additional weight. There is a kind of prison pallor synonymous with a person who spends all his time in windowless surroundings, under artificial light, and who smokes chronically.

He was prepared to die while in prison and likely always knew he would not survive into old age. With a renewed engagement in religion, he believed that a higher being would determine his fate, and that whatever happened to him was meant to be and part of the will of society at large. He told the judge at his sentencing that he preferred a death sentence and that he "wanted death" for himself. His eventual sentence was sixteen life sentences in Ohio and Wisconsin (941 years).

Aside from some members of Dahmer's family who mourned his loss, a handful of specialists and individuals in law enforcement who study serial killers believe that the things that made Dahmer unique from other killers was his readiness to answer questions, his participation in evaluations and discussions, and his willingness to take complete responsibility for his crimes. All of this is helpful to those who hunt killers.

In the first weeks of December 1994, when news of Dahmer's death made its way around the world, *People* magazine's article about his murder was headlined The Final Victim: Haunted by His Grim Legacy of Murder and Cannibalism, Jeffrey Dahmer, Like the Families of Many of His Victims, Felt He Deserved to Die.

According to this article, Jack Levin, noted professor of criminology at Northwestern University in Boston, was quoted as saying, "Most serial killers are pathological liars. Dahmer was different. He was willing to reveal his experiences with murder, and we could have learned more from him."

But the article also suggests that though he had confessed and the state had punished him for his crimes, Dahmer didn't deserve to die in prison. He was sentenced to spend the rest of his life there and natural causes should have ended his life. While it is understandable there were many who felt that justice, outside of what had been decided in that Milwaukee courtroom, had been served with Dahmer's murder at the hands of another, there were people who mourned his death at age thirty-four. His family, those who came to befriend him in prison, and indeed even Kennedy (who learned so many terrible things about Dahmer) felt the loss. His mother Joyce was quoted at the time of his murder as saying, "Now is everybody happy? Now that he's bludgeoned to death, is that good enough for everyone?"

Most serial killers fight to stay alive—by appealing a death sentence and often staying in solitary confinement if they and others fear for their life in general population, with the desire to live as long a life as possible, even if it is behind bars. Dahmer wished to die and didn't fight back when he was attacked. Apparently, Dahmer's last words as he was being beaten were, "I don't care if I live or die. Go ahead and kill me."

It was clear that while Dahmer always intended to plead guilty, his lawyers felt they had a strong case of insanity, and the world's media did little to dissuade the public that anyone capable of such atrocities clearly had to be sick. It seemed that Dahmer's depravity caused most rational people to question his sanity and his state of mind.

For Kennedy, the question of whether Dahmer was sane or insane was simple. He believed, based on what he knew and learned about Dahmer, that he suffered from mental disease that unfortunately led to the deaths of his many victims. He believed that Dahmer could function to a degree, but that he had to be mentally insane in order to commit such crimes against so many people.

Most sexual predators have dual personalities (not to be confused with multiple personality disorder), which is a necessity for a sexual predator to function in the real world with family, friends, co-workers, clients, neighbors, etc., while the true self's world is filled with sexual fantasies, stalking potential victims, and preying on those they perceive as weak, deserving, available, or simply unaware of the danger the predator presents until it is too late.

There was a genesis of Dahmer's deviancies as diagnosed by many psychiatric professionals at his sanity trial, including Dahmer's defense. They argued that he suffered from a mental disease as defined by law, driven by obsessions and impulses he was unable to control and therefore not responsible for, and thus he was eligible for treatment in a psychiatric hospital. Defense experts argued that Dahmer was insane due to his necrophilic drive—his compulsion to have sexual encounters with corpses.

Defense expert Dr. Frederick Berlin testified that "Dahmer was unable to conform his conduct at the time that he committed the crimes because he was suffering from paraphilia, or, more specifically, necrophilia." Dr. Judith Becker, a professor of psychiatry and psychology, also diagnosed Dahmer as insane for acting on his necrophilic drive. Final expert witness Dr. Carl Wahlstrom diagnosed Dahmer with borderline personality disorder.

The prosecution argued that Dahmer had the ability both to appreciate the criminality of his conduct and to resist his impulses despite any mental disorders he suffered. The prosecution's expert witness, forensic psychiatrist Dr. Phillip Resnick, testified that he believed Dahmer did not suffer from primary necrophilia because he actually preferred live sexual partners, as evidenced by his initial efforts to create submissive sexual partners devoid of rational thought and to whose needs he did not have to cater. However, Dahmer did resort to necrophilia with almost every victim once he strangled them, having sex with the corpses several times after death. Resnick also diagnosed Dahmer with borderline personality disorder.

Dr. Fred Fosdal also testified to his belief that Dahmer was without mental disease or defect at the time he committed the murders; Fosdal did state his belief, though, that Dahmer was not cruel or a sadist, characteristics common among sexual serial killers. Common among this type of killer is often the sexual torturer, whose pleasure is derived from degradation, physical torture, a deep-seated desire to inflict pain, most often comorbid with deviant appetites, perversions, and sexual thrill-seeking, generally geared toward creating pain and fear. Dr. Fosdal, like many others, felt that Dahmer was unique among many sexual serial killers in that regard. He also diagnosed Dahmer with borderline personality disorder.

The final witness to appear for the prosecution was forensic psychiatrist Dr. Park Dietz, who testified that he did not believe Dahmer suffered from any mental disease or defect at the time he committed the crimes. He stated, "Dahmer went to great lengths to be alone with his victim and to have no witnesses." He believed Dahmer's habit of becoming intoxicated prior to committing each of the murders was significant in terms of the kind of killer Dahmer was. Typically for sexual serial killers, the activity before, leading up to, and during the actual killing is what drives them, for reasons including fear, dominance, anger, hatred, sadism, and revenge. Dahmer actually deplored killing, choosing to dispatch his victims as easily as possible by drugging them first and then strangling them while they lay unconscious so that their deaths, in his mind, would be painless. Dahmer's sexual predilections were specific and overriding. The sexual gratification came from what he chose to do to the bodies after—from dismemberment, to cannibalism, to saving parts of the bodies and the skulls. In short, his compulsion was necrophilia—killing in order to obtain a corpse, according to Dietz.

Dahmer chose to kill young men whom he found attractive because he wanted to engage in sexual acts with an unconscious partner. While he had developed several unusual and eventually dangerous paraphilias, and he ultimately acted upon them despite the risk and with no thought to the life of others—almost everything vile, unconscionable, monstrous, and disrespectful was done postmortem.

Dr. Dietz stated, "If he had a compulsion to kill, he would not have to drink alcohol. He had to drink alcohol to overcome his inhibition, to do the crime which he would rather not do." Dr. Dietz diagnosed Dahmer with substance use disorder, paraphilia, and personality disorder with borderline and schizotypal features.

In addition to the specialists who were asked to testify for each side, there were also two court-appointed mental health professionals testifying independently of either prosecution or defense: forensic psychiatrist Dr. George Palermo and clinical psychologist Dr. Samuel Friedman. Dr. Palermo suggested that the murders Dahmer committed were the result of "a pent-up aggression within himself. He killed those men because he wanted to kill the source of his attraction to them. In killing them, he killed what he hated in himself." Dr. Palermo diagnosed Dahmer with borderline personality disorder.

Dr. Friedman, who also diagnosed Dahmer with borderline personality disorder, testified that it was a longing for companionship that caused Dahmer to kill. He stated, "Mr. Dahmer is not psychotic." He spoke kindly of Dahmer, describing him as "amiable, pleasant to be with, courteous, with a sense of humor, conventionally handsome, and charming in manner. He was, and still is, a bright young man."

***

Trying to comprehend Dahmer is to attempt to understand the power of loneliness and alienation at its absolute core. Too often, fantasy is the severely lonely person's internal coping mechanism, and it can occasionally become external and homicidal. Dahmer's personality and low self-esteem manifested itself early in the mostly self-harming action of drinking too much, but eventually this seemed to develop into troubling external actions against others—crimes of murder, which, like his drinking, he was incapable of stopping on his own.

In Dahmer's case, it was alcohol and abnormal sexual compulsion, not anger or rage, that drove him as a killer, and he confessed to every murder he committed.

Patrick Francis Kennedy (1954–2013)

Patrick Francis Kennedy was born February 17, 1954, in Detroit, Michigan. One of ten children born to Catherine and Angus Kennedy and the eldest of the boys, Pat eventually followed his father's footsteps into law enforcement and became a police officer. He was raised in Detroit, where he was active in sports, primarily football and basketball. His size (over two hundred and fifty pounds) and height (six feet, seven inches) were considered assets. Athletics were always an important part of his life, and he later added cycling to his list of physical passions, even after undergoing knee surgery and painful rehabilitation in 2008.

Pat was raised in a devout Roman Catholic family. Feeling the pull of the Catholic faith early, he studied theology with the intent of attending seminary and becoming a priest. He followed that path to St. Lawrence Seminary at Marian College of Fond du Lac (now Marian University), a Roman Catholic liberal arts university where he met his three closest, lifelong friends: Bill Holly, Greg Jarouch, and James Simmers. He began his studies there and was on the basketball team when he met Mary Lynn, a young woman from the area, and the two began dating. He always joked that he would have become a priest, but could not keep the vow of poverty when it was actually the vow of chastity that ended his pious journey. Within a few months of dating, Mary Lynn discovered she was pregnant and in 1974, they married and started their family. The Catholic faith was the lifelong focus of his spirituality, and the church an important part of his life, but with a young wife and a baby on the way, his new area of study became the community and social work/public service. The couple started their new life together in Milwaukee and at the age of nineteen, Pat was a father for the first time. He found employment in social work, and was involved with a group home located in a small town in northern Wisconsin.

He became director of a not-for-profit group that helped low- and middle-income families purchase their first homes, as well as giving ex-convicts an opportunity to learn a legitimate skill while gaining valuable work experience and making money to live. They purchased run-down foreclosed homes in downtown Milwaukee, and hired former prisoners who were determined to leave their criminal lives behind them. He had them learn a trade through apprenticeship in the construction fields, including building, painting, remodeling, plumbing, electrical, etc. while getting paid legitimately. The houses were fixed up and sold, with any profits made put back into the organization.

Pat also attended Lakeshore Technical College in 1977 and played basketball there, but for the most part, he held a variety of jobs in order to provide for his family. They moved a few times and even tried a move southwest when he relocated his family to Texas. He later admitted to many people that the adventure was a complete disaster.

Pat and Mary had three children (two sons, Patrick and Alexander, and a daughter, Maureen) and to keep up with a growing family, he turned to a new career that he was familiar with, having grown up as the son of a police officer. He entered the academy in 1979. At age twenty-five, he was quickly hired as an officer of the Milwaukee Police Department and a percussionist in the Milwaukee Police Band. He was active as much as possible; when spending time with him, one expected to be biking, hiking, skiing, or swimming.

Alcohol was a problem for most of his adult life, but he successfully managed sobriety thanks to treatment programs and his Catholic faith. As Patrick put it, he isn't sure if he drank because his marriage was starting to break down or if the marriage began to break down because of his drinking—likely a little of both. He attended Alcoholic Anonymous meetings but admitted that he struggled with it from time to time because of pressures on the job, as well as stress at home and in the marriage. Mary and Pat divorced, remarried, and then divorced a second time.

The Police Athletic League (sometimes called Police Activities League), or PAL, helped Pat cope with the struggle of alcoholism in many ways and on many occasions. As a young man, he was involved with PAL through his father's work as a cop, and it was an organization to which he devoted energy and countless hours. He worked to bring the program to new communities, strengthened chapters in established neighborhoods, and promoted and encouraged the program wherever he went. His participation also gave him the chance to get him onto his beloved basketball court.

Pat received his master's degree from the University of Wisconsin-Milwaukee in 2000 and retired from the Milwaukee Police Department that same year. He spent several months in the Peace Corps in Ascension, Paraguay, working with youth. His hope was to bring the success of the PAL program with him, and he committed to working with young people and police officers to prevent crime by bringing communities together. Pat quickly came to recognize first-hand the massive problems facing the country's law enforcement community because of corruption, violence, and poverty, as well as physical assaults, guns, and threats against police on the streets. He returned from Paraguay, and it didn't take long before Pat landed a job as program chair at Marian University.

He married his second wife, Patricia Leal Kennedy, a nurse and the mother of a grown son. Pat's three grown children were all married, and he had six grandchildren living all over the country.

"When I first met Pat, it seemed that he was entering into one of life's many transformative stages. We were friends, as he was in the midst of separating from his wife, and I would learn later the trials and tribulations of his younger days as we got to know each other. With Pat came his family, and some of them, the most extraordinary people you would want to meet. His mother Catherine was one of the most beautiful people I've ever known," says Patty Kennedy.

According to Patty, Pat loved and admired his mother and always spoke of how strong the Kennedy women were. Pat acquired many traits from his mother, including kindness and generosity of spirit. He made others feel as though they were the most important person in the room. He always complimented their efforts, no matter what they were doing. He found good in everyone, and the rare moments of rehashing old wounds left him asking for forgiveness in doing so. Patty only saw him down a couple of times in the twenty years that he was in her life. It was in stark contrast to what she experienced most in their time together.

He had a great way of summarizing his day. After a day of doing whatever he wanted to do, he sat down and announced, "I had a great day today," and listed what he did that day in the order that it happened. Then he said, "If I wasn't me, I would envy me." He was a significant presence when in a room, usually moving, snapping his fingers to music, commenting on something he was reading or watching on television, or choosing a topic for debate depending on who was present.

While attending St. John's Cathedral in Milwaukee, Pat became involved in an outreach ministry called the Open Door Café, where the homeless and other hungry folks could have a hot, sit-down meal. Pat was a serving volunteer, and faithfully attended the Sunday meal after 9:30 a.m. mass. He shared the Sunday newspaper with others who were waiting in line to be served their meal. Ever the cop, Pat not only maintained order in the line, but also always had conversations with those waiting, and he came home to tell Patty many interesting stories. He got to know many people, and when Pat and Patty drove around town, he stopped occasionally to yell out, "Say, pal, you need a ride?" In this way, Patty got to know some of these same people, and now she volunteers with Open Door Café. She still hears stories about how Pat touched the lives of people from all walks of life. Whenever he could, he had his friends or relatives help out at the café.

Pat also developed a street basketball league in collaboration with Gingerbread Land, Inc., a Milwaukee-based nonprofit organization. During the summer, he arranged through the city to have certain streets blocked off and organized a basketball league of kids from the local neighborhood. Kids and their parents came from all over the inner city on summertime Saturday mornings to play basketball on the closed streets. Parents set up their chairs and watched their kids play, with Coach Kennedy running up and down the various courts the entire day. Patty remembers stopping one Saturday to drop off some team shirts. She watched as kids walked over from all directions, bouncing their basketballs as they walked, talked, and met their friends. This was a regular summer event the kids could count on, and Pat worked on the project tirelessly. Pat saw the value in organized play and community involvement. He absolutely loved to coach kids, including his granddaughter's middle school team, along with his son, Alex.

While teaching at Marian University, his former alma mater, Pat drew many new students to the program by virtue of his reputation as a homicide detective for MPD and the infamous Dahmer case. One year, he was successful in obtaining a significant grant from the US Marshals, and through liaisons with the Fond du Lac law enforcement community, took the program and student population to new heights.

While at Marian and teaching criminal justice at other colleges, he continued his push to educate and engage students in the importance of community involvement when working in law enforcement. He was invited to speak at many law enforcement conferences and was sought for many interviews for documentaries about his work obtaining Dahmer's confession.

Pat found his work in academia very rewarding. He conducted research in his main area of study, critical race theory (CRT). This work became a crucial part of Pat's continued studies and provided an opportunity to transfer what he learned into new training criteria for new police recruits. It improved and modified education for all officers regardless of their rank and/or tenure.

In 2009, he received the University of Wisconsin-Milwaukee's School of Education's Dissertation of the Year Award for his research, "Critical Race Theory and the Experience of Police Recruits: A Milwaukee Experiment."

***

On April 18, 2013, Patrick Kennedy died suddenly at home from a major heart attack. He was fifty-nine. I found out about Pat's passing a day or two later while in the midst of reading his manuscript.

***

"Grief does not change you. It reveals you."
—John Green, *The Fault in Our Stars*

2016

After communicating with Patty Kennedy after Pat's death, we decided his story deserved to be published, that it was still worth preserving and sharing, despite the fact Pat wouldn't be here to see the project to its conclusion.

According to Patty, "I was glad that I had two years to put this letter in writing (to Robyn), because it took that long to come to grips with the grief I felt at Pat's loss. When I first met Pat's mother, I fell in love with her too, and I believe that the Lord presented me to this woman when I needed it. She taught me by offering me an example of how to deal spiritually with loss and grief. To this day, at certain times of the day, I think about him and what we would do right now. I feel his spirit very heavily some days and nights. At first, I felt a heavy heart and sadness, but now it feels more like a pull to prayer; a prayer for peace and serenity, a prayer for Pat."

Appendix

The 911 emergency telephone call between a civilian and dispatcher regarding the presence of a naked boy on the street was made available to the media and was played during Dahmer's trial, becoming part of the official court transcript.

The recording between the officers and dispatch after the incident was recorded and made public. The second telephone exchange between a civilian and MPD was recorded, and after Jeffrey Dahmer's capture, the conversation was then heard around the world. It seemed to demonstrate that when given two different stories by two people of different races in a given situation, the police inclination at that time was to believe the Caucasian male rather than the African American female who actively tried to get involved in order to save a boy's life, but faced a brick wall of ambivalence and indifference. The killing of Konerak Sinthasomphone took place two months before Dahmer's capture and a further four men would be killed in that interim.

— Don Davis, *The Jeffrey Dahmer Story: An American Nightmare*

Definitions

Borderline Personality Disorder (BPD) is a mental illness marked by essential symptoms and signs including a pattern of impulsivity and instability of behaviors, of interpersonal relationships, and of self-image. There may be uncontrollable anger and depression. The pattern is present by early adulthood and occurs across a variety of situations and contexts.

Other symptoms usually include intense fears of abandonment, sensitivity to feelings of rejection, extreme anger, and irritability, the reason for which others have difficulty understanding. People with BPD often engage in idealization and devaluation of others, alternating between high positive regard and great disappointment. Self-harm, suicidal behavior, and substance abuse are common. There is evidence that abnormalities of the frontolimbic networks are associated with many of the symptoms.

The disorder is recognized in the Diagnostic and Statistical Manual of Mental Disorders (DSM, now in its fifth edition), published by the American Psychiatric Association. Since a personality disorder is a pervasive, enduring, and inflexible pattern of maladaptive inner experiences and pathological behavior, there is a general reluctance to diagnose personality disorders before adolescence or early adulthood. However, some practitioners emphasize that without early treatment, the symptoms may worsen. There is an ongoing debate about the terminology of this disorder, especially the suitability of the word "borderline."

Necrophilia is a pathological fascination with dead bodies, which often manifests as a desire to engage with them in sexual activities. Considered a sexual deviancy, it is prohibited by the law in many countries. Necrophilia, also called thanatophilia, is a sexual attraction or sexual act involving corpses. The attraction is as an "Other Specified Paraphilic Disorder" by the DSM-V, published by the APA. The term was coined by the Belgian psychiatry pioneer Joseph Guislain, who first used it in a lecture in 1850. It derives from the Greek words νεκρός (*nekrós*; "corpse") and φιλία (*philía*; "love"). Rosman and Resnick reviewed information from thirty-four cases of necrophilia describing individuals' motivations for their behaviors: these persons reported the desire to possess a non-resistant and non-rejecting partner (68%); reunions with a romantic partner (21%); sexual attraction to corpses (15%); comfort or overcoming feelings of isolation (15%); or seeking self-esteem by expressing power over a homicide victim (12%).

Bibliography

Chin, Paula. "The Door of Evil." *People*. August 12, 1991.

Gleick, Elizabeth. "The Final Victim." *People*. December 12, 1994.

Mohammed, Susan. "Retired Teacher Perishes in Fire." *Trinidad Express*. October 12, 2012.

Terry, Don. "Jeffrey Dahmer, Multiple Killer, Is Bludgeoned to Death in Prison." *New York Times*. New York City, NY. November 29, 1994.

Rosman, J.P., and P.J. Resnick. "Sexual Attraction to Corpses: A Psychiatric Review of Necrophilia." *Bulletin of the American Academy of Psychiatry and the Law* 17. February 1989: 153-63.

Dahmer, Lionel. *A Father's Story*. New York, NY: William Morrow and Company. 1994.

Davis, Don. *The Jeffrey Dahmer Story: An American Nightmare*. New York, NY: St. Martin's Press. November 15, 1991.

Fisher, Hart D. *An American Horror Story: As Lived by Hart D. Fisher*. Los Angeles, CA. American Horrors. 2011.

Ressler, Robert K., and Tom Schactman. *I Have Lived in the Monster: A Report from the Abyss*. New York, NY. St. Martin's Press. 1997.

Diagnostic and Statistical Manual of Mental Disorders: DSM-5. Arlington, VA. American Psychiatric Publishing. 2013.

Detectives Kennedy, Patrick and Murphy, Dennis. Milwaukee Police Department. Jeffrey Lionel Dahmer Confession. Milwaukee: Milwaukee Police Department, District 3. July–August 1991.

Detective Nowicki, Joseph. Milwaukee Police Department. Jeffrey Lionel Dahmer Incident Report. Milwaukee: Milwaukee Police Department, District 3. July 12, 1991.

"Jeffrey Dahmer FBI Files." Internet Archive. Last modified March 16, 2015. https://archive.org/details/JeffreyDahmer.

Administrative Office of the US Courts, PACER Service Center. Public Access to Court Electronic Records. https://www.pacer.gov/.

Wikimedia Foundation. "Jeffrey Dahmer." Wikipedia. Last modified December 17, 2017. http://Wikipedia.org/wiki/Jeffrey_Dahmer.

"Jeffrey Dahmer - Full Trial - Serial Killer." Video file, 1:33:42. YouTube. Posted by Jesusmalaark11. December 5, 2012. https://www.youtube.com/watch?v=hnuSl8PNYqc.

Ballard, Natalie. "question re: former case and client." Email message to Wendy Patrickus. December 17, 2016.

Fisher, Hart D. "Dahmer lawsuit." Email message to Natalie Ballard. January 2–3, 2017.

Masters, Brian. "Dahmer." Email message to Natalie Ballard. November 28, 2017.

Patrickus, Wendy. re: question re: former case and client. E-mail message to Natalie Ballard. January 4, 2017.

Author Biographies

Former Milwaukee Police Department Homicide Detective **Patrick Kennedy, PhD**, spent several months engulfed in a serial killer case that made headlines around the world. After spending several more years as a detective and after returning from Paraguay after spending time with the Peace Corps, he returned to college and later taught criminal justice at two Wisconsin universities. He was featured in the documentary film *The Jeffrey Dahmer Files* in 2012. An active PAL (Police Athletic League) participant, Patrick Kennedy passed away in April 2013.

Robyn Maharaj is a freelance journalist, grant writer, and former arts director based in Canada. Since 1991, she's published feature articles, profiles, poetry, and book and film reviews in numerous Canadian newspapers, magazines, and literary journals. Co-founder of Thin Air: the Winnipeg International Writers Festival, one of her literary essays was published in the anthology *The Winnipeg Connection: Writing Lives at Mid-Century*. In 2014, CrimeMagazine.com published her feature article, "Exorcising Dahmer's Ghost."

For More News About Patrick Kennedy and Robyn Maharaj, Signup For Our Newsletter:
http://wbp.bz/newsletter

Word-of-mouth is critical to an author's long-term success. If you appreciated this book please leave a review on the Amazon sales page:
http://wbp.bz/grillingdahmera

AVAILABLE FROM KEVIN SULLIVAN AND WILDBLUE PRESS!

THE ENIGMA OF TED BUNDY by KEVIN SULLIVAN

http://wbp.bz/enigmaa

AVAILABLE FROM JONI JOHNSTON, PSY. D. AND WILDBLUE PRESS!

JONI JOHNSTON, Psy.D.

SERIAL KILLERS

101 QUESTIONS
TRUE CRIME FANS ASK

SERIAL KILLERS by JONI JOHNSTON, Psy.D.

http://wbp.bz/serialkillersa

AVAILABLE FROM CARL DENARO, BRIAN WHITNEY, AND WILDBLUE PRESS!

THE 'SON OF SAM' AND ME by CARL DENARO and BRIAN WHITNEY

http://wbp.bz/sonofsama

Printed in the USA
CPSIA information can be obtained
at www.ICGtesting.com
LVHW051501291124
797957LV00004B/172